FAITHFUL DELIBERATION

FAITHFUL DELIBERATION

Rhetorical Invention, Evangelicalism, and #MeToo Reckonings

T J GEIGER II

THE UNIVERSITY OF ALABAMA PRESS
Tuscaloosa

The University of Alabama Press
Tuscaloosa, Alabama 35487-0380
uapress.ua.edu

Typeface: Scala Pro / Avenir

Cover image: Detail from *The Ecstasy of Mary Magdalene* by Albrecht Dürer (German, 1471–1528), woodcut, 1501–1504
Cover design: David Nees

Cataloging-in-Publication data is available from the Library of Congress.
ISBN: 978-0-8173-2120-8
E-ISBN: 978-0-8173-9396-0

This book is dedicated to all survivors of sexual abuse and domestic violence and to the people creating more survivor-affirming communities of faith.

CONTENTS

Preface ix

Acknowledgments xvii

Author's Note: On Researcher Positionality and Responsibilities xxi

Introduction: From Proverbs of Ashes to Invention for Faithful Deliberation 1

1. Naming Those Sins: A Brief History of Rules, Boundaries, and Responses 24

2. Wake Up, Sleepers: Cheap and Costly Rhetorical Grace Before #ChurchToo 46

3. More Than Platitudes: Casuistically Tightening Forgiveness 65

4. Letters to Their Brothers: Southern Baptist Women and a Rhetoric of Reconciliation 84

5. A Fellowship of Survivors: Archiving Abuse, Inviting Healing, and Drawing Lines 104

Conclusion 120

Notes 129

Works Cited 157

Index 175

PREFACE

"Go home." John MacArthur, a longtime influential preacher in evangelical circles, uttered this phrase in the fall of 2019 when invited to free associate with the name "Beth Moore."

Moore, a Houston-based ministry leader, founded the women-centered Living Proof Ministries in 1994. An important figure with a distinctive persona within evangelicalism, Moore belonged to the largest Protestant denomination in the United States, the Southern Baptist Convention (SBC), until March 2021. After *Faithful Deliberation* had entered the production process, Moore announced that she was leaving the SBC. With an accessible, down-home presentation style, Moore shares life stories, research, and scriptural interpretation to convey spiritual messages as she instructs her audience, primarily composed of women. A survivor of childhood sexual abuse, Moore often shares her story. She is among the evangelical women growing increasingly vocal regarding how church communities should approach sexual abuse, harassment, and gender-based violence.

Gathered to commemorate MacArthur's fifty years of ministry, the audience laughed and applauded at his reply. MacArthur's expressive command actually proposed a course of action that might put some folks at risk of violence. Despite *home*'s association with escape and respite, safety and belonging, home actually operates as a decidedly unsafe space for many: children facing abuse from family, intimate partners subjected to domestic violence. This point was driven home during the early days of the COVID-19 outbreak in the United States as populations sheltered-in-place at the urging of public health officials and the orders of government leaders. Advocacy centers, hotlines, and shelters circulated contact information intended to help anyone forced into sheltering with an aggressor. When MacArthur made his impromptu comment, Moore was heavily engaged in advocacy against abuse, violence, exploitation, and practices that enable these destructive dynamics.

Faithful Deliberation focuses on arguments forwarded by Moore and other prominent women within or closely associated with the rhetorical enclaves (i.e., groups of mostly like-minded people) that constitute predominantly white US evangelicalism. Through a series of case studies, I examine rhetorical work that reinvents evangelical commonplaces (i.e., typical statements and ideas) related to sexual objectification, harassment, assault, abuse, and domestic violence. This rhetorical invention that reformulates readily available ideas facilitates a form of in-group-directed discussion that I refer to as *faithful deliberation*, that is, deliberation intended to mobilize evangelicals around these issues.

Even as recent faithful deliberations continue a long history of Christian argument, I focus on efforts that arose just before and following the mainstreaming of the #MeToo movement, a movement dedicated to breaking silences around sexual harassment and sexual assault through expressions of survivors' solidarity with each other. Since 2017, the movement has expanded and intensified deliberation on the need for more survivor-affirming responses in many domains. These deliberations unfold within political, social, cultural, professional, and religious contexts. One such context is evangelicalism: a multifaceted, transdenominational Christian movement constituted through participants' mutual recognition of personal experiences with God and through participation in the circulation of shared histories, discourses, literacies, and rhetorical practices.

This book contributes to rhetorical studies by examining the dynamics of enclave deliberation in some evangelicals' recent rhetorical action in the lead-up to, and in light of, the #MeToo movement. Specifically, I analyze evangelical women's rhetoric about sexual and domestic violence on its own terms to theorize about deliberation within a highly religious enclave. An outsider to evangelicalism, I care about what happens within it for many reasons, including its significance as a cultural force connected to political and social movements. My interest also stems from living the last decade as a Christian actively involved in local churches and in a mainline Protestant denomination. While evangelicalism intriguingly attends to affect, personal experience, intellectual engagement, and literacy-rich environments, some contemporary manifestations of this Christian tradition confound outsiders such as myself. One confounding episode in recent evangelical history came with the 2016 US presidential election, which witnessed a supermajority of voting white evangelicals casting ballots for a candidate whose sexual ethics, stated lack of repentance for sin, and sexually coercive language were surely at odds with evangelicals' long-held refrain that personal morality, religious status, and character matter.

On election night in November 2016, as soon as it became clear that Donald J. Trump would be the forty-fifth US president, a line from the Episcopal Church's 1979 *Book of Common Prayer* traditional language confession came to me: "We acknowledge and bewail our manifold sins and wickedness."[1] The only language that seemed to adequately address the unfolding situation was language that spoke in terms of virtue, vice, and ultimate concerns. This line from a religious rite of corporate confession holds together threads of personal grief and collective lamentation over the state of the world and the speakers' role in the situation. Like many people of faith, when confronted with uncertainty, crisis, or trouble, I turn to religious practices—such as confession and prayer. Writing this book became an extension of my election night prayers.

The morning after the election, I struggled to understand the voting breakdowns. While exit polls showed that a strong majority of white evangelicals cast ballots for Trump (81 percent), majorities of white Roman Catholics (60 percent)[2] decided similarly, as did Protestants (58 percent) and white voters (58 percent) generally.[3] In other words, most white Christian voters chose Trump.

In the month prior to the election, I wrote a blog post about how writers popular among evangelicals, Moore and Jen Hatmaker, pushed back against outspoken leaders within their community who had offered apologias for Trump's comments in the infamous *Access Hollywood* recording: "When you're a star, they let you do it. You can do anything," he boasted. "Grab 'em by the pussy. You can do anything." Writing an article version of that blog post, I focused on how highly esteemed women within evangelicalism helped to reframe their audience's priorities. After the election, continuing to write about that episode took on more urgency, because I wanted to highlight what I perceived as a moment from that preelection period that might continue to reverberate into the future. Then, a year later, the popularization of the #MeToo movement occurred, in October 2017.

#MeToo persists as a force re-constellating elements of the US public sphere, sponsoring diverse instances where survivors confront the many forms violence takes and discuss the trauma that follows. Evangelical-oriented #MeToo corollaries also appeared in 2017: #ChurchToo and #SilenceIsNotSpiritual. These movements for survivors connected to Christian and evangelical communities likewise worked to reconstitute elements of evangelicalism. They generated alternative ways of thinking about assault, abuse, harassment, and other forms of violence, shifting the default commonplaces. As the episodes examined in *Faithful Deliberation* unfolded, many prominent evangelicals embraced elements of the broad reimagining of public discourse underway regarding sexual violence—particularizing #MeToo conversations for theologically conservative Christian communities. Of course, as Michel Foucault observes, increasing discursive volume does not necessarily disrupt hegemonic power relationships or habitual practices.[4] More talk and more silence-breaking around violence does not, in itself, produce anti-violence social change. Even explicitly feminist projects can result in outcomes decidedly not liberatory for all, or even most, women.

Given that projects aimed at increasing life options may achieve mixed outcomes, my analysis of episodes within evangelicalism before and after the mainstreaming of #MeToo relies on scholarship about literacy, rhetoric, and healing that points to the sponsored and negotiated nature of healing projects. In *Rhetorical Healing: The Reeducation of Contemporary Black Womanhood*, scholar of rhetoric Tamika L. Carey studies efforts to manage US Black women's wellness, efforts she calls "rhetorics of healing."[5] The contemporary rhetorical healing that Carey identifies authorizes action but often limits that action to community-sanctioned, commercialized scripts. Enabling/constraining tensions likewise attend the deliberative invention studied in this book. I see in some evangelicals' work elements of Carey's observation that "many have accepted the challenge" to undertake robust healing work not beholden to neoliberal market, reactionary antifeminist, and philosophically individualist agendas. Carey cites as an example the women described in Beth Daniell's *A Communion of Friendship: Literacy, Spiritual Practice, and Women in Recovery*.[6] When naming the reading, writing, and speaking habits of these Al-Anon members (a program for friends and family members of those who misuse alcohol), Daniell notes that many of the texts that this group of presumably white women discussed together were authored by Black women (e.g., *Beloved, for colored girls who have considered suicide / when the rainbow is enuf, The Temple of My Familiar, The Color Purple*). These works present powerful women in contexts of brutality, and "the theme of spirituality as a source of confidence" is central.[7] Authored by leading writers of what has been called the late-twentieth-century Black women's literary renaissance, these works also deal with sexual violence, abusive relationships, and healing practices. Reading and discussing these texts generated opportunities for Al-Anon members to identify practices that roused their sense of agency over their healing, such as journaling or writing letters to God in the tradition of Celie in Alice Walker's *The Color Purple*.

Rhetoric that might promote healing work in response to diverse forms of trauma is informed by sponsoring networks and by preexisting discourses, as well as by reformulations of those networks and discourses. For example, even as works, such as Walker's, from an earlier period created highly visible opportunities for Black women to foreground the development of a political awareness that valued both individual consciousness and gendered experiences, more recent wellness campaigns do not always fulfill their liberatory potential. While such campaigns may assist participants in developing a quality of life and agency, Carey argues that they often embody status quo and anti-feminist ideologies that end up circumscribing Black women's options, especially as they take on commodified forms for market consumption. Likewise, Daniell observes how Al-Anon materials enact conservative gender roles and obscure class issues.[8]

Without ignoring the differences between them, I believe the sponsored and reformulated rhetoric of women connected to predominantly white evangelicalism, on the one hand, and Carey's rhetorical healing, on the other, have certain similarities. Two questions that are important to these projects suggest these similarities: one asked by a fictional character and one by Jesus. In Toni Cade Bambara's novel *The Salt Eaters*, healing figure Minnie Ransom asks ailing community activist Velma Henry, "'Are you sure, sweetheart, that you want to be well? . . . I like to caution folks, that's all. . . . No sense us wasting each other's time, sweetheart. A lot of weight when you're well.'"[9] Carey invokes this question to describe the community-involved, labor-intensive, lengthy process of developing knowledge and connections that heal psychological, emotional, and spiritual wounds.[10] This question resonates with one Jesus poses to a man lying near a pool of healing waters where people with disabilities and illnesses often gathered. Translations render variously the question in John 5:6, put to a man who had lived with paralysis for thirty-eight years: "Do you want to get well?" (NIV), "Do you want to be healed?" (ESV), and "Wilt thou be made whole?" (KJV). Following an explanation that he was unable to access the healing waters because he lacked assistance and because others cut ahead of him, Jesus orders him to collect his mat and go on his way. The man does so, illustrating a substantial change in his condition.

Moore used this gospel text in a teaching session in 2016. She discussed its question in terms of the relationship between an individual's patterns of ongoing behavior that contribute to diminished options in life (i.e., sin), the importance of providing an honest account of one's own self (i.e., confession), and the necessity of personal cooperation with the divine in one's restoration to social life (i.e., repentance and healing).[11] Moore and the other women whose work I examine urge evangelicals to apply this kind of program, which enables a moral accounting of habitual practices that cause harm, to their patterns of discourse, action, and inaction around sexual and domestic violence.

I am not a psychiatrist, psychologist, counselor, social worker, criminal justice researcher, minister, or theologian. Trained not in clinical therapeutic techniques or pastoral care but in rhetoric, I am alert to the messages generated in the wake of interpersonal trauma and to what messages yield some forms of healing. Even as my study of discourse about violence draws insight from clinical and carceral approaches, other means of addressing trauma exist. "Healing" and "trauma," while problematic terms, prove useful, because "the category of trauma" creates "space for accounts of pain as psychic, not just physical. As a name for experiences of socially situated political violence, trauma forges overt connections between politics and emotion."[12] This connection-drawing is especially true in the context of multiple, overlapping traumas: One participant in Daniell's study addressed how her participation in Al-Anon and in an incest survivor group mutually reinforced her healing through writing practices. The rhetoric at the center of my study shares in Cvetkovich's goal of "creat[ing] a collective audience for trauma rather than consigning its representation to therapeutic contexts."[13] *Faithful Deliberation* consequently builds on previous insights about the contextual, negotiated, group-oriented, and sponsored nature of rhetorics designed to stimulate transformation in response to oppression.

Instances of faithful deliberation also provide occasions to think through the relationship between spiritual concepts, like grace and forgiveness, and rhetorical concepts, such as agency, in regard to trauma and trauma discourses. From a Christian's standpoint, grace is a ground of agency that arrives from beyond the self but that also enables individual and collective action in response to changing circumstances. This both/and dynamic of dependence and power is not contradictory but paradoxical, and it can give rise to action.

While analyzing rhetoric at the intersection of paradox and action, I ultimately respond to a question I share with Jeffrey M. Ringer and Sharon Crowley. After a conference panel where Ringer and others responded to Crowley's work analyzing the rhetoric of reactionary, politicized Christianity, Crowley asked, "Okay. So what do we do?"[14] I, like Ringer, take that as a genuine question. I respond by studying instances of women reinventing theological and cultural commonplaces within evangelicalism to promote robust enclave deliberation about how to respond to sexual and domestic violence, deliberation that goes beyond merely providing information about the problems and that engages with values shared within an enclave.

Many religious and nonreligious people assume that religious leaders simply need more information to respond appropriately to situations of abuse. However, in a 2018 reflection on her book *Woman-Battering* (1994), radical feminist Carol J. Adams recalls a pastoral care professor identifying a flaw with her project: Adams assumed that pastors lacked knowledge about how to help women in abusive relationships. This respondent suggested that pastors may well know what they could do but still fail to act.[15] While closing the knowledge-action gap constitutes a central challenge of the #MeToo movement and its evangelical counterparts, histories of evangelical activism, preferences for community-internal alliances, and doctrinal line-drawing have shaped how recent efforts unfolded—indicating the need for a rhetoric that does more than inform audiences with generalized best practices or statistics about a problem's prevalence.

This is a book about women like Moore who strive to close that gap; who ground their work in a vocabulary of shared faith and values; who are "not going home," in the words of a social media image filter that appeared in the wake of MacArthur's dismissal; who keep asking the church and the broader public, both rife with the long-lasting effects of trauma and trauma-minimizing commonplaces, "Do you want to get well?"

ACKNOWLEDGMENTS

My thanks to the folks at the University of Alabama Press who made this book a thing in the world. Special thanks to Dan Waterman for taking an interest in this project.

I am grateful beyond measure for Beth Daniell's work and her support. My work builds on hers. For more than a decade, she has mentored me as a writer and a teacher. Beth's feedback strengthened and refined my ideas.

Trish Roberts-Miller provided a much-appreciated note of encouragement when a version of chapter 3 appeared as an article.

I owe a lasting debt to faculty associated with the composition and cultural rhetoric (CCR) doctoral program at Syracuse University (SU). First among them is my mentor, Rebecca Moore Howard, better known as Becky. My career has been shaped by Becky's fierce commitment to writing and rhetoric research as a means of transforming social conditions. Alongside Becky, Lois Agnew and Eileen Schell helped focus my intellectual passions. Many other faculty whose time in CCR overlapped with mine informed my thinking: Minnie Bruce Pratt, Patrick Berry, Iswari Pandey, Gwendolyn Pough, Margaret Himley, Steve Parks, Collin Brooke, Krista Kennedy, Kevin Browne, Tony Scott, Adam Banks, Louise Wetherbee Phelps, and Carol Lipson. M. Gail Hamner of the religion department has also been an important mentor. Thanks also to many SU graduate students, especially those in CCR, English, and religion.

Hugh Burns and AnaLouise Keating at Texas Woman's University gave me a vision of academic work filled with spirit, joy, and love. When I was an undergraduate student at Lamar University, Stephanie Yearwood, John Yearwood, Steve Zani, and Pat Heintzelman made majoring in English seem like a good idea, and John Storey made me aware of Baptist history as a topic (one I wouldn't pursue until more than a decade later).

A number of groups and individuals at Baylor University have made this book possible through various forms of support. Baylor University provided generous financial support through a research leave during the fall 2019 semester. Many colleagues in the English Department have offered their tireless support and advocacy, especially those who teach in the professional writing and rhetoric major: Coretta Pittman, Lisa Shaver, Kara Poe Alexander, Danielle Williams, Mike DePalma, and Lauren Short. Thanks also to the students in the spring 2019 graduate seminar on religious rhetorics: Anna Beaudry, Shannon McClernon, Stewart Riley, Kelly Sauskojus, and Luke Sayers.

Some of my weekly happy hour friends—Jerry Bradley, Barrie Scardino Bradley, Terri Davis, Gretchen Johnson, Bill McDonald, J. P. Nelson, Don Price, Jim Sanderson, Liz Richardson Sanderson, Thomas Sowers, Diana Vitanza—have kept me on my toes, yet grounded.

Much gratitude to the folks who commented on the ideas presented here. Mostly importantly, Jeff Ringer and Jess Enoch served as the reviewers for the book manuscript, and their feedback improved my work tremendously. Attendees at a 2017 session of the College English Association, especially Margaret Downs-Gamble, were helpful conversation partners. Redoubtable colleagues in two writing groups read portions of this book and provided support: Katie Calloway, Sarah Crover, Nicole Kenley, Annie Mendenhall, Erika Claire Strandjord, Julia Voss, and Jacob Babb. Participants in a session at the University of Louisiana at Lafayette's 2020 Rhetoric Symposium were generous in their engagement with my ideas, especially Keith Dorwick, James McDonald, Clancy Ratliff, Lisa Graley, and Taylor Clement.

The Rhetoric and Religious Traditions Standing Special Interest Group of the Conference on College Composition and Communication has served as a space for me to explore and develop connections with people who have informed my work on this project.

My conversation partners include Elizabeth Vander Lei, Melody Pugh, Jeffrey Ringer, Paul Lynch, Heather Thomson-Bunn, Vicki Tolar Burton, Emily Cope, GPat Patterson, Geoffrey Clegg, Teresa Hooper, Joonna Trapp, Brandon Morgan, Brandon Barnes, Paul T. Corrigan, Jim Beitler, Will Duffy, and the students in Will's ENG 7/8001 seminar.

Dear friends have encouraged my work, contributing to the emotional and material support needed to write a book; among them are Gaby Miller, Ian Nicoll, Christopher Pieper, Zachary Sanger, Chris Moore, Mary Z. Moore, Lilly Ettinger, Rob Bradfield, Max Brewer, Stephanie Drum, Kyndall Rae Rothaus, Christopher Williamson, Kody Bartley, Frank Gentsch, Missy Gentsch, Joanne Spitz, Geoffrey Davidson, Maddee Schrader Barbier, Cameron Barbier, Sharyl West Loeung, Stephen Swanson, Nate Myrick, Casey Lea Ford, Sarah Tinker Perrault, Doug Downs, Hilary Sarat-St Peter, Seth Kahn, Cam Armstrong Conn, Patrick Conn, Bekah Meek, Grayson Meek, Lisa Mastrangelo, Ryan Skinell, Brian Bailie, Tamika L. Carey, Justin Lewis, and so many more.

Very little of this book was written in an office or at home. I composed much of it in third spaces. I am grateful for these Waco businesses-cum-community spaces: Dichotomy, Pinewood, Dancing Bear, Common Grounds, One Day, and Starbucks on Valley Mills. Whether I wrote with coffee, a cocktail, or a pint by my side, I always had a clean well-lighted place and was tended by professionals, such as Hayden Smith, Leighton Bagley, Chris Henderson, Mellen Julsen, Ryan Payne, and Lauren Jameson.

The soundtrack that helped me meet daily word counts includes Sweet Honey in the Rock, Nina Simone, Harry Belafonte, Odetta, and Jessye Norman. In particular, Bernice Johnson Reagon's versions of "Come an' Go with Me to that Land," "Come by Hyar," and "In My Hands" were often set on repeat, as was "Joan Little," Reagon's song supporting a Black woman ultimately acquitted of murder charges after killing a white jailer who attempted to rape her.

Social media communities have been sources of encouragement.

I wish Daddy, Jerry Don Geiger, were here to see this moment. I am grateful for the support of Barbara Jean Geiger; Mama is always my biggest advocate.

Thanks to Jen Wingard and the reviewers at *Peitho* for their feedback and support in the publication of an earlier version of chapter 2 under the title "Forsaking Proverbs of Ashes: Evangelical Women, Donald Trump, and Rhetorical Grace," *Peitho* 20, no. 2 (2018): 315–37. Thanks also to Susan Jarratt and the reviewers at *Rhetoric Society Quarterly* for their feedback and support in the publication of an earlier version of chapter 3 as "Forgiveness Is More Than Platitudes: Evangelical Women, Sexual Violence, and Casuistic Tightening," *Rhetoric Society Quarterly* 59, no. 2 (2019): 163–84.

AUTHOR'S NOTE

On Researcher Positionality and Responsibilities

Writing about the communities and arguments that I do presents several challenges related to positionality. First, I am a cisgender man writing about the community-based rhetoric of women in ways that will professionally and personally benefit me. Second, as a non-evangelical writing about evangelicals, I may fall prey to the pitfalls of misrepresentation and inaccuracy that sometimes accompany the project of writing about communities of which one is not a part. In response to these first two limitations, the primary stance I adopt is one of solidarity with the women at the center of this study. Consequently, I surely miss opportunities to examine how the rhetoric productively challenging discourses surrounding sexual and domestic violence within predominantly white evangelicalism may not adequately address the experiences of women of color—the original focus of #MeToo—or LGBTQ+ people.

While my relationship to the figures at the center of this study in no way resembles that between Beth Daniell and her research participants (i.e., preexisting friendships and relationships), I find instructive her methodological note about the decision to not focus on class issues. Daniell thought that to collect data on class differences among participants might risk compromising the relationships necessary to conduct this research.[1] While I do not have a personal relationship with Moore, Hatmaker, Rachael Denhollander, or Karen Swallow Prior, I teach at a university where many students and faculty come from evangelical backgrounds. Friends of mine at the seminary connected to my university likewise come from such backgrounds. I hope that, beyond contributing to scholarly understandings of the rhetoric involved in contemporary evangelical efforts just before and following the mainstreaming of the #MeToo movement, *Faithful Deliberation* may also be of use in my immediate teaching and living contexts.

When I began work at my current university in the fall of 2016, I had no intention of researching the intersection of sexual violence, domestic violence, religious rhetorics, and evangelicalism. However, as former and current student survivors of sexual assault continued to come forward with their stories, as lawsuits persisted, as high-profile figures left the university over how these incidents were handled, and as a candidate who bragged about sexual assault and characterized such talk as ordinary language won the number of electoral college votes necessary to become president, I knew that there was something I could contribute to my university, local, and disciplinary communities and that I was accountable to these communities. My sense of responsibility also comes with an accountability to history, to those who have come before, and to the future, to those yet to come.

My early understanding of Christianity came from what I saw on the Sunday morning political talk shows, and I didn't much care for it. It seemed abrasive, overly dramatic, and narrow-minded. During my middle school and high school years, I would often lie about attending church for the sake of getting along with classmates, just so they wouldn't keep pestering me about it. The earliest point of contact with church that I remember came when I was four years old through a program called "Mother's Day Out" held at First Baptist Church in Colorado City, Texas. This program title leveraged both the gender ideology that configured childcare as "women's work" and the material reality that much caring labor is done by women on whom gendered work expectations are placed. Setting aside the fact that Mama and Daddy were both out working every day, I will simply say that the program provided a space for little ones like me to play and be kept busy. In February 1990, the group I was a part of wrote a Presidents' Day letter to George H. W. Bush. Each of us four- and five-year-olds contributed a question, and a local newspaper, the *Big Spring Herald*, published our listicle epistle.

The topics ranged broadly: Bush's church attendance, belief in God, how he liked his job, the quality of his government housing. Out of fourteen questions, eight related to the topic of children, five of them were about Bush's own children. However, there were three in our bunch who had a clear sense of social concern in connection with children: "What about homeless kids? . . . Why do kids sleep on the street? . . . What about poor children, crying children, if one of them are hurt, where do they go?"[2] I'm pretty sure these questions came from the much more mature five-year-olds—that extra year makes all the difference. These children may or may not have come from religious homes, but they clearly didn't view the church-informed context of their writing as disinviting questions about poverty, homelessness, and social responsibility. My question would seem less about politics or religion and more about aesthetics and nature: "Mr. President, do you like flowers?"[3] In this question, though, are themes that continue to inform my political, rhetorical, and religious sensibilities. Given that my parents were not fans of the Bush administration, I hoped to build on some potential point of connection between my family and him. My maternal grandmother, whom I called Granny, was an extraordinary gardener who could always grow the most gorgeous flowers; my maternal grandfather, whom I called Papa, was an accomplished nature photographer who could capture the most exquisite flower pictures. They both dedicated themselves to cultivating, capturing, and sharing beauty—flowers in particular. So I just knew that if President Bush liked flowers, we could all find a way forward. My faith in flowers has been surely and sorely tested in the intervening decades.

As I drafted *Faithful Deliberation,* I purchased a used copy of *The Courage to Heal,* a popular self-help book from the 1980s for survivors of childhood sexual abuse. When I got home, I discovered in it several folded, torn-out notebook-paper pages with handwriting on them. After reading the first line, I realized that this was a survivor's story of being abused by her father. At first, I didn't know what to do. I didn't know if I should keep reading. Following consultations with other researchers on the ethics of the situation, I determined to read it and write about the fact of its discovery while avoiding direct quotation and specific description of the contents.

I suspect the writer left her story in the text deliberately. She likely imagined the next owner(s) as survivors who would discover and read this story. Those future readers would know they weren't alone and would encounter a model of survivor storytelling. While this might not be the kind of book-sharing that Anne Ruggles Gere observes among clubwomen[4] and Daniell describes among Al-Anon women,[5] this passing along of one's own story to the next survivor echoes their insight that sharing texts facilitates sharing individual perspectives in ways that generate community. The writer imagined an empathetic reader receiving her words; the reader would imagine a writer who saw the narrative's recipient as a figure capable of healing. Even though I have read many survivors' stories, holding handwritten pages I didn't expect to encounter struck me in a way I did not anticipate. Words from Marilynne Robinson's novel *Gilead* came to mind: "Precious things have been put in our hands and to do nothing to honor them is to do great harm."[6] Holding this artifact of abuse and healing made tangible ever-present responsibilities.

Faithful Deliberation is the result of those responsibilities. My religious faith as a convert to Christianity, my normative vision as a progressive feminist, and my commitment to deliberative democracy as a scholar and teacher of rhetoric compelled me to support what I perceived as positive developments within US evangelicalism. Witnessing the same arguments unfold over and over again frustrates me, yet an orientation toward deliberative democracy compels me to remain engaged. Witnessing moments where promising shifts occur within enclaves and across community lines fuels my determination and hope.

FAITHFUL DELIBERATION

Introduction

From Proverbs of Ashes to Invention for Faithful Deliberation

> Your maxims are proverbs of ashes;
> your defenses are defenses of clay.
> —**Job 13:12**

In the cause of wellness, some feminist theologians have drawn from the biblical book of Job to name the theological-cultural problems that both justify trauma and prevent action to address it. Following their lead, I begin with Job, literature of ancient wisdom that explores issues of divine justice and human suffering. Readers encounter a story about God granting Satan permission to test the faith of the title figure, a religiously observant and highly moral person. In a single day, Job's livestock and fields are devastated through disaster and theft, his servants are murdered by thieves or killed by fire from the sky, and his children are killed in a violent wind.[1] Job is then beset with physical ailments.[2] After these calamities unfold, Job sits with friends who have sought him out, keeping silence for seven days as Job grieves. When Job begins a mournful lament, his friends reply with traditional theological assertions. Various explanations of Job's sufferings and his responses to those explanations constitute the bulk of the text. Job's interlocutors present, for instance, claims about the righteousness of God, the sinfulness of those who suffer, the release from pain that will come by repenting of sin and simply trusting in the Lord, and the inevitable improvement of circumstances with time's passage.[3] Zophar the Naamathite says to Job, "You will surely forget your trouble, recalling it only as waters gone by. Life will be brighter than noonday, and darkness will become like morning."[4] Not in itself a terrible sentiment, these words might not top the list of insights to share following a friend's loss of everything he valued and virtually everyone he loved. Deployed in this moment, such wisdom might actually compound the trauma—that is, the overwhelming experience that leaves a person without a stable sense of self or a way to understand the experience.[5] Rejecting Zophar's advice, meant perhaps more to quiet Job's lamentation than to comfort him, Job responds with a speech that includes the epigraph above.

While one who long endures trouble without complaint is said to "have the patience of Job," this common expression, perhaps more indebted to another biblical text than to Job itself,[6] captures the popular imagination around this character as a paragon of endless endurance in the midst of suffering. However, Job's own words resist ready-made answers to the problem of pain and stock depictions of him as the silently suffering servant. He hears these defenses of God as platitudes offering death and brokenness: "proverbs of ashes" and "defenses of clay."[7] In this moment, these statements function not as sources of healing but as clichés for shortcutting the process of meaning-making. Beyond arguing with friends and with God,[8] Job also charges God as cruel,[9] unjust, and unloving.[10] Job's anger and grief are unrestrained.[11] Eliphaz attempts to justify Job's suffering by appealing to God's divine justice: "Consider now: Who, being innocent, has ever perished? Where were the upright ever destroyed?" and "Blessed is the one whom God corrects; so do not despise the discipline of the Almighty."[12] When God finally addresses Job and his conversation partners, the divine expresses anger toward Job's friends because of their stock language about suffering and sin: God "said to Eliphaz the Temanite, 'I am angry with you and your two friends, because you have not spoken the truth about me, as my servant Job has. . . . My servant Job will pray for you, and I will accept his prayer and not deal with you according to your folly. You have not spoken the truth about me, as my servant Job has.'"[13] Even as God proceeds to address Job in grand and poetic language about the vast nature of creation and Job's place in it, the divine refrains from directly answering Job's specific charges. Indeed, perhaps that is the wisdom: No direct response adequately answers the reality of suffering and trauma. And yet, God's reply let Job know he was heard. Somebody was listening. The God who hears also appears to favor expressions of anger and instances of vigorously emotional deliberation over platitudes; the divine condemns trauma-minimizing, victim-blaming commonplaces.

Attending to this divinely sanctioned tradition of deliberation about trauma and religious commonplaces, I argue that, just before and following the mainstreaming of the #MeToo movement for abuse survivors, a number of women prominent within evangelical circles undertook theologically reflective invention to promote a form of enclave deliberation I call "faithful deliberation." Deliberation involves interlocuters who have a sense that they mutually participate in a shared reality engaging in reciprocal listening so as to make decisions and take actions, often across lines of difference. Enclaves are groups of "the relatively like-minded."[14] Invention for faithful deliberation, then, involves practices of thinking, reflecting, storytelling, and acting within an enclave that might foster community-internal change through a recommitment to shared values. The inventive work identified in the case study chapters that follow promoted enclave deliberation about appropriate responses to the discourses surrounding sexual and domestic violence.

This deliberation emerged against a background steeped in commonplaces that reinforce the rape culture endemic to the dominant US public sphere and the purity culture that circulates within some evangelical communities. A descriptive label generated by feminist activists and theorists, "rape culture" names those attitudes and practices that work to trivialize sexual trauma and normalize violence.[15] "Purity culture" names those practices and beliefs that reinforce religious norms related to sexuality and gender, deeply racialized norms shaped by an inclination toward nostalgia for the virtues of piety, purity, domesticity, and submissiveness that characterized the nineteenth-century cult of true womanhood. In keeping with this historical vision, recent iterations of evangelical subculture came to define women's purity as a supposed defense against men's sexual advances. As sexual gatekeepers responsible for not stimulating male desires, women should dress and behave modestly.[16] Operating from an all-or-nothing view that configures sexual activity as contamination, purity culture perceives women's bodies and experiences as shameful. Given the vaunted status of virginity within this framework, mixed with an all-or-nothing view of sex that often fails to distinguish between coercion and consent, survivors' contexts shape their experiences of shame and self-blame.

Significantly, much religious rhetoric works in the wake of sexual violence to silence, dismiss, ignore, or minimize trauma. There are surely examples enough of Christian aggressors quoting scripture to justify their abuse, but certain commonplaces within white evangelical subculture constrain members' compassion and action. If a notion of purity that conflates violence and sex holds a privileged place within evangelicalism, then staying silent about harassment preserves the survivor's status within a church community. When a religious leader, such as a pastor, a *man* after God's own heart (the gendered language is intentional here), takes no action following reports of abuse by congregants, it is assumed that this clearly esteemed figure with proximity to God and the divinely authoritative words of scripture is doing the right thing, and not simply silencing survivors to preserve a congregation's reputation. These silences, forced and enforced, indicate the obstacles that faithful deliberators face and the stakes their arguments involve.

Rape and purity cultures molded the rhetorical terrain that faithful deliberators navigated as they inventively reconfigured what I, following the lead of feminist theologians, refer to as "proverbs of ashes": theologically inflected commonplaces that minimize trauma and normalize violence. This language, of course, comes from Job. Employing this vocabulary and opening with Job act as gestures of accountability to the community whose rhetoric I analyze: contemporary, predominantly white evangelicalism. Grounding discourse in scripture is an important literacy practice among many evangelicals, and it can establish ethos. In common parlance, I want them to know that "I read my Bible." Dwelling with Job also locates my work alongside that of feminist theologians and ministers who use this text to call attention to the intersection of religion with discourses of sexual and domestic violence. By rejecting religious justifications of traumatic events, Job offered inspiration for Rita Nakashima Brock and Rebecca Ann Parker's project in *Proverbs of Ashes: Violence, Redemptive Suffering, and the Search for What Saves Us*. They share stories of interpersonal violence justified through appeals to scripture or divine providence, emphasize domestic and sexual violence done to women in the church, and reflect theologically to challenge religious positions that are accepting of gendered and racialized violence.

More broadly, Brock and Parker find a particular theological concept implicated in many justifications of trauma, a concept that is also at the heart of Kenneth Burke's theorizing about rhetoric through the lens of Christian tradition: the explanation of Jesus of Nazareth's death as a substitutionary atonement for the sins of humanity. In this theological stance, which is widely subscribed to by Christians within many denominations, Jesus suffered and died in the place of humanity so as to restore divine order. Jesus's death became, variously, a ransom paid to the forces of evil, a satisfaction of God's own divine order, a manifestation of moral love through sacrifice, or a penal substitution. Applied to human relationships and systems, atonement theology has worked to sacralize sacrifice in ways that consecrate ongoing suffering—that is, suffering serves as a divine test or a preparation for later blessings, likely after death, while shoring up existing hierarchies. When Brock and Parker critique the suffering-justifying functions of atonement theology, they are not alone.

Other contextual theologians offer similar evaluations, such as some womanist perspectives informed by the lived experience, history, and cultural practices of Black women. Delores Williams contends that focusing on Jesus's suffering and death on the cross as the (or even *a*) saving event historically encouraged accommodation to, and justification of, unjust conditions, such as the forced sexual exploitation of Black women in slavery and their enduring labor exploitation.[17] Fellow womanist theologian JoAnne Marie Terrell concurs that associating divine sacrifice with human systems risks sacralizing differential distributions of suffering. However, Terrell argues for the salvific power of the cross and Jesus's blood—and, indeed, the blood of all the unjustly killed, such as the many victims of domestic violence—not by their status as sacrifices but by creating sacramental witnesses of the living who reflect on "how they exercised or did not exercise their moral and creative agency."[18] In contrast to these assessments, a belief in Jesus's death on the cross as an atoning sacrifice (i.e., crucicentrism) is a historically defining feature of evangelicalism, though perhaps a less emphasized feature.[19] Despite these divergent readings of the cross, feminist and womanist assessments of religiously supported violence provide guidance for thinking about and developing rhetorical theory based on instances of evangelicals' inventive theological reflection for deliberative purposes.

I follow in the tradition of building rhetorical theory from religious rhetorics generally and from feminist theological engagements with Job specifically. Burke memorably articulated his logological description of how human language and symbolic action operate through an assumed analogical relationship to theological language. His analysis takes the atonement on the cross as a given within Western Christianity, the religious tradition upon which he theorizes. Drawing on feminist and womanist theology, scholar of rhetoric Kristi Maddux observes how Burke's logological account, which views sacrificial atonement as an inescapable impulse in human symbolic systems, minimizes human agency by limiting the available responses to injustice. Rather than imagining the supposedly restorative violence of sacrificial atonement to necessarily follow violations of orderly systems (human or divine), Maddux proposes "recommitment to core values" as an agency-affirming and theological alternative to a sacrifice-oriented rhetorical order; she cites the Hebrew prophets' recurring calls for a return to the righteous path and Jesus's way of life, which championed reconciliation (i.e., another kind of return) over a system of exacting retribution.[20] This focus on values and practices similarly resonates with Williams's focus on Jesus's life of ministry as salvific and with Terrell's view of the cross as redemptive when it promotes reflection and action. Values recommitment as an exercise of agency—especially in the face of violence and injustice—is at the center of this book.

In the following section, I define rhetorical invention for faithful deliberation as an exercise in values recommitment within evangelical enclaves. The next three sections present terms that are key to understanding my analysis of the case studies. Then, I explain the feminist rhetorical ethics of hope and care that guides my analysis of theologically conservative women's reflective invention. In chapter 1, I provide a brief overview of the history of discursive rules for deliberation in White Christian America. In chapters 2 through 5, I present the case studies of invention for the faithful deliberation described.

INVENTION FOR FAITHFUL DELIBERATION WITHIN EVANGELICALISM

The foundational canon of classical rhetoric, invention traditionally entailed collecting topics, terms, and arguments in common use. Sharon Crowley advocates this orientation to invention within political environments shaped by affective attachments to reactionary religious discourse. Despite championing invention as a form of improvising with common language (particularly within potentially contentious circumstances), Crowley ultimately laments her self-perceived inability to invent paths toward productive conversation between an imagined liberal, secular public and participants in evangelical subculture.[21] Searching for such paths, Jeffrey Ringer finds that evangelical millennials can approach argument with an everyday creativity that resembles invention: socially situated improvisation in light of traditions and changing circumstances. Ringer draws on Peter Simonson's description of invention as "*generating rhetorical materials*," a distributed process that involves forging new formulations from extant materials.[22] Invention for enclave deliberation, then, describes the contextually engaged process of generating rhetorical materials, with special attention to shared traditions, in order to aid decision-making and practical action through community-internal discussion.

I examine enclave deliberation through case studies of the rhetorical invention that women in, or long-associated with, evangelicalism practiced as they forwarded arguments about fellow evangelicals' responses to sexual and domestic violence. These arguments took place in social media posts, blog entries, published interviews, news commentaries, victim impact statements, petitions, and other genres. The inventive practices I identified include the following:

- employing ethos-dependent values articulation to disentangle potentially competing commitments through a costly rhetorical grace;
- casuistically tightening the concept of forgiveness to promote new actions;
- appealing to denomination-specific traditions and values as a rhetoric of reconciliation that maintains community bonds while also pursuing reform; and
- composing archives of abuse and healing through an invitational rhetoric that fosters solidarity (i.e., fellowship) with survivors.

I also understand these practices as emerging from a history of Christian discursive rules, community boundaries, and alternative responses at the intersections of gender, sexuality, and race. The four practices that occurred within evangelical-to-other-evangelical deliberative discourse will be of interest to scholars of rhetoric for at least two reasons. First, they provide further opportunities to test Catherine M. Pavia's recent assertion that religious enclaves hold important "possibilit[ies] for civic and critical work."[23] As more or less insular spaces, enclaves and the discourses that circulate within them are often viewed as having relatively limited reach beyond their own boundaries. Furthermore, absent norms to mitigate in-group thinking, enclaves tend toward factionalism and polarization.[24] Instances of enclave deliberation where genuine differences exist among participants, such as the instances examined in chapters 2 through 5, provide occasions to understand what reach such deliberations might achieve.

Second, by locating these attendant case studies as recent moments in longer US public and evangelical histories of deliberation involving gender, sexuality, and race, I bring into view some of the ways enclaves and the dominant public sphere interact. Discussions of sexual and domestic violence have been hyper-visible in the general public and in religious communities in recent years. Although these issues periodically arise as central concerns within evangelical and mainstream platforms, public silence had until recently been the most common evangelical position. A 2014 survey conducted by the evangelical group LifeWay Research found that Protestant senior pastors seldom preached about domestic or sexual violence: 42 percent "rarely" or "never" and 22 percent approximately once a year.[25] Even as these sensitive topics are surely difficult to address in sermons, Sunday school classes, Bible studies, and elsewhere, conditions are changing. As a solidarity movement for survivors of sexual abuse initiated by social justice organizer Tarana Burke in 2006 on the social media platform MySpace and popularized by actor Alyssa Milano in 2017 on Twitter, the #MeToo movement gave rise to parallel developments in religious contexts: #ChurchToo and #SilenceIsNotSpiritual. Many evangelicals today prioritize more deliberation and healing rhetoric.

Long a cultural mainstay within the United States, evangelicalism is diverse. While not religiously oppressed, many evangelicals still grapple with their late-twentieth-century loss of proximity to cultural hegemony. Mainstream and academic representations of their communities frequently fail to adequately capture their imaginative efforts, their lifeworld's texture, and their rhetorical projects. Consequently, they often come across as cartoonish or conspiratorial characters.[26] Moreover, rhetorical studies scholars observe the difficulty of even defining evangelical.[27] Historically, evangelicals were Christians who subscribed to a high sense of biblical authority, promoted sharing religious faith through language and activism, emphasized the life-transforming experience of coming to faith, and highlighted that salvation occurs through God in Jesus Christ's death by crucifixion.[28] Anthropological research highlights the role of feeling and affect, particularly intimacy, within evangelicalism. Evangelicalism demonstrates a religious-historical imagination oriented toward an "intimate, relational spirituality."[29] Emotional practices foster evangelicals' feelings of closeness with God.[30] This intimate spiritual movement is not, however, a conflict-free zone. Historian Molly Worthen defines US evangelicals through the recurring tensions that arise as they strive to blend seemingly competing religious, emotional, and intellectual authorities. These conflicts produced a community ethos defined by a "crisis of authority" that arises "from a deep disagreement over what the Bible means, a sincere desire to uphold the standards of modern reason alongside God's word—and the defensive reflexes that outsiders' skepticism provoke."[31] Despite this defensiveness, many evangelicals deeply engage with dominant cultural trends, developing "an increasingly professionalized ethos and an infrastructure wired to consecrate culture wherever possible."[32] This cultural consecration serves as just one of many ways evangelical enclaves and the larger public interact with each other, presaging the way #MeToo helped reshape evangelical communities.

Despite evangelicalism's theological and political diversity, both historically and recently, affect-laden histories of social, cultural, and political alliances contribute to public perceptions of these religious communities as conservative and reactionary. These histories are shaped by "White Christian America" and the "White Christian Strategy." The former describes the long-standing cultural hegemony of white mainline and evangelical Protestantism in the United States and the social institutions built primarily to benefit their members; the latter describes a political alliance between conservative politicians and religious leaders to harness white Christian anxiety about increasing diversity during the second half of the twentieth century.[33] Recall that the majority of voting white Christians cast ballots for Trump, with a supermajority of voting white evangelicals doing so. Religious Right arguments in the 1970s were not static but evolved through strategic (if idiosyncratic) collaborations among evangelical leaders, corporate interests, conservative politicians, and activists; these networks framed as morally superior those arguments that supported business interests, resisted federal government-enforced school desegregation, defunded welfare opportunities, and opposed the legal recognition of women's rights.[34] Participants in these networks imagined themselves as preserving both religious and cultural traditions in the midst of social change. Echoing much of this narrative, Randall Balmer identifies the mobilizing issue for politically engaged evangelicals as resistance to forced private school desegregation. He laments the ironies of evangelical subculture's selective traditionalism, which neglects evangelical histories of activism for many progressive causes, including women's political autonomy.[35] The women whose arguments I analyze similarly lament a perceived inconsistent engagement with Christian values in conversations and policies related to assault, abuse, and harassment.

Significantly, deliberation about how to enact Christian values may involve reinventing proverbs of ashes, which means working with commonplace statements, ideas, and verses of scripture that faithful deliberators may hold as true, as dear, and as sacred. What they might view as otherwise beneficial Christian commonplaces become proverbs of ashes depending on the context or on what other ideas are tightly bundled together with a given expression. Christian survivors of sexual assault may well believe in, for instance, the imperative to forgive, but for another Christian to invoke that idea in a specific moment (such as when survivors disclose their assault or seek counseling) may result in further harm. In this way, proverbs of ashes function in a manner comparable to essentialist and universalizing feminist claims about the nature of women's shared political situation. For example, even if a particular person held as true the notion that *rape is a political act* or *sisterhood is global*, if deployed without contextual awareness, such phrases may ring hollow, doing more harm than good—promoting transwomen's exclusion from global sisterhood or relying on racist tropes in a political analysis of rape. Several relationships shape the possibilities for reinventing proverbs of ashes and for the prospects of values recommitment: the relationship of evangelical enclave deliberation to the public sphere, of rape culture to purity culture, and of trauma and healing to rhetoric and deliberation.

THE PUBLIC SPHERE, ENCLAVE DELIBERATION, AND THE COMMON GOOD

Evangelical enclaves exist in dynamic relationship to the dominant public sphere. Jürgen Habermas describes the emergence of the eighteenth-century European bourgeois public as "the sphere of private people come together as a public . . . to engage them [public authorities] in debate over the general rules governing relations."[36] An ideal emerged about a space where people could engage in discussion of shared concerns in a rational-critical way without succumbing to factionalism. Of course, this Enlightenment-birthed liberal vision is not the only model of the public sphere.[37] Many theorists have complicated and extended Habermas's public sphere with accounts of multiplicity, affect, positionality, and discursive forces. When Michael Warner charts the general features establishing *a*—rather than *the*—public, he argues that a "*public is poetic world making.*"[38] By "poetic," Warner explains, "I mean not just that it is self-organizing, a kind of entity created by its own discourse, or even that this space of circulation is taken to be a social entity, but that in order for this to happen all discourse or performance addressed to a public must characterize the world in which it attempts to circulate and it must attempt to realize that world through address."[39] Evangelical world making occurs in relationship with—sometimes in contradistinction to—the dominant public's lifeworld. Reciprocally, evangelicalism now and historically has informed the dominant public sphere.

The US public sphere is shaped by, and evangelical world making occurs in light of, a historically contingent lifeworld that includes what moral philosopher Charles Taylor terms "a secular age." Religion within the US context is increasingly understood as a private affair (i.e., as separate from public life); religious faith is not the default stance but only one option.[40] The "nones," a fast-growing population, affiliate with no faith tradition and do not identify as religious.[41] Writing and rhetorical scholarship often demonstrates a perceived incommensurability between strong conservative religious commitments and equally strong commitments to discourse across lines of difference and to intellectual investigations.[42] Such assumptions divest much religious discourse of its potential contributions to the search for the common good within and across diverse constituencies, a central concern in deliberative models of the public sphere. Consequently, it might seem counterintuitive to look toward a conservative religious enclave for insights into contemporary deliberation. However, writing and rhetorical scholarship increasingly acknowledges how religious traditions provide resources for undertaking the kinds of intellectual, reflective, critical, and productive work valued within the discipline and for orienting the public sphere toward robust democratic deliberation.[43] In short, within an increasingly secular public sphere, religion—even absolutist and largely in-group-focused religion—can still hold value for scholars of rhetoric when religion contributes to deliberation for the common good.

While political theorists and rhetoricians variously describe deliberative discourse, pursuit of the common good is a central feature of—or at least a defining alibi for—a deliberative public sphere. Despite how much this concept might sound like the ghost of liberal publics past where all participants would set aside their particularities to pursue the obviously right course of action, determining the common good within an ambitiously democratic arrangement breaks down notions of liberal universalism and instrumental rationality. As Patricia Roberts-Miller observes, this "is the paradox" of the Habermasian project: "The more the public sphere became democratized, the less it could be an area of rational-critical argument. That is[,] . . . ratiocination and participation are necessarily in conflict."[44] Discursive expansion appears endemic to an increasingly democratic society: More participation means more kinds of arguments. However, democracies might end up preserving a common sense that merely restates existing hierarchies, like hyper-skepticism of women's testimony about assault or accepting an expanding law enforcement response to domestic violence without addressing police and state violence. Even as democracies and deliberative arrangements in themselves may not achieve just remedies to long-standing inequities, counterpublics increase the number of available argumentative options by placing taken for granted ideas into public contest.[45] For example, nineteenth-century evangelical women challenged ubiquitous sexual double standards that limited women's life options, and civil rights workers testified to the sexualized brutality they encountered in southern jails years long before the modern anti-rape movement emerged.

To achieve something other than simple bargaining, prematurely claiming consensus, using the embodied authority of lived experience in over-universalizing and expressive ways, or allowing privileged people's fantastical (if genuinely believed) claims of oppression to circulate without scrutiny, deliberation must include a number of conditions. It concerns itself with practical action for the future, with what decisions a community should make.[46] Deliberation involves argumentation that features reciprocity through mutual listening and response informed by that listening,[47] intersubjectivity through access to a sense of a shared social world,[48] and a recognition of the value of narrative as well as emotion.[49] Roberts-Miller puts the proposition of deliberative democratic discourse starkly: "The question is not whether or not it will go well, but whether or not it will go at all."[50] There is no guarantee.

Even though deliberation is typically understood as an exercise occurring among diverse constituencies with differing views, deliberative rhetoric also occurs within enclaves. These groups may be more or less tightly insulated. Enclaves form around many elements: opinions, structural locations (e.g., occupations), and identities.[51] Despite relatively high levels of homogeneity within such groups, "enclave deliberation" understood as "discussion among like-minded people" occurs.[52] Enclave deliberation presents challenges, prominent among them "groupthink" and group polarization. With groupthink, preserving community cohesion becomes paramount and includes an overestimation of group rightness and unanimity.[53] Group polarization involves the development of more extreme positions within the enclave.[54] While a group's "affective ties can be expected to diminish dissent" within an enclave, in-group deliberation does not "automatically" intensify an enclave's insularity and extremism.[55] Predominantly white US evangelicalism constitutes one identity-based enclave engaged in deliberation about sexual and domestic violence.

Religious adherents engaged in deliberation certainly view their traditions as containing resources that would help them identify the common good and conditions impeding that good. Noting the historical connections between liberation theology and critical pedagogy, Shari Stenberg suggests that religious discourses may aid critical reflection on injustice.[56] Although religious language directed at nonreligious or mixed audiences is sometimes too packed with insider-speak,[57] when deliberation occurs within a relatively like-minded group, shared vocabularies, values, traditions, and histories serve as important assets. As faithful deliberators reevaluate common beliefs, attitudes, and language surrounding sexual trauma and domestic violence, they draw on shared points of reference within the broader public and within their enclave. In so doing, they navigate discursive terrain shaped by the rape culture of the dominant US public sphere and the pronounced purity culture in some strands of evangelicalism.

RAPE CULTURE AND SEXUAL PURITY

The term "rape culture" signifies attitudes and practices that work to trivialize sexual trauma and normalize violence.[58] The term first appears in the early to mid-1970s, associated with New York Radical Feminists, the DC Rape Crisis Center, and Prisoners Against Rape, Inc.[59] Susan Brownmiller is credited with redefining rape as a political issue about power rather than an idiosyncratic, individual, or sexual problem. Rape culture practices include blaming victims for their assault, doubting survivors' stories, forgiving aggressors with ease, and asserting that only certain women are sexually victimized.[60] Examples include questioning victims about what they were wearing, why they were where violence happened, what happened during an assault, and why an attack took place. Even the terms that name violence themselves function as sites of knowledge, resistance, and struggle. Indeed, "rape," "victim," and "survivor" are evolving labels.[61]

Important from a rhetorical standpoint when addressing rape culture commonplaces is the just-world hypothesis, a cognitive heuristic or mental shortcut that leads a person to rationalize events—positive or negative—as the consequences that rightly follow a person's choices or personal characteristics. In short, good people who do good things are rewarded, and bad people who do bad things are punished. First theorized by Melvin Lerner, research documents this phenomenon in many contexts, including when evaluating accounts of rape and intimate-partner violence.[62] Consequently, as rape culture stringently regulates women's behavior and circumscribes social responses to violence, a rationalizing cognitive bias justifies and minimizes trauma. Situating discourse about sexual violence within this cultural context is important, because survivors' experiences alone fail to define trauma. Trauma also involves the perceptions of "others, directly or indirectly, and the extent to which others are able to listen empathetically to a survivor's testimony."[63] In other words, the social and political context shapes opportunities for healing.

Given that patriarchy, racism, classism, homophobia, transphobia, ableism, and other systemic forms of oppression shape the reception and circulation of survivors' stories (indeed, work to define who counts as a survivor), rape culture mitigates against the reception of survivors' narratives and limits what kinds of social change survivors might achieve. When the stories of domestic violence survivors are "examined against a masculine epistemological framework, the woman's narrative is perceived as fragmented, disconnected, incoherent, invisible."[64] Rape survivors' discourse has been variously banned, misunderstood, and disbelieved; many survivors find their accounts delegitimized.[65] Existing structures amplify problems for women of color and LGBTQ+ survivors.[66] For example, when a lesbian raped by her partner calls a rape crisis hotline, the counselor may repeatedly default to masculine pronouns for the aggressor; when she calls a hotline for anti-LGBTQ+ violence, the respondent may not be equipped for this interpersonal violence.[67] Feminist activists have long made gendered violence a key issue, and anti-rape activists have sought to revise the reception of survivors' stories.[68] Despite these long-standing efforts, many survivors still meet with wariness.

In fact, survivors of sexual and domestic violence may find healing undermined in precisely the spaces where they seek it. Domestic violence victims sometimes report feeling stigma when they encounter helping professionals, including judicial, law enforcement, and mental health representatives.[69] Many Black and transgender women experience daily interactions with the police as sites of sexualized violence.[70] Although therapy promotes important forms of healing, it may not provide ways to alter everyday patterns of individualized thinking and language that work to shore up rape culture.[71] That is, a therapeutic focus on the individual may end up reinforcing common shame-inducing and depoliticizing beliefs. In attempts to nurture positive self-regard, psychiatric practices may actually foster victim-blaming.[72] Turning to religious and church communities may likewise prove nonrestorative for survivors. In religious communities, where survivors might hope to find comfort, support, and advocacy, they are as likely to find rape culture attitudes blended with theological sentiments of the sort expressed by Job's friends. For example, an assault is God's punishment for misdeeds, God's will or plan, merely a cross or burden to bear, or something to forgive because that's what good Christians do.

Within evangelicalism, impediments to creating survivor-sensitive healing spaces arise in connection with racialized cultural preservation work that some community participants and their networks perform around gender and sexuality. For example, from 1979 to 1993, the SBC, a denomination formed from a split over slavery in the lead-up to the Civil War, adopted numerous resolutions stringently defining gender roles—especially the roles of women.[73] During roughly the same period, a variety of efforts designed to prevent the recognition of LGBTQ+ people's rights were spearheaded by evangelical leadership.[74] Beginning in the late 1970s, evangelical activists began in earnest trying to restrict access to abortion, a campaign focus that emerged in connection with the larger goals of promoting a strong social order and of countering the 1960s and 1970s sexual revolution.[75] Balmer ties these efforts to nostalgia for the "cult of true womanhood."[76] Barbara Welter uses this term to name the interrelated operations of piety, purity, domesticity, and submissiveness in nineteenth-century periodicals' construction of womanhood. In tandem with prevalent stereotypes of Black women's insatiable sexual desire as jezebels, this regime also defined true womanhood as the province of white women.

A late-twentieth-century manifestation of this sexual, gendered, and racial nostalgia was purity culture. Dianna Anderson argues, "Sexual purity has become the one means by which the evangelical church separates itself from 'the world.'"[77] Within evangelicalism, purity culture regulates adherence to culturally prescribed gender norms—especially norms for women. Indeed, purity culture amplifies the general double standard in US culture that more stringently regulates women's sexuality in contrast to men's while also configuring (white) women as less desiring of sex than men. The normative vision for sexuality within a purity culture paradigm reserves all expressions of desire and physical intimacy for heterosexual, monogamous marriage between two cisgender people of the opposite sex.[78] This purity culture vision finds support from a variety of social practices and popular culture sources that blend sexuality with rigorously enforced, naturalized, and racialized gender roles, roles tied to religiosity and the binary organization of private and public spheres. A generation of evangelicals received instruction in this purity-oriented sexuality through virginity pledges, statements committing the signatory to abstain from sex until marriage; purity balls, formal ceremonies with wedding imagery where young women accompanied by their fathers commit themselves to abstinence; promise rings, tokens worn as symbols of a commitment to abstinence; curricula (e.g., True Love Waits); and popular books and media.

Important in institutionalizing and widely disseminating this perspective was Joshua Harris, who published *I Kissed Dating Goodbye* in 1997. He would be professionally mentored within the church community at the center of what Rachael Denhollander refers to "as one of the worst, if not *the* worst, instances of evangelical cover-up of sexual abuse."[79] At twenty-one, Harris, the son of a major Christian homeschooling proponent, published his teen relationship advice book and found a mentor in Sovereign Grace Churches (SGC) founder C. J. Mahaney. From 2004 to 2015, Harris pastored the denomination's longtime flagship church, taking over Mahaney's old position. During Harris's last few years there, his church and the SGC denomination faced lawsuits alleging sexual abuse and cover-ups dating to the 1980s and 1990s and the sexual abuse criminal conviction of a former church volunteer from roughly that same time.

The years prior to #MeToo as a public-altering cultural force witnessed an ongoing reevaluation of Harris's book and its legacy. When Harris stepped down from his pastorate and announced his intention to go to seminary in 2015, he contributed to this reevaluation. The summer of 2016 saw the author seek feedback on social media about how people had been influenced by his work. The Toast, an online feminist humor site, hosted a roundtable with women affected negatively by the book. Then, in July, a digital conversation took place under the label #KissShameBye. Later, Emily Joy, a cofounder of the #ChurchToo effort to call attention to abuse within evangelicalism, used the #KissShameBye label to express anger at how her experiences failed to mirror the purity-proffered ideal. In 2018, Harris issued a statement that his thinking about dating and sexuality had changed and asked that publication of the book be discontinued. In July 2019, Harris announced that he was getting a divorce and leaving Christianity and apologized for the harm his work had done, especially to LGBTQ+ people. It is important to note that one of The Toast's founders, Danny M. Lavery, was instrumental in the 2019 to 2020 process of holding accountable his father, John Ortberg Jr., the evangelical pastor who resigned from Menlo Church after it became clear that Ortberg knew that another one of his sons, John Ortberg III, had confessed to an attraction to minors and Ortberg Jr. had nonetheless failed to remove Ortberg III from a church volunteer position that gave him access to children.[80] The interrelated operations of rape and purity cultures within general public and enclaved discourse, along with community and institutional preservationism, have contributed much in the way of trauma and shame.

TRAUMA, AFFECT, AND RHETORIC AS HEALING

Against this rape and purity culture background that normalizes violence and delegitimizes survivors' own experiences, faithful deliberators generate trauma-informed arguments that facilitate forms of healing. Trauma has a complicated intellectual history, filled with fits and starts, forgettings and reclamations, individual figures and collective movements. Definitions vary widely, but they tend to acknowledge that trauma involves overwhelming experiences that are difficult to fully integrate into one's view of the world or sense of self.[81] More generally, intellectual histories of trauma observe the relationship between trauma study, war, and the aftermath of violence.[82] As psychiatrist Judith Herman seeks to historicize clinical understandings of trauma, she provides a feminist approach that links the violence of war with the violence of sexual trauma, and she positions trauma within the context of political and social movements: "Not until the women's liberation movement of the 1970s was it recognized that the most common post-traumatic stress disorders are those not of men in war but of women in civilian life."[83] Indeed, appeals to a framework of rape as war commonly appeared in statements by feminist and anti-violence activists. Drawing connections between social change movements and combat contexts enables an understanding of sexual violence as a form of collective trauma.

With Ann Cvetkovich, I view the sources of trauma and their remedies as "diffuse, . . . opening up the need to change social structures more broadly rather than just fix individual people."[84] Sexual trauma and its related affects have contributed to the production of diverse cultural material. Cultural and rhetorical productions informed by trauma may contribute to forms of healing that resist the familiar problem of pressuring survivors into any specific developmental process, the conventions of therapeutic self-disclosure, or the teleology of a whole or fully healed self.

This cultural publics approach opens space for rhetoric responding to trauma and its discourses, such as Beth Moore's social media writing. Writing and rhetoric have certainly contributed to therapeutic and other healing approaches.[85] However, Daphne Desser considers trauma and healing in relationship to "the rhetorical dimensions of civic discourse and practical political action."[86] Her rhetorical approach to writing and trauma captures some of the healing sponsored by faithful deliberation. Resisting quick movements toward a superficial closure, the strong pulls of a dominant ideology to appropriate healing into narratives of a well-functioning community, and binary distinctions between writing as a healing activity and writing as a political resource, Desser argues that critique through rhetorical analysis and action through rhetorical practices can contribute to healing.[87] This framework resembles the rhetorical program employed in the case studies I consider throughout this book: The faithful deliberators resisted the premature closure of easy forgiveness, the call to a superficial reconciliation, the forced preservation of community cohesion, and the idea that advocating change means a departure from a primary mission (from ministry or evangelism) or from orthodox theology. The position Desser advances, configuring rhetorical activism as a source of healing, resonates with Cvetkovich's claim that "trauma cultures are actually doing the work of therapy."[88] I view deliberative rhetorics informed by trauma or that respond to trauma discourses as sites of potential healing that co-implicate the affective and the political when rhetors seek to alter feelings, relationships, and typical modes of action within the dominant public or an enclave.

Emotional work is political and social, but the links among oppression, justice, and emotion are complicated. For example, in chapter 4, I describe how longtime SBC leader Paige Patterson told a story in which he advised a woman to stay with her husband despite her disclosing what Patterson characterized as "some abuse," saw her at church with two black eyes, and expressed happiness about the situation because her enduring that abuse caused her husband to follow her to church and accept Jesus. An eighteen-year-old recording of this story, which surfaced several times, eventually provoked change-producing actions in 2018, following the mainstreaming of the #MeToo movement. Emotion plays an important role here in both the preservation of oppressive relations and the pursuit of justice. Patterson encouraged the woman to share in his happiness about a conversion in a way that reinforced a marriage relationship where abuse existed; this is the kind of religious encouragement to sanctify sacrifice that Williams, Terrell, and Brock and Parker critique. While Southern Baptists ultimately found this advice unacceptable, they reached this conclusion only after cultivating increased empathy and solidarity with survivors. Such transformation helps keep in focus the tensions and discrepancies between categories that often serve as tools for organizing the affectively charged terrains of personal and social life: public/private, emotional/intellectual, safe/unsafe, religious/secular. A deliberative orientation within publics and enclaves acknowledges these tensions, allows them to exist without rushing to an ultimate resolution, and engages in reflective reading, writing, speaking, and listening with others about possible courses of action—all while keeping in mind that answers to deliberative questions are tentative, partial, and open to revision. These practices appear throughout my case studies of faithful deliberations.

While reinventing categories for thinking about, and emotional responses to, unjust conditions is not the ultimate arrival of justice, it can be part of the process. For example, Herman describes how as a trauma survivor works through rage-filled fantasies of retaliatory revenge in a supportive environment, these thoughts and feelings may be transformed into a righteous indignation that fuels advocacy for aggressor accountability.[89] Following Sara Ahmed,[90] I accept that injustice involves maintaining certain forms of feeling toward power arrangements that foster traumatic experiences and toward inequitable distributions of suffering, such as advising an abused spouse be a happy long-sufferer. Consequently, rhetorical invention for deliberation that seeks to dismantle hierarchical social relations entails addressing affective life.

One affect that emerges as important in public cultural work by evangelical women generally, and in rhetorical action to address sexual and domestic violence specifically, is shame. According to Kate Bowler, shame is a frequent topic of conversation among evangelical women's conference attendees, and lines from social work researcher Brené Brown's TED Talk on shame "always manage to worm their way into the conclusion."[91] Brown defines shame as feelings of unworthiness that stymie relationships and connections; she addresses shame in connection with personal as well as social dysfunction.[92] For abuse survivors, shame can mean a sense of blame for an assault, negative self-image (sometimes derived from religious concepts of sinfulness or purity), and distrust of bodily/emotional responses.[93] Shame, likewise, receives attention for the productive work it has enabled. Capable of emotionally shaking a person out of unthinking and creating an occasion for reflection, shame is a marker of both interest and its disruptions, which can become sources of cultural production and creativity.[94] Scholars in the humanities, cultural studies, affect studies, and queer theory reveal this reflective and productive capacity through attention to shame-related cultural activity, such as the performative nature of camp and the advocacy of ACT UP. Elspeth Probyn links shame to feelings of intense interest and the perception of others. Shame is thus bound up with an experienced desire, disruption of that desire, and others' perceived and actual reception of that desire.

By "writing shame," Probyn argues that writers "provide an argument against considering expressions of shame as merely a personal affliction."[95] Shari Stenberg applies this framework to sexual assault survivors' social media writing and describes the rhetorical action performed when writing shame: changing survivor relationships to the dominant public and resisting rape culture commonplaces.[96] As participants in an enclave that frequently considers shame as a site for personal reflection and public vulnerability, the faithful deliberators whose work I study reflect on the conditions that enable sexual and domestic violence, critique the shaming that surrounds sexual trauma, and produce new arguments that center—rather than further isolate and shame—survivors.

A FEMINIST RHETORICAL ETHICS OF HOPE AND CARE AND THEOLOGICAL REFLECTION

To analyze the critically reflective, inventive work of faithful deliberators who address trauma discourses within rape and purity cultures, I employ what Jacqueline Jones Royster and Gesa E. Kirsch call a feminist rhetorical "ethics of hope and care."[97] Such an ethics requires a capacity that is simultaneously analytical and imaginative and that links scholarly investigation with practices of accountability to the writers whose work I study. An ethics of hope and care also means patiently dwelling among rhetorical performances without preconceptions that might limit the scope of inquiry by focusing on familiar figures or readily understood goals.[98] Practicing this ethical stance as a researcher blends feeling, thinking, and acting: "The goal with an ethics of hope and caring is to learn to listen and speak, not just with our heads but with our hearts, backbones, and stomachs."[99] Applying an ethics of hope and care to the rhetorical invention for faithful deliberation underway within evangelicalism leads me to pay attention to practices of theological reflection.

Theological reflection occurs in diverse ways, including situated responses to lived experience—how people think, talk, and pray about what happens to them and others. Such reflection may contribute to the disentangling of multiple values, beliefs, and traumas. Both deliberative discourse and healing from trauma rely upon reflective practices, like attentive listening. When survivors and their communities strive "to keep a certain understanding of the world,"[100] trauma may go unacknowledged, without language to name it. Trauma becomes "unclaimed experience" that indicates the porous epistemological boundary between knowledge and uncertainty.[101] As survivors and advocates navigate this boundary and come to voice, "trauma stories" involve a form of sharing that necessitates a particular kind of listening.[102] Listening in response to trauma disclosures not only enables trauma's revelation but also survivors' ability to represent the experience at a remove, or through a "departure" from it, aided by an empathetic other.[103] Consequently, listening serves as an encounter that may support survivors in their healing endeavors. Given that listening to others is foundational to deliberative discourse, efforts to foster deliberation within evangelicalism that begin with carefully attending to the stories and experiences of trauma survivors may contribute to personal and social healing. Religiously conservative women's theological reflection furthers these possibilities for listening and healing within evangelicalism.

When religious adherents think about their beliefs, their views about God, and the relationship of those beliefs and views to life as they experience it, they engage in theological reflection. Such contemplation of experience leads to renewed vitality around the task of making sense of Christian messages within particular circumstances. "Local theology" poses "*new questions*" to analyze the context in which believers live, rejecting "*old answers*" to the concerns raised by contextual analysis and forging "*a new kind of Christian identity.*"[104] Others term this and similar practices "contextual theology."[105] This process describes aspects of the work that Moore, Hatmaker, Denhollander, Prior, and others undertook. They asked anew questions about conservative Christian life, practices, and institutions by centering the perspective of trauma survivors. In a context reconstellated by #MeToo, #ChurchToo, #SilenceIsNotSpiritual, and other campaigns, faithful deliberators rejected previously standard trauma-minimizing commonplaces as defenses for typical practices and attitudes. While the women at the center of this book might not say their Christian identity has changed as a result of their theological reflection, invention, and deliberation, they have certainly worked to renovate Christian institutions and practices.

As I examine instances of religious insiders working for change, I also strive to honor the commitments of religiously conservative women who may or may not claim feminist identities. Charlotte Hogg asks feminist scholars of rhetoric, "Aren't conservative women's rhetorical practices also worthy of study?"[106] My affirmative response is informed by cultural anthropologist Saba Mahmood's account of agency. Since norms are not merely resisted but also diversely inhabited, Mahmood pushes feminist thinkers to examine gender performances that endorse ostensibly nonfeminist agendas and that form subjects who experience flourishing and dignity in ways not readily intelligible within liberal or progressive feminists' normative vision.[107] Religiously conservative women's practices do, indeed, pursue objectives that challenge patriarchal violence and affirm the dignity of those shamed by rape and purity cultures.

CASE STUDIES AND DISCURSIVE RULES

I examine theologically reflective invention to reinvigorate proverbs of ashes and advance faithful deliberation in four case studies, each the focus of a chapter. A long history of discursive rules and community line-drawing informs my analysis of these recent events. Following M. Jacqui Alexander,[108] I understand time as palimpsestic. Like a sheet written on repeatedly with old inscriptions not completely covered over, the past inscribes itself in the practices of the living. Time-as-palimpsest invites an understanding of supposed polarities—religiosity and secularity, preservation and innovation—as scrambled together, not clearly demarcated. Consequently, the first chapter introduces relevant discursive rules, community boundaries, and alternative responses as they have emerged in the history of White Christian America, evangelicalism, counterpublics addressing sexual violence, and the dominant public sphere.

The first case study (chapter 2) examines divergent evangelical responses to Donald Trump's discourses of sexual assault in the historical moment immediately prior to the mainstreaming of the #MeToo movement and relies on theologian Dietrich Bonhoeffer's distinction between "cheap grace" and "costly grace." Through their social media writing in October 2016, Beth Moore and Jen Hatmaker, who were both prominent at the time within evangelical circles, enacted a *costly rhetorical grace* to counter a *cheap rhetorical grace* stemming from proverbs of ashes that permitted misogyny and rape culture to go unchallenged. That is, whereas leaders supportive of an evangelical-Religious Right-Republican establishment used their religious positions to extend a grace that left religious-political alliances intact, Moore and Hatmaker modeled a message of grace that located God's action in solidarity with survivors—a solidarity that might come at the cost of typical alliances, modes of thinking, and patterns of feeling. In addition to leading Living Proof Ministries, Moore, who appears in every chapter, regularly reaches audiences through the Trinity Broadcasting Network broadcasts of her Living Proof Live events. As of August 2020, her Twitter account shows more than 950,000 followers. Moore took to Twitter shortly after the release of Trump's comments with a thread that confronted, without naming, Christian leaders who fail to take seriously stories of sexual assault. At the time, Hatmaker was a bestselling author and a frequent headliner at influential evangelical conferences and had starred as an HGTV miniseries personality. She confronted Trump by name on Facebook, made additional statements indicative of increasingly progressive politics, and experienced major pushback from other evangelical leaders. Employing costly rhetorical grace, these rhetors made Christian values the subject of deliberation, focusing on commonplaces related to sexual violence, forgiveness, and community membership.

In the second case study (chapter 3), I examine how Denhollander and Moore critiqued evangelical Christians' responses to sexual violence by calling for theological reflection on grace and forgiveness. The occasion for their rhetorical action arose from Denhollander's victim impact statement at the criminal sentencing of former USA Gymnastics doctor Larry Nassar on charges of sexual assault against minors and possession of child pornography. Denhollander was one of the first of Nassar's victims to come forward. Both survivors of childhood sexual assault, Moore and Denhollander confront a latent-yet-operative antinomianism. A debated theological position in the history of Christianity, antinomianism here means an understanding of God's forgiving grace as a kind of in-group license entitling Christian abuse aggressors and enablers to human forgiveness. Moore, in a blog post, and Denhollander, in an interview with leading evangelical magazine *Christianity Today*, employed a form of rhetorical-ethical invention I call "casuistic tightening" to facilitate theologically informed deliberation about forgiveness. Rather than casuistically stretching apparent oppositions so that a broader third value might cover them, a well-understood rhetorical practice, Denhollander and Moore tightened or narrowed the larger categories of sin, sinner, grace, and forgiveness, so as to generate more survivor-sensitive responses to abuse.

In the third case study (chapter 4), I articulate the ways Southern Baptist women engaged in denomination-specific enclave deliberation about appropriate responses to comments from a religious leader that appeared to permit domestic violence and to sexualize a teenager. Specifically, this deliberation emerged out of the 2018 controversy involving longtime denominational leader Paige Patterson, an architect of the campaign that resulted in conservative dominance within the SBC. It would be hard to imagine a more institutionally secure figure than former SBC president Patterson. And yet these deliberations resulted in his seminary presidency ouster. The primary materials include two open letters: a blog post by Moore that describes her encounters with misogyny in conservative Christian communities and a collaboratively authored petition designed as a collective expression of Southern Baptist women's concerns over Patterson's advice to abused spouses and his apparent objectification of a teenager. A spokesperson for the collective, Karen Swallow Prior was a longtime English professor at Liberty University (founded by Jerry Falwell and led, until August 2020, by his son Jerry Falwell Jr.). I argue that Moore and these other religiously conservative women employed a robust rhetoric of reconciliation that involves accountability for individuals and social change that confronts violence-enabling discourses. Given that Patterson's controversy-sparking comments had been reported several previous times without incident, #MeToo, #ChurchToo, and #SilenceIsNotSpiritual were changing the public sphere and evangelicalism.

The fourth case study (chapter 5) focuses on Moore's Twitter exchanges with survivors of sexual abuse following an investigative report documenting twenty years of sex crimes involving seven hundred victims abused by 380 SBC-connected pastors, leaders, and volunteers. This chapter also attends to backlash Moore has experienced over a perceived softening of her complementarianism (that is, the belief that men and women each have distinct, divinely ordered natures with different roles in domestic, church, and social affairs) and of her theology of lesbian, gay, bisexual, transgender, and queer (LGBTQ+) sexuality. At stake in these rhetorical situations is the theological notion of "fellowship." Drawing on insights about the emotionally connected healing that can occur in groups that mutually exchange interpretations of traumatic experiences and on Moore's thinking about fellowship, I articulate how Moore initiated a Twitter thread that came to function as a widening fellowship of survivors and advocates established through an archive of abuse and healing. This moment of connection contrasts with moves to construct a narrowing fellowship of believers through doctrinal line-drawing that reinforced conservative orthodoxy around gender, sexuality, and race that policed acceptable expressions of evangelical beliefs.

The faithful deliberators in these case studies assert the existence of absolute truths as revealed through their sacred scriptures. Likewise, they describe personal experiences with those truths and how their traditions shape them. While they challenge perceived misapplications or subordinations of ultimate truths derived from scripture, faithful deliberators mostly see themselves as working within existing frameworks for thinking, believing, and acting. Their rhetorical action, rather than breaking bonds, demonstrates and reaffirms community commitments. Their task is not creating an entirely new system, nor rejecting all previous expressions of evangelicalism, but rhetorically inventing to support deliberation aimed at a recommitment to core values.

1

Naming Those Sins

A Brief History of Rules, Boundaries, and Responses

"We especially deplore the intimate acquaintance and promiscuous conversation of *females* with regard to things 'which ought not to be named,' by which that modesty and delicacy, which is the charm of domestic life, and which constitutes the true influence of woman, is consumed". . . . This is a false position.

—Sarah Grimké, "Social Intercourse of the Sexes"

I love Jesus. I love Scripture. I like people. I like diversity. My interactions and follows do not equal endorsements or reflections of doctrinal alignment.

—Beth Moore

To understand contemporary evangelical women's invention for faithful deliberation as reformulations of extent traditions, this chapter historicizes the current moment by examining episodes from the history of White Christian America. Turning to selected moments that act as precedents for twenty-first-century faithful deliberators' calls for a recommitment to core values, as well as the resistance they encountered, readers will notice that US Christian deliberation about sexual violence, trauma, and affect is nothing new. Affective regimes intended to shame and silence did not begin with twentieth-century rape and purity cultures; deliberations to address trauma and facilitate healing did not commence with #MeToo; white Christian institutional resistance to the changes such deliberations portend did not start with telling Beth Moore to go home. For example, Sarah Grimké's nineteenth-century detractors baselessly speculated that she would appear naked in public, speculations that followed her and her sister Angelina Grimké's work to lay bare the ideological and rhetorical operations of slavery and patriarchy.

In their campaign against slavery, the Grimkés named white enslavers' rape of Black women as one systemic evil. This directness about sexual violence led conservative white *clergymen* (I use the gendered form intentionally) in the north to strike back in the name of protecting white womanhood. Touring New England in 1837 and spreading the message of abolition, the Grimkés became unnamed targets in a Massachusetts clergy statement challenging the appropriateness of public lectures by women abolitionists. The first epigraph above quotes a portion of "The Pastoral Letter of the General Association of Congregational Ministers of Massachusetts," which Sarah Grimké excerpts and roundly disputes. Asserting that women's proper influence rests with the home and fretting over the preservation of white women's apparently fragile moral purity, the clergy behind the statement opposed the vigorous campaign of moral reform the sisters undertook. They also criticized women who named "things 'which ought not to be named,'" a reference to abolitionists' discussions of sexual violence against enslaved Black people. For women to publicly address this subject, in the minds of political and religious status quo figures like these ministers, put the speakers' own chastity at risk.[1] Indeed, one opponent predicted that Sarah Grimké would soon walk city streets naked.[2] Other minister-detractors likewise labeled abolitionist Abbey Kelly a "Jezebel" and "fornicator."[3] Sexual scandalization tropes persisted into the twentieth century, surfacing in contrived southern and national accounts about Black and white civil rights activists. Segregationists charged freedom workers with holding interracial orgies in churches, flaunting Jim Crow sexual norms, and receiving payment for their activism in the form of unlimited sex.[4] Of course, attacking a speaker's chastity is a common theme in the history of women's rhetoric.[5] Ideologies of racial and sexual purity have persistent legacies that shape current deliberative possibilities—deliberation-shaping legacies such as purity culture's nostalgia for the cult of true womanhood and enduring discursive rules from the history of White Christian America.

Gendered, sexualized, and racialized anxieties are particular versions of a more general notion expressed variously throughout the history of rhetoric: that closely engaging with those ideas or people imagined as deplorable, dubious, or morally diseased hazards persuasion by them. This is the logic of purity culture. Grimké responds explicitly to the clergy's articulation of this contamination concern when they reference those invoked-yet-unnamed "things" and to the charge that rhetorically promiscuous abolitionist women's speech addressing sexual violence would result in moral corruption:

> So far from woman losing any thing of the purity of her mind, by visiting the wretched victims of vice in their miserable abodes, by talking with them, or of them, she becomes more and more elevated and refined in her feelings

> and views. While laboring to cleanse the minds of others from the malaria of moral pollution, her own heart becomes purified, and her soul rises to nearer communion with her God. Such a woman is infinitely better qualified to fulfil [*sic*] the duties of a wife and a mother, than the woman whose false delicacy leads her to shun her fallen sister and brother, and shrink from naming those sins which she knows exist, but which she is too fastidious to labor by deed and by word to exterminate.[6]

Critiquing male Christian leaders' vision of white womanhood as "*false delicacy*," Grimké refuses to "shrink from *naming those sins*" of violence and exploitation that are white supremacist, patriarchal, interpersonal, state-sanctioned, and religiously permitted. By articulating her view that sexual exploitation in slavery is part of a sinful system defended by the white Christian establishment, Grimké sought to uphold an absolute standard for Christian moral obligations. These moral obligations take shape through connections with others and may involve hearing survivors tell their stories, sharing survivors' stories with others, and engaging in activism.

While significant differences exist between historical instances of Christian deliberation and the deliberative discourse about sexual violence undertaken by contemporary evangelical women, there are also similarities in these faithful deliberations: redefining community commonplaces through invention grounded in theological reflection, resisting an imposed false consensus, contending with community rules for discourse, and redrawing boundaries for group membership. There is also a sense that, as Cvetkovich asserts about publics that form around everyday and sexual traumas, "trauma is far from a straightforward experience and no simple prescription, whether therapeutic or political, or both, can heal it."[7] Grimké posits a relationship between habitual *actions* taken with or on behalf of those victimized by an oppressive system (i.e., visiting, talking, laboring) and *affective dispositions* (i.e., refining feelings, purifying the heart). That is, acting in certain ways disposes the person toward particular feelings. This model of Christian women's deliberative rhetorical action links feelings and practices with an analysis that attends to harms sexual violence survivors incur while also confronting overlapping traumas from an intersectional stance. The clergy statement and Grimké's rejoinder, which come roughly midway in an approximately four-hundred-year history of White Christian America, illustrate that when gendered, sexualized, and racialized contamination anxieties are prevalent, community boundaries (e.g., who counts as a Christian or a moral woman) will be more narrowly drawn, and discursive rules (e.g., how should Christians speak and act) will become more numerous. Some group members will attempt to more strictly enforce these boundaries and rules, and others will invent alternative ways of responding to them. Discursive rules and boundaries at work throughout the history of White Christian America that are relevant to contemporary evangelical women's confrontations with sexual and domestic violence include:

- preserving community cohesion is of the utmost importance;
- acting within accepted gender norms provides a relative measure of limited freedom;
- preserving community cohesion and exercising gendered freedom depend upon traditions that privilege whiteness and heteronormativity.

These rules and boundaries are not exclusive to historical or contemporary evangelicals. Rather, they cooperate with general operations of public discourse.

Engaging in rhetoric that works within or against these rules and boundaries, Christian and evangelical women invented alternative responses as they joined community deliberations to confront exploitive sexuality:

- insisting upon consistent moral standards sometimes entails exceeding established gender expectations or fulfilling them in new ways;
- building connections outside the enclave while maintaining community and ideological commitments is possible but sometimes risks a perceived loss of purity;
- centering the experiences of survivors is critical and involves recognizing the emotional dimensions of advocacy-informed deliberation.

These responses are often informed by the dominant public sphere and activist counterpublics as well as by their own enclaves.

In the rest of this chapter, I do not offer a detailed genealogy of these rules, boundaries, and responses within US-based Christian and evangelical rhetorical action around sexual violence. I do, however, examine a few historical moments that bring into focus the operations of discursive line-drawing for marking community boundaries (especially within predominantly white evangelicalism) and of discursive rulemaking (especially for rhetoric dealing with gender, sexuality, and violence). This account of discursive line-drawing, rulemaking, and response-generating is not meant as an exception-free, totalizing explanation of any given historical or contemporary situation; rather, I mean to suggest durable-yet-evolving patterns that help situate the case studies in the following chapters within longer histories. My highly compressed illustrations include examples from colonial Puritanism, nineteenth-century evangelical women's activism, twentieth- and twenty-first-century feminist and Black anti-violence movements, gender and domestic violence politics within evangelical feminism, and the emergence of #ChurchToo and #SilenceIsNotSpiritual as enclave-oriented versions of #MeToo. The theoretical frameworks established in the introduction (the public sphere and enclave deliberation, purity and rape cultures, trauma and affect) inform my telling of this history. By locating recent evangelical women's rhetorical invention within a history of enclave and public arguments, I also respond to Caroline Dadas's recent contention, building on work by critical legal scholar Kimberlé Crenshaw, that #MeToo conversations require increased intersectionality and feminist analysis oriented toward remedying structural oppression.[8]

COMMUNITY, HIERARCHY, AND PURITAN BEGINNINGS

Debates about the proper form of Christian community obligations date to arguments between the Apostle Paul and other early church leaders. One well-known dispute in the early days of White Christian America provides enduring insights into discursive line-drawing and rulemaking, particularly the importance of preserving group cohesion and the relative freedom achieved within gender norms: the 1636–1638 Antinomian Controversy. At the risk of oversimplification, this political and ecclesial Puritan struggle that roiled life in the Massachusetts Bay Colony consisted of two sides: elite colonial authorities, on the one side, and Anne Hutchinson and her supporters, on the other. In 1634, Hutchinson and her family left England, following her favorite minister, John Cotton, to New England. Like many other colonists, Hutchinson held meetings at her house, where attendees discussed the Bible and sermons delivered within the settlement. Conversations apparently veered into criticisms that prominent ministers' sermons focused on outward behavior as central to Christian salvation—that is, a doctrine of works. Colonial authorities, in turn, charged Hutchinson and her compatriots as antinomians, who saw the observance of moral law as utterly irrelevant to discerning one's election (that is, salvation) and whose positions would lead to moral depravity. A century earlier, Reformation leader Martin Luther had coined the term "antinomian" as a label to denounce a German reformer who thought the laws of scripture were immaterial to true Christian faith. Puritans' religious and social disputes were also political, resulting in maneuvers to influence elections, control leadership positions, and exercise dominance. Without addressing the correctness of labeling Hutchinson and her supporters antinomians or of labeling the authorities' position a doctrine of works, I would note that Puritan authorities had theological and practical reasons for perceiving Hutchinson's supporters as a potential threat. The Puritan establishment had an interest in maintaining a high level of social order and group cohesion, an interest indicated by their promoting the doctrines of signs and preparation: that behaving in accordance with religious law might, respectively, signal the possibility of election or prepare believers to experience their election.

Although colonial authorities viewed Hutchison as the instigator of division, they pursued charges against her last. By the time they dealt with Hutchinson, many of her supporters, including minister John Wheelwright, had already been banished, disenfranchised, or disarmed or had voluntarily left the colony (as in the case of one-term governor Henry Vane). Wheelwright preached a dissident sermon at an occasion dedicated to cultivating unity. When charged with sedition, Wheelwright's supporters circulated a petition on his behalf. These signatories faced the various consequences listed above or recanted their previous positions. Hutchinson eventually faced two trials: one civil, one ecclesial. Since she had not signed the petition, keeping her comments within her house meetings, Hutchinson initially defended herself ably against some charges. The private domestic sphere provided a measure of freedom. However, upon claiming access to divine revelation, including that God would will retribution upon the court if they acted against her, her banishment became a certainty. One opponent told Hutchinson, "You have stept out of your place, you have rather bine a Husband than a Wife and a preacher than a Hearer; and a Magistrate than a Subject."[9] Departing from the accepted social scripts for a Puritan subject and a woman, and thereby exceeding her allotted freedom, drew harsh reprisal. In short, this episode elucidates two recurring patterns. First, Christian women's community-disrupting rhetorical action that stays within normative gendered forms can frustrate (at least temporarily) religious authorities' efforts to dismiss them. Exacting discipline follows perceived departures from such forms. These patterns anticipate the different forms of backlash that Beth Moore and Jen Hatmaker experience (see chapters 2 and 5). Second, many evangelical women today respond to religious controversies using theologically conservative, denominationally accepted conventions: emphasizing evangelism, privileging scripture in arguments, acknowledging local and institutional authority, and operating within gender norms. The following chapters also show the reprisal that comes with perceived departures from an orthodoxy that collapses evangelical identity into specific theological positions with political and social implications.

Sexuality, theology, and community maintenance surface in the way authorities narrated the antinomians' story and identified the dangers they posed, illustrating abiding concerns with in-group purity and with believing in a just world. John Winthrop titled his version of events *A Short Story of the Rise, reign, and ruine of the Antinomians, Familists & Libertines, that infected the Churches of New England.* Winthrop would also refer to Hutchinson as "this American Jezebel."[10] Winthrop and others would point to pregnancies of Hutchinson and her supporter Mary Dyer that resulted in "monstrous" births as providential signs confirming their heretical status. In keeping with the just-world hypothesis, tragic circumstances became evidence of righteousness's absence. Charges of scandalization (i.e., associating Hutchinson's apparent opposition to community-preserving doctrines with sexual libertinism) and concerns about destructive contamination (i.e., oppositional positions "infecting" religious bodies) anticipated later arguments: those used in slavery-sustaining northern ministerial attacks on the Grimké sisters two centuries later, in mid-twentieth-century southern segregationists' propaganda against Black liberation, and in some contemporary Southern Baptists' insinuations linking advocacy on behalf of racial justice and of sexual abuse survivors with the concern that the analytical frameworks of critical race theory and intersectionality will undermine evangelical biblicism and complementarianism (more on this last point in chapter 5). Of the Antinomian Controversy, David D. Hall observes that the argumentative pattern of both groups involved a "sharply dualistic understanding of the good and the bad: orthodoxy and heresy, the forces of God on the one side, the forces of Satan on the other."[11] Roberts-Miller relies on this point to note the difficulty of assessing arguments about intention, especially intention discerned through a perceived shared position or group membership, with one's own position or group viewed as holding virtuous intentions.[12] Setting aside questions about the accuracy of either side in this controversy, both camps reveal the importance that Christians generally and evangelicals specifically place on theological concepts in ideas about group membership.

The value placed on preserving community and hierarchy included constructs of sexuality and race, as well as of gender—anticipating the cult of true womanhood's conflation of womanhood with whiteness, a conflation that purity culture would propagate in the twentieth century. Colonial court documents contain comments construing girls under ten as sexually wanton; these documents record that the real victims in rape cases were male relations, fathers and husbands, whose property had been damaged.[13] Eighteenth-century Massachusetts records show that, while the overwhelming majority of accused rapists were white, the five men sentenced to death were white laborers, Native American, and Black.[14] Throughout colonial and early republic America, between 1700 and 1820, Black men made up more than 80 percent of documented executions for rape charges, white women made up more than 90 percent of rape victims whose claims resulted in prosecutions, and "white men were only very irregularly convicted of rape."[15] Early on, the dominant public understanding of sexual violence reinforced patriarchal white supremacy as a community norm, perennially placing people of color outside the category of victim and inside the category of aggressor.

Despite colonial-era Puritan laws stringently criminalizing same-sex intimacy, the impulse toward maintaining community cohesion was also a powerful and sometimes countervailing influence against enforcement, even when a colonial citizen had a reputation for abusive sexual advances toward members of the same sex. Richard Godbeer offers the case of Nicholas Sension, a well-regarded man with relative wealth who settled in Windsor, Connecticut, around 1640. He was arrested in 1677 on sodomy charges, convicted, and sentenced to a public beating. This resolution followed two previous informal censures by town elders in the 1640s and 1660s. The final investigation documented the open secret of coercive sexual incidents decades in the making: Sension often grabbed men's genitals and forced himself on others, especially on younger men and servants. Connecticut Puritan reluctance to charge Sension earlier likely stemmed from his position within the town and from town members' desire to uphold social order through community maintenance.[16] While this story may offer evidence of temporary forbearance against a violently enforced compulsory heterosexuality, it equally suggests indulgence of esteemed community members exploiting more vulnerable members, illustrating how rape culture minimizes trauma and delays accountability until further delay becomes untenable. Exemplifying patterns that endure throughout the centuries, Sension's community sought to preserve unity by dealing with abusive behavior quietly, anticipating what Beth Moore refers to as "the church's silence." Once the situation came into public discussion, the concern rested not on exploitation and aggression but on general violations of sexual norms, anticipating the logic of purity culture.

EVANGELICAL WOMEN'S ACTIVISM THROUGHOUT THE NINETEENTH CENTURY

Fulfilling their moral obligations as Christians, many nineteenth-century women undertook social action based in their religious convictions, including using emotionally engaged deliberative rhetoric to produce opportunities for healing trauma and remedying conditions that produced trauma. Their actions resemble those of contemporary faithful deliberators who practice a costly grace that challenges a status quo–maintaining cheap grace, who address sexual violence as a social problem with attendant moral responsibilities to both survivors and aggressors, who insist on a reconciliation of reality with a just biblical standard rather than conflict avoidance, who extend the circle of community concern, and who risk perceived purity rather than uphold strict community boundaries. For example, Lisa Shaver argues that evangelical women of the period understood themselves as "moral agents accountable to God's word rather than man's interpretation of it," an understanding that stirred them to activism.[17] Susan Zaeke demonstrates how religious sentiments fueled a sense of social concern, which informed women's political efforts, specifically their petitions campaigns; as their Christian convictions motivated many women to write and sign petitions, they also sought to leverage the special moral status ascribed to them by the period's gender ideology so as to further social causes—all while not violating the period's gendered notions of propriety.[18] This intertwining of religion and collective action, of personal salvation and social reform, exerted profound and lasting influence on the dominant public sphere and subsequent counterpublics. Indeed, Nancy A. Hardesty traces the development of US feminism to nineteenth-century evangelical revivals that stirred social activism as well as souls.[19] In this way, dominant public, activist counterpublic, and enclave interactions are dynamic and mutually informing: Intensely religious communities and their practices have contributed to the evolution of the dominant public sphere. These interactions anticipate contemporary faithful deliberators who reinvent trauma-enabling proverbs of ashes and find help in the #MeToo movement's reshaping of the dominant public discourse on sexual violence.

Contributing to a sense of participatory democracy that wedded personal morality, social action to fulfill moral obligations, and emotional connections to exploited women, nineteenth-century evangelical women frequently addressed issues of family violence and sexuality in ways that risked social cohesion and others' perceptions of their purity. Shaver describes the way the American Female Moral Reform Society (AFMRS) used public discussion of sexuality to direct a civic-minded and righteous anger toward a social arrangement that enabled men to pursue sexual relationships—sometimes leaving their families economically devastated—with relative impunity through a double standard that produced social stigma and economic ruin for women.[20] Like the Grimké sisters, these evangelical reformers, who saw themselves as fulfilling their divinely sanctioned roles as women upholding a consistent moral standard, often faced criticism from establishment men in business, politics, and the clergy[21]—criticism that anticipated the resistance Beth Moore faced when told to "go home." Like petitioners and the AFMRS, the Woman's Christian Temperance Union (WCTU) did not simply maintain the established order unthinkingly or merely offer critique. By framing temperance as women righting men's wrongs, including the social wrongs of physical, emotional, and financial abuse,[22] they jeopardized a general social comity while still fostering identification through appeals to emotion and fulfilling gender roles in new ways. These efforts anticipate the reconciling rhetoric examined in chapter 4.

The WCTU championed the late-nineteenth- and early-twentieth-century campaigns to raise the age of consent across the United States. Temperance advocates brought the experiences of survivors into public deliberations, defined those experiences as exploitive, blurred clear demarcations between the deserving virtuous and the undeserving degenerate for the sake of remedying oppressive conditions, and disrupted a general consensus to expose harmful practices. The age of consent ranged from zero to twelve but was generally set at ten. This campaign against childhood sexual exploitation constituted a moment filled with the potential for cross-class and multiracial solidarity, because of the demographic configuration of the girls and women whose lives this legislation might alter. For example, age-of-consent reform opponents claimed broad rights for white men to have sex with most women, circulated racialized tropes about the sexual voraciousness of women of color, opined about working-class women's morally compromised status (e.g., "especially typewriters"), and asserted the perpetual availability of girls who turned to survival sex.[23] Arguing for age-of-consent changes consequently meant that middle-class, white evangelical temperance women confronted rape culture and supported a broad cross section of women in positions quite different from their own. Unfortunately, the organizing happened mostly on white women's terms. While Black women's clubs engaged in their own programs to defend against sexual exploitation, they mostly opted out of WCTU age-of-consent campaigns, because temperance leaders had such a milquetoast stance on anti-lynching efforts and because of the ways expanding categories of sexual crimes could be policed in racially biased ways.[24] These concerns certainly make sense given the earlier description of historic racial disparities in sex-related crimes. Tensions between white and Black activist women persisted into the modern anti-violence movement: White-dominant frameworks would stifle coalition-building through universalizing assertions and definitions of violence that downplayed racist state violence.

THE ANTI-VIOLENCE MOVEMENT: POSSIBILITIES AND MISSED OPPORTUNITIES

If the AFMRS's emotionally charged activism put sexual exploitation and double standards on the public agenda and the WCTU's age-of-consent campaign served as an effective vehicle for policy change that missed an opportunity for thoroughly intersectional organizing, then these white evangelical women-led efforts prefigured developments to come in the twentieth-century anti-violence movement. Possibilities for addressing trauma discourses and violence today derive in part from the anti-violence movement—the sometimes overlapping, sometimes parallel campaigns to address rape and domestic violence—that emerged out of 1960s and 1970s feminism. The anti-violence movement was also anticipated by the organizing against sexual violence that had long been part of the Black liberation struggle. Feminist and Black liberationist counterpublic activism created public space for experiences laden with shame, viewed emotion as a resource, generated opportunities for healing trauma through analysis and action, and informed dominant public and evangelical ways of discussing violence.

Twentieth-century anti-rape activists built on the strategies of the movement to destigmatize and decriminalize abortion, a movement that centered the voices and experiences of abortion recipients. People of faith and religious spaces were at the heart of early local, national, and international networks that connected patients with abortion providers, and these efforts contributed to the political emergence of the anti-rape movement. Shortly after Texas Baptist Howard Moody assumed the senior pastor position at Greenwich Village's Judson Memorial Church in 1957, women seeking abortions contacted him. A decade later, he served as the founding spokesperson for the Clergy Consultation Service, a network of fourteen hundred clergy who would refer abortion-seekers to doctors, leveraging the respectability and privilege afforded religious leaders in order to circumvent the law. Just as some churchgoers and clergy worked to ensure the sacrament of bodily autonomy, churches served as spaces for the sacred liturgies of radical feminist storytelling and consciousness-raising. Judson hosted consciousness-raising sessions where women told their stories of acquiring illegal abortions.[25] In February 1969, radical feminist protesters forced a New York legislative committee hearing about abortion into a closed-door session. The witness lineup that provoked outrage? A panel of men and one Catholic nun. As a follow-up action later that year, the feminist group the Redstockings organized the historic Abortion Speak Out at Washington Square United Methodist Church in Greenwich Village where women told their stories about abortions. These events inspired the New York Radical Feminists' (NYRF) 1971 Rape Speak-out at St. Clement's Episcopal Church in Manhattan, an occasion for publicly discussing experiences of sexual violence in a supportive environment.

Just as the AFMRS and the WCTU centered exploited women in their religiously motivated social vision, the public voicing of experiences that connect women's and survivors' lives with social conditions is also the through line that links feminist attention to sexuality and gender within the development of the anti-violence movement. Local domestic violence shelters and programs developed throughout the 1960s and 1970s. By 1976, efforts included state-based advocacy networks and legislative campaigns. Decade's end witnessed national developments, including the establishment of a national crisis hotline, the National Coalition Against Domestic Violence, and hearings on domestic violence by the Commission on Civil Rights.[26] A similar pattern followed in the anti-rape movement with the creation of rape crisis centers in the early 1970s. Legal changes recognized marital rape, made victims' sexual histories inadmissible in trial proceedings, and expanded legal definitions of sexual violence. In both domestic violence and anti-rape work, the local programs began as peer-to-peer community efforts that often had connections to radical feminist politics.[27] However, Stonewall uprising veteran and transgender activist Sylvia Rivera explained in a 1973 speech that women's and lesbian organizations generally failed to aid transgender women, poor women, incarcerated women, and sex workers.[28] So, initially, anti-violence programs operated as alternatives to state indifference toward women's safety and to state hostility toward women's self-determination. However, through gaps in their vision, they overlooked vulnerable populations; institutionalization, professionalization, and reliance on state funding softened their radical edge. Social services took the place of self-advocacy.[29] These gaps in feminist anti-violence visions resemble problems that contemporary faithful deliberators address: cheap grace that maintains political alliances, antinomian forgiveness that lets in-group members off the hook while vigilantly policing out-groups, and firm community boundaries that resist change wrought by intersectional analysis.

That early radical edge appears in feminists' and anti-rape activists' frequent appeals to the emotionally powerful framework of rape as war. Susan Brownmiller compared rapists to guerrilla soldiers.[30] In 1985, Andrea Dworkin leveraged a connection between war and rape—comparing knowledge about sexual violence to seeing "piles and piles of bodies"—in a speech to a group of politically radical men: "Even in wars, there are days of truce. Go and organize a truce. Stop your side for one day. I want a twenty-four-hour truce during which there is no rape."[31] As useful as this lens proved for mobilizing public attention and resources, Kristin Bumiller argues that this gender war perspective created an artificial unity among women's experiences, emphasizing gender to the exclusion of other identities and narrowing the range of feelings about trauma into an "expressive justice" that required appropriate expressions of certain feelings in response to violence.[32] Furthermore, this expressive justice cooperated with an expanding, racially discriminatory criminal justice system and with the bureaucratic management of survivors' everyday lives in social service domains.

Consequently, even groups dedicated to a common good defined by affirming survivors and seeking feminist social transformation may end up reenacting dominant, damaging beliefs, such as those that reinforce racist stereotypes and whiteness as a standard. In *Women, Race, and Class,* Angela Davis argues that many architects of the 1970s anti-rape movement replicated beliefs in keeping with dominant racial attitudes, namely, that men of color are particularly prone to sexual violence and that "women" is the appropriate organizing category for resisting sexual violence. Specifically, Davis points to Brownmiller's interpretation of historical incidents that are important in the development of the civil rights movement, such as the freedom campaign for the Scottsboro Boys and the kidnapping-murder of Emmett Till by white supremacists; another of Davis's several examples included Diana Russell's selection of survivor narratives involving men of color aggressors.[33] Davis made the same critiques earlier on her Pacifica Radio program in 1976.[34] On another Pacifica program in 1977, in conversation with socialist and lesbian activist Martha Shelley, Brownmiller and Russell responded. Brownmiller reasserted her criticisms of radical leftists in the United States for their dismissive stance toward rape survivors, insisted upon the growing specter of interracial rape as an instrument of racial militancy and political retribution, and defended her belief in the common political predicament of Black and white women within a patriarchal system. Russell defended her collection of voluntarily submitted rape survivors' stories, and she implored listeners to not dismiss the recent emergence of the anti-rape movement, even if they accepted Davis's premise that its supporters exemplified racism.

Of course, that this emerging anti-violence movement within white-dominant feminism replicated the racial attitudes of the prevailing culture was exactly Davis's point. Organizing against sexual and sexualized violence, by this point, had long been part of Black women's activism throughout and prior to the twentieth century. Davis points to Ida B. Wells and other Black women's campaigns to combat lynching.[35] An oratorical champion who frequently criticized WCTU president Frances Willard's racist statements, Wells named rape as the complementary tool of lynching in the white supremacist architecture of the post–Civil War United States. When Wells suggested that Black men and white women might have consensual sex, she dismantled the common invocation of the Black male rapist and exposed this racist specter as an instance of cunning projection used to conceal white men's everyday sexual violence against Black women. In the mid-twentieth century, decades before the modern anti-rape movement emerged, the justice campaign for Recy Taylor further attests to Black women's long-standing social movement organizing against rape culture. In 1944, a group of white men abducted and gang-raped Taylor as she and others walked home from church one evening. NAACP activist Rosa Parks, who had been active in the campaign to support the Scottsboro Boys, investigated the attack and led efforts to form the Committee for Equal Justice for the Rights of Mrs. Recy Taylor, which generated local advocacy groups across the United States.[36] Years before the NYRF's Speak Out on Rape, listening campaigns in 1963 organized by civil rights and women's rights leaders, principally president of the National Council of Negro Women Dorothy Height, solicited the stories of Black and white civil rights activists who encountered police brutality and sexual violence in the US South.[37] Other groups emerged because of gaps in the civil rights as well as the feminist movements, including the Black lesbian socialist Combahee River Collective (CRC). The CRC prioritized responding to violence against women in 1979 as the murders of a dozen Black women and one white woman went unsolved in Boston. Since the victims were allegedly sex workers whose deaths were simply a cost of doing business, the CRC charged police and reporters with placing too little attention on this violence.[38] These divergent histories contributed to agendas for Black women and other women of color that differed from what became the mainstream anti-violence movement.

As the anti-violence movement grew and expanded survivors' access to resources, the movement also came to participate more thoroughly with state power. That is, as an activist counterpublic reshaped the state and the general rules of operation within the dominant public sphere, the state also reshaped that counterpublic. Establishment politicians, law enforcement, and regulatory social agencies claimed an element of feminist discourse while not consistently moving forward a liberatory agenda for social transformation.[39] In other words, activist efforts to secure historically marginalized peoples' freedom from violence in the United States were appropriated in ways that expanded state power and interventions, frequently contributing to forms of state violence that generally distributed disproportionately among communities of color, working-class people, and other vulnerable groups racialized policing, immigration, family regulation, and warfare. In a moment in 2018 when the diffuse interconnectedness of racialized state violence and sexual trauma converged with religious rhetoric used to shore up White Christian America's boundaries, US attorney general Jeff Sessions quoted the biblical text Romans 13 as justification for a family separation policy that exponentially increased the vulnerability of migrant children from elsewhere in the Americas to sexual abuse.[40]

Long before this Romans 13 moment of using scripture to sanction an immigration policy, racialized exercises of state power had already shaped the institutionalization of anti-violence activism. For example, the Violence Against Women Act (VAWA) was passed in connection with the Violent Crime Control and Law Enforcement Act of 1994.[41] While VAWA expanded funding for survivor services, the civil rights protections it extended in the form of survivors' abilities to sue their aggressors were struck down by the Supreme Court. Furthermore, this landmark legislative achievement reinforced the criminal justice framework as the primary mode for understanding violence. Even before the 1994 legislation, incarceration intersected with feminist and anti-violence concerns. From 1970 to 2014, the number of women in jail grew by "14-fold," and today, the majority of women in jail have experienced some kind of sexual violence (86 percent) or intimate-partner violence (77 percent).[42] While the criminal justice system offers an avenue for some survivors to find justice, turning to it as the primary space for addressing violence obscures the historically interrelated operations of interpersonal violence and state violence, including the legacies of sexual violence that are part of state-sanctioned programs of colonization, slavery, and segregation.

From the early instances of these sanctioned forms of violence to the contemporary moment, activist counterpublics have pursued campaigns that centered survivors' voices, leveraged emotion for advocacy, and fulfilled or disrupted gendered expectations to reconfigure the general public's responses to sexual and gendered violence. Just as many nineteenth-century white evangelical women crossed lines that risked their perceived purity while also reinforcing their middle-class and white positions as the cultural default, the modern anti-violence movement likewise seized and missed opportunities for solidarity. The next section illustrates how boundaries and resistance to robust intersectional action likewise informed mainstream and feminist evangelicalism during roughly the final quarter of the twentieth century.

EVANGELICAL FEMINISM AND GENDER BOUNDARIES

While feminist counterpublic activism that contributed to the general discourse around sexual and domestic violence found direct precedent in abortion politics, this is less true for both mainstream evangelicalism and evangelical feminism. Popular beliefs and evangelical leaders' own retrospective accounts locate the full political emergence of evangelicals into modern public life with the 1973 *Roe vs. Wade* Supreme Court decision legalizing abortion access. However, the record actually exposes a more complicated story. Many evangelical figures and institutions expressed silence at, or moderate endorsement of, *Roe* at the time. Randall Balmer's study of evangelical political mobilization locates the origin story in white Christians resisting federal action to desegregate church schools and colleges in the 1970s.[43] Not until the late 1970s did abortion galvanize evangelical activists. The issue then touched a larger agenda: strengthening social order, rolling back the sexual revolution, and reinforcing racist hierarchies.[44] Balmer locates in this agenda a fondness for the "cult of true womanhood," that racialized code for defining gender norms.[45]

Even as nostalgia bred resentment toward the larger feminist movement and its sexual revolution, an evangelical version of this public exploration of sex took place in the 1970s with the publication of sometimes quite explicit sex and marriage guides, like Marabel Morgan's *The Total Woman* and Tim and Beverly LaHaye's *The Act of Marriage: The Beauty of Sexual Love.*[46] Typical of an evangelical ethics that defines morality in personal rather than social terms and reminiscent of the age-of-consent opponents who accused working-class women of lax sexual morals, these guides framed an audacious sexuality within Christian marriage as wives' defense against the threat of working women who would steal away their husbands. Problems of power, harassment, coercion, and violence in the workplace and the lack of economic opportunity for women fail to even register as concerns in these accounts—in contrast to their evangelical ancestors in the AFMRS and WCTU.

Just as evangelical uptake renovated, instead of simply rejected, the sexual revolution for their own purposes, a modern evangelical feminist movement emerged during the early 1970s and saw itself as following in the tradition of the faith-motivated activism described earlier. In 1973, Evangelicals for Social Action (ESA) formed and composed a statement on social and political issues. The resulting "Chicago Declaration" addressed war, poverty, abuses of government power, violence, and sexism. When this group's next meeting occurred the following year, the Evangelical Women's Caucus (EWC) formally organized.[47] On the one hand, given that the sprawling Chicago Declaration issues list would ostensibly reflect ESA's engagement with the wider culture's interest in social change and protest, the formation of EWC would surely seem to suggest the influence of modern feminism on these evangelicals. On the other hand, while socially and theologically conservative evangelicals generally blame any departure from traditionalist gender norms on the encroachment of secular values, fundamentalist and evangelical traditions are dynamic and have always included elements that advocate for gender equality.[48] Leading participants in evangelical feminism roundly rejected the notion that their politics came from recent cultural influences.

Evangelical feminists found their identity in the Bible and their history in the tradition of earlier activist evangelical women. For example, Letha Scanzoni wrote of nineteenth- and early-twentieth-century evangelical women's faith and biblicism: "It is profitable to explore the message the early Christian feminists have left for us." She further asserted that EWC was "much more than a warmed-over, imitative, Christianized version of secular feminism."[49] Various scholars note the centrality of arguments about gender roles among evangelical feminists and the extensive attention EWC figures paid to biblical exegesis and hermeneutics.[50] Andrea Smith describes the substantial energy spent debating issues of inerrancy and infallibility as well as the diverse positions on these issues within evangelical feminism, observing that reactions within the mainstream evangelical community ranged from a default position that these groups were heretical to a willingness to engage in conversation depending on a particular woman's approach to scripture.[51] As evangelical feminists claimed support for their egalitarianism through appeals to history and scripture, they insisted on consistent moral standards for Christians of all genders. Yet they eventually faced internal disruptions, and some drew new boundaries over questions of sexuality.

The story of EWC demonstrates the kind of boundary work and community line-drawing that stymies broader coalition-building out of a need to maintain doctrinal purity, to preserve the limits of freedom within gendered expectations, and to ensure that community cohesion relied upon heteronormativity. According to Weddle and Aldredge-Clanton, in 1975, EWC held a conference independent of ESA; over the next few years, local chapters formed and EWC published a newsletter.[52] Over the next decade, momentum continued with a growing membership and an expanding agenda. However, divisions over how to read scripture, especially in regard to gay and lesbian rights, had become increasingly apparent by the 1984 conference. At the 1986 gathering, group unity became harder to preserve with the adoption of resolutions on challenging racism, confronting violence against women, and affirming the civil rights of "homosexual persons."[53] Many leaders in the group had been moving in a progressive and affirming direction for years. Scanzoni and Mollenkott published *Is the Homosexual My Neighbor? Another Christian View* in 1978. Despite having written the foreword to Scanzoni's 1973 advice book for parents planning to discuss sex with their children, James Dobson retracted his endorsement in 1982.[54] Following the vote to affirm gay and lesbian civil rights, some members left EWC. After this split, some of these breakaway members and others began meeting in 1987, and in January 1988, they founded Christians for Biblical Equality

(CBE). As CBE organized, an evangelical group formed that was dedicated to defending complementarianism: the Council for Biblical Manhood and Womanhood. Despite conversations about a joint 1994 statement condemning abuse within marriage, these two new organizations ultimately could not reach agreement, elucidating boundaries lines between them. The fracturing of the EWC and the formation of these new groups revealed how connection with the broader evangelical community would require endorsing heteronormativity. The unsteady relationship between the complementarian CBMW and the egalitarian CBE suggests the fragility of some evangelical-internal coalitions.

Impediments to coalition-building within evangelicalism around feminist concerns and gender politics also involve histories of racial politics. Andrea Smith concludes, "Evangelical feminism often forecloses alliances with nonevangelicals, particularly women of color, rather than providing openings for new coalitions."[55] The racial politics at play within evangelicalism have long worked to authorize white women's rhetorical endeavors through missionary and evangelizing work. Ingersoll observes that theologically conservative Christian communities empower US white women through the missionary impulse to evangelize elsewhere in the world.[56] This sense of empowerment commonly surfaced in support of nineteenth-century white missionary women who endured hardship and desired real connections with indigenous peoples while at the same time often maintaining racist beliefs about the supremacy of white culture and the English language.[57] A contemporary women's mission pamphlet declares: "We can rescue their [oppressed Third World women's] souls from continuing to live in hell, not just here, but for all eternity!"[58] These racialized evangelical appeals to a universalizing, global mission rely on constructing patriarchy and gendered violence as the province of a *them* located *over there*. Such constructs contribute to the between $2.5 and $5 billion spent annually on religious mission trips,[59] predominantly to countries that former president Donald Trump disparaged as "shithole countries" while his administration acted to remove fleeing gang and domestic violence as grounds for seeking asylum.[60] These dynamics caution against overgeneralizing about the condition of "women"—which privileges white, heterosexual, cisgender, middle-class, US Christian women with citizenship—but also highlight the potential power that arguments among this consistency might carry.

In the US context, as indicated by the efforts of the WCTU, AFMRS, and other groups, evangelicalism's attention to issues of sexual and domestic violence is not new, nor has evangelical women's critique of patriarchy targeted only distant "others." Practicing an atypical reliance on a non-evangelical expert, 1990s evangelicals drew on United Church of Christ minister Marie Fortune's publications in the 1980s that were designed to generate among Christians greater concern around abuse.[61] Much popular evangelical writing on these issues appeared during this historical period.[62] In April 1994, CBE held a conference dedicated to women, abuse, and the Bible. At the same time, despite the official hardening of complementarian gender lines within various corners of evangelicalism, for the SBC, the legacies of evangelical feminism brought about changes in both the descriptions and the practices of complementarianism, blurring its boundaries with egalitarianism.[63] Specifically, arguments related to, and women's experiences of, "domestic and sexual violence within evangelical communities" informed these changes.[64] In other words, growing discourse about gendered and sexualized violence loosened some boundaries regarding evangelical gender policing. These appear to be precisely the dynamics that motivate some criticism of Beth Moore, which I examine in chapter 5.

The general resistance to broader coalitions speaks to a widespread (and not evangelical-specific) conflation of arguments and identities, a conflation that contributes to boundary policing. Within evangelicalism, for example, holding a position in common with secular feminists may sometimes result in charges of leaving the properly orthodox fold, as in the 1980s split within EWC. In a recent example, Moore's Twitter profile, which serves as an epigraph to this chapter, reads, "I love Jesus. I love Scripture. I like people. I like diversity. My interactions and follows do not equal endorsements or reflections of doctrinal alignment." This language indicates an effort to preempt attacks grounded in the historical tensions between evangelical belonging and out-group relationships. Such tensions persisted as the broad #MeToo cultural shift began.

#METOO, #CHURCHTOO, #SILENCEISNOTSPIRITUAL, AND EVANGELICAL WORLD MAKING

Like their ancestors in faith, contemporary evangelical women who address domestic and sexual violence interact with both the dominant public sphere and the evangelical subculture. This interaction and the discursive line-drawing that enables enclave deliberation (even as it can also circumscribe coalition-building across lines of difference) contributed to evangelical-oriented efforts following the mainstreaming of #MeToo: #ChurchToo and #SilenceIsNotSpiritual. On October 15, 2017, when actress Alyssa Milano tweeted the statement that would make the #MeToo campaign go viral, she participated in world making that increased survivors' visibility and that highlighted the pervasiveness of violence: "If you've been sexually harassed or assaulted write 'me too' as a reply to this tweet." Within a day, the hashtag appeared in more than 500,000 tweets. This poetic world making occurred in relationship to material realities, preexisting discourses, and earlier efforts to establish a public sphere shaped by visibility for, and mutuality among, survivors.

Foregrounding the experiences of survivors and emotional connections among them, Tarana Burke describes the inception of the name given to the movement she initiated long before accusations of coercive conduct by a Hollywood producer or other media personalities came into full public light. Burke recounts a story from her time working as a counselor with youth of color at a camp. A girl around the age of thirteen, whom she calls Heaven and who was a youth identified as having behavioral difficulties, wanted to speak to Burke. Heaven told Burke about the sexual abuse inflicted by her mother's boyfriend. After listening for only a few minutes, Burke directed Heaven to another camp counselor. Despite the fact that Burke, too, was an assault survivor, she could not bring herself to voice empathy with the young survivor during this disclosure. Haunted by the memory of Heaven, in 2006, Burke launched an online effort through the social media site MySpace to bring attention to sexual violence against women and girls of color, an effort encapsulated in the phrase she wished she had spoken to Heaven: "Me too."[65]

Just as the #MeToo movement and its popularization have reshaped the dominant public sphere, so too have they contributed to a reshaping of evangelicalism—opening new opportunities for enclave deliberation and new possibilities for evangelical lifeworlds. Still, important distinctions mark different discursive movements bringing about change. In November 2017, #ChurchToo was launched by Emily Joy and Hannah Paasch as a way to build on the #MeToo movement, highlighting the stories of survivors whose abuse took place in connection with church contexts. These two former evangelicals met at Moody Bible Institute when Joy was an undergraduate student and Paasch was a seminarian. During her time there, Paasch frequently experienced shaming by other Christian students who felt her appearance did not match the gendered expectations of feminine modesty, which ostracized her in ways that she saw as contributing to a clinical depression; while her own sexual assault did not take place in connection with a religious community, she attributes the shame she felt and the silence she kept to lessons learned from the purity culture of her church upbringing. Joy had experienced an abusive, manipulative, grooming relationship with an older male church leader when she was sixteen; her peers and family held Joy equally responsible when the relationship became public knowledge. In their statements describing the rationale for the #ChurchToo label and the primary issues they hope to address, both of these former evangelicals specifically critique evangelical theology about sexual purity and complementarianism.[66] While theologically diverse evangelicals endorse church-specific conversations to confront sexual and domestic violence, this more revolutionary than revisionist approach gives some theologically conservative women pause.[67]

A month after #ChurchToo launched, on December 20, 2017, Belinda Bauman and Lisa Sharon Harper launched #SilenceIsNotSpiritual. Two figures deeply invested in evangelicalism, Bauman is the founder of a peacemaking group that works with women in conflict zones and Harper works with many evangelical groups on a range of progressive issues. Harper is a Black woman who has spent much of her life working and worshiping in white evangelical communities, which was the context of her Christian conversion. The founding statement of the #SilenceIsNotSpiritual campaign acknowledges #MeToo and #ChurchToo and seeks to build on what these efforts are accomplishing. As a rhetorical endeavor, this campaign appeared to take an invitational approach, asking evangelical churches to move beyond silence and inaction in regard to sexual- and gender-based violence and to find forms of solidarity with survivors. A call to repent of—or to turn away from—those systemic problems that harm women and girls recurs throughout the founding statement.[68] Their stance echoes the one Mattingly describes among temperance women—motivated as many of them were by religiosity—who presented "women's rights by emphasizing wrongs women endured."[69] However, unlike Joy and Paasch, distinctly evangelical theological configurations that might contribute to abuse and silence are not named or critiqued.[70] Rather, it works more as a jeremiad, naming the group's failure to live up to a promise and calling on them to better fulfill that promise moving forward. In the year that followed, the list of evangelical leaders who stepped down, retired, or were fired over allegations or proven instances of harassment, abuse, or poor handling of such cases (e.g., Bill Hybels, Andy Savage, and Paige Patterson) indicated that significant renovations were taking place within evangelicalism.

These different-yet-interrelated efforts, the lines of community demarcation they signal, and the world making they enable were on display in December 2018 during the lead-up to an evangelical summit on the #MeToo movement. With a speaker lineup that included Beth Moore, the Billy Graham Center at Wheaton College hosted a #ChurchToo summit under its programming label GC2, which references two of Jesus's charges to his followers: the Great Commission, about the imperative to evangelize, and the

Great Commandment, about religious obligations being contained in the love of God and of others. This event name and its intertextual references work to bind historic evangelical concerns with conversionism, biblicism, and activism. As an effort to engage in an enclave-specific way with the anti-violence work of #ChurchToo, from the standpoint of the hashtag initiators, the GC2 uptake seemed too limited. While seeking to embrace the power of the #ChurchToo label and to enter the anti-violence conversation, GC2 organizers established an all-evangelical lineup that didn't veer from established orthodoxy or generate space for those whose trauma had led them entirely away from the faith. Consequently, #ChurchToo architects and others hosted a social media event concurrent with the Wheaton conference.

These evangelical-oriented campaigns were clearly made possible by reworkings of the dominant public sphere facilitated by the #MeToo movement. Despite evangelicals' claims to be set apart from the dominant US culture while also engaged with it, world making in the dominant public sphere helped to sponsor evangelical invention and deliberation. While agency in the public sphere relates to movement within the dominant lifeworld, evangelicals generally set themselves in opposition to that configuration of social life—even as they take it up and reconfigure it. Evangelical women's agency within their enclave derives from varied sources, but when exercised for the purpose of community maintenance and reform through deliberation, agency relies on evangelical rhetors' ability to position themselves as insiders who exist within evangelicalism's lifeworld. Consequently, throughout the remainder of this book, I address how rhetors inhabit, mobilize, and reinvent evangelical commonplaces much more than I examine how they disavow such commonplaces.

Addressing the conditions that gave rise to pervasive violence and the regulatory regimes of rape and purity cultures requires deliberative discourse that is dependent upon listening to survivors' voices. The following chapters examine deliberative discourse that strives for attentive listening within contemporary evangelicalism. Each chapter examines an aspect of inventive practice that aims at survivor-sensitive, evangelical world making with special attention to theological concepts at play within a given case study. In the next chapter, I examine a pre–#MeToo mainstreaming episode of enclave deliberation. Looking at one case study before October 2017 helps bring into focus the possibilities that #MeToo and #ChurchToo would create.

2

Wake Up, Sleepers

Cheap and Costly Rhetorical Grace Before #ChurchToo

I just start kissing them. It's like a magnet. Just kiss. I don't even wait. And when you're a star, they let you do it. You can do anything.

—Donald J. Trump

Wake up, Sleepers, to what women have dealt with all along in environments of gross entitlement & power. Are we sickened? Yes. Surprised? NO.

—Beth Moore

Days before the second US presidential debate in 2016, a recording surfaced of then-Republican presidential nominee Donald J. Trump offering boastful comments about how his fame provided him with license to commit sexual assault against women. The tape had been recorded in 2005 prior to an interview for the entertainment news program *Access Hollywood*. The first epigraph comes from that candid "hot mic" moment. Asked about these comments during the second debate with Democratic nominee Hillary Clinton, Trump repeatedly characterized his remarks as "locker room talk." Even as Trump here describes and endorses sexually coercive behavior, he has long appealed to fears about racialized sexual violence in order to promote a law-and-order society that more stringently polices marginalized and vulnerable people of color. In fact, he did so the day news of the recording broke, revisiting his role as a prominent New Yorker who stoked public sentiment against the Central Park Five, Black and Latinx teenagers wrongfully convicted of raping and beating a white woman.

Decades earlier, little more than a month following the 1989 attack and arrests, Trump took out a full-page advertisement in leading New York City newspapers. That published statement called for reinstating the death penalty for violent crimes such as rape (i.e., "BRING BACK THE DEATH PENALTY!"), urged support for the police (i.e., "BRING BACK OUR POLICE!"), and encouraged expressions of public hatred toward the Central Park Five, who were ultimately exonerated in 2002 after spending years in juvenile detention and prison. Despite their innocence, the day the *Access Hollywood* recording was released, Trump reasserted his belief in their guilt and criticized their release. Trump's 1989 call for tougher law enforcement responses to sexual assault actually resonated with many late-twentieth-century legal feminists' arguments, which sought structural remedies for patriarchy through what sociologist Elizabeth Bernstein terms "carceral feminism," "drift[ing] from the welfare state to the carceral state as the enforcement apparatus for feminist goals."[1] In contrast, feminist and civil rights lawyer Ruth Bader Ginsburg had served as the lead author of an American Civil Liberties Union brief in the 1977 Supreme Court case that ruled the death penalty unconstitutional in rape cases. The brief argued that death penalty statutes for sexual violence were a holdover from a system that regarded women as the property of fathers or husbands and were state tools for the maintenance of white supremacy.[2] Messages such as Trump's surely capitalize on these histories and hierarchies—a pattern he enacted at the opening of his presidential campaign in 2015, which mobilized fears of racialized sexual violence, linking immigrants from Mexico with drugs, crime, and rape.

Prominent evangelicals' reactions to the *Access Hollywood* tape illustrate White Christian America's long-standing discursive rules, boundaries, and alternative responses to sexual trauma. Many Trump supporters offered only modest criticism (some even provided apologias, asserting their moral leadership and maintaining a political alliance with the Republican Party). Privileging community preservation and cohesion, this stance blessed a regime of permissiveness for expressions of coercive sexuality from a powerful political ally who had repeatedly touted rigorous law enforcement measures (often selectively targeting people of color) against sexual violence as a way to protect white womanhood. In contrast, social media responses from several leading evangelical women centered survivors' experiences, risked perceived purity, and insisted on consistent moral accountability within their community. Their responses suggested the possibility of a renegotiation of evangelical identity and political priorities in regard to rape culture. Popular evangelical writer and speaker Beth Moore offered a series of four tweets that were widely perceived as responding to the sexualized language and abusive acts Trump described. Jen Hatmaker, an author, speaker, and HGTV miniseries personality, confronted Trump on Facebook. Her post called on readers to not vote for Trump and expressed compassion for those who have experienced the kind of assault he described.

News and editorial reports in the lead-up to the election covered these reactions as signs pointing to shifts within evangelicalism. Writing for the *New York Times*, Laurie Goodstein cited Hatmaker's Facebook post as evidence of political "rifts" within evangelicalism.[3] In a piece for *Politico*, Laura Turner noted divisions within evangelicalism regarding how to feel about Trump.[4] *Slate* contributor Ruth Graham collected numerous comments from evangelical women responding to the Trump tapes and observed, "If Moore's and Hatmaker's names aren't familiar to you, however, that's not because they're not important."[5] Sara Groves, a celebrated Christian musician, commented for a piece in the *Daily Beast*: "Someone like Beth [Moore] can go a long way in helping Evangelicals recognize these major blind spots" around misogyny and sexual violence.[6] Katelyn Beaty, the then-print managing editor for *Christianity Today* and the first woman to hold that position, published an opinion piece in the *Washington Post* that gathered a number of comments from prominent evangelical women and lamented, "It's actually hard to know which stung worse: Trump's words or our leaders' defense of him."[7] These reports echo calls within feminist and rhetorical studies to pay more attention to religious women engaged in literacy and rhetorical activity even when they may not appear wholly reflective of the contemporary moment's progressive politics.[8] This sort of scenario seems to be what scholar of rhetoric Jeffrey Ringer imagines when he argues that vernacular Christian rhetoric may provide the basis for evangelicals' deliberative democratic engagement. The vernacular in Ringer's account focuses on the everyday rhetorical activities of undergraduate students, thus working to distance evangelicalism from often-polemical, public personalities. While I focus on prominent figures within evangelicalism, Ringer's analysis of how evangelicals out of the limelight address non-evangelical audiences inspires my attention to values as part of the rhetorical invention that enables faithful deliberation.

During the period before the popularization of #MeToo, the deliberative Christian rhetoric employed in divergent evangelical responses to sexual violence within rape and purity cultures present different theological orientations to the notion of grace. To examine these divergent responses for evidence of rhetorical invention that might inform faithful deliberation, I draw on scholarship about women's rhetoric that theorizes grace in terms of community practices of literacy and rhetoric and on Nazi-resister Dietrich Bonhoeffer's distinction between "cheap grace" and "costly grace," a vocabulary of grace shaped in part by his six months of worshiping in a Black Baptist church in Harlem. A theological explanation of grace valued by both liberal and conservative Christians, cheap grace involves extending the church's blessing without concretely confronting practices that destroy life, promote violence, and diminish hope. Costly grace involves both substantial individual change and substantial collective change undertaken as part of the religious life.

Moore, Hatmaker, and other evangelical women practiced theological reflection to produce what I call a "costly rhetorical grace" to counter the "cheap rhetorical grace" stemming from proverbs of ashes (i.e., religious-cultural commonplaces that reinforce rape culture and minimize trauma). More precisely, Moore and Hatmaker generated rhetorical materials that created opportunities for a relational openness that might produce new understandings of survivors' painful experiences and for community transformation in light of those experiences and understandings. These rhetors used costly rhetorical grace to facilitate faithful deliberation about what Christian communities should value by fashioning new formulations out of the following proverbs of ashes: viewing instances of assault and coercion as primarily about sex rather than power and violence (i.e., Trump was merely lewd), promoting instant forgiveness (i.e., Trump is a sinner just like all of us), and appealing to in-group trust that diminishes the need to confront rape culture (i.e., Trump is a real Christian). While "cheapness" in this configuration rests with those who demean and dismiss survivors and their stories, I wish to acknowledge the often too close association of "cheap" with women—a dominant and detrimental understanding that often sponsors sexual violence: She's cheap, disposable, and deserved it. It is precisely this commonplace thinking that is rhetorically cheap and that Moore and Hatmaker confront with a costly rhetorical grace.

GRACE, BONHOEFFER, AND LITERACY AND RHETORICAL STUDIES

In secular terms, "grace" indicates a task artfully accomplished, a tumult endured with relative composure, an attack peaceably met. As a theological concept within Christianity, grace is God's forgiveness toward humanity for our sinfulness. While substantial differences exist among Calvinist, Arminian, Lutheran, and other traditions that still inform strands of US evangelicalism, the historic consensus is that "sin" names an ontological condition experienced by all humans, namely, the predisposition to resist God's will and disobey divine law. Not a problem overcome by effortful exertion, sin describes a common condition. The remedy for sin, within many Protestant traditions, comes solely in the form of grace received through faith in Jesus Christ; grace is God's divine forgiveness that comes to believers through trust in the life, death, and resurrection of Jesus. While this articulation of grace's saving power is a contested notion even within Protestantism, salvation from one's sinful condition is often understood to rest not on behaviors undertaken by the believer but on the agency of God, who works through grace—that is, independently of a person's particular actions. At the same time, grace becomes a source that enables and supports human action.

Dedicated to supporting Christian action, German pastor and theologian Dietrich Bonhoeffer wrote about the problem of "cheap grace" and the need for "costly grace" against the background of rising Nazism in Germany. In 1937, Bonhoeffer wrote, "Cheap grace is the grace we bestow on ourselves. Cheap grace is the preaching of forgiveness without requiring repentance, baptism without church discipline, Communion without confession."[9] Theologian L. Gregory Jones explains, "Cheap grace offers consolation without any change of life, without any sense of either dying or rising in Christ."[10] This language about a ubiquitous-yet-non-transformative grace illustrates Bonhoeffer's debt to the time he spent at Abyssinian Baptist Church, a historically Black Baptist church in Harlem.

The year before publishing his thoughts on cheap and costly grace in *Discipleship* (eventually published in the United States after his death as *The Cost of Discipleship*), Bonhoeffer celebrated his thirtieth birthday in 1936 with students he instructed at the underground seminary Finkenwald. On that birthday, Bonhoeffer led this anti-Nazi Christian community in singing the Black spirituals "Go Down Moses," "Swing Low, Sweet Chariot," and "There is a Balm in Gilead," which he learned during his 1930–1931 time in the United States. He shared with them the story of his friendship with fellow Union Theological Seminary (UTS) student Frank Fisher and of how Fisher brought Bonhoeffer to worship at Abyssinian during the German theologian's six-month period at UTS.[11] As a congregant, Sunday school teacher, and one-time preacher at Abyssinian, Bonhoeffer would hear senior pastor Adam Clayton Powell address the "cheap grace" of American Christianity and its "tangled web of apostasy," which led to "the accommodating of the church to the hypocrisy, racism and greed" of the dominant culture.[12] Shaped by this socially involved, Black theology, Bonhoeffer's own thinking about cheap grace turned to how, as Christianity became part of the general background of Western life, monasticism arose as an effort to resist "the secularization of Christianity."[13] However, Bonhoeffer claimed that the movement ended up reinforcing worldly hierarchies of meritorious achievement and self-possession; the monk's attempt to flee worldliness yielded to a subtle form of worldly love.[14] Exercising cultural separation from worldly influences, evangelicalism has achieved something quite similar in its construction and elevation of purity culture.

If Bonhoeffer argued that cheap grace leaves the person and community unchanged in its wake, then a partial explanation of why that grace is ineffectual comes from its neglect of *repentance*, namely, the need for individuals and the community to turn from one reality to another. While Priscilla Perkins observed two decades ago the guilt- or shame-inducing dimensions of the term "repentance"—dimensions that might limit its potential as a rhetorical resource for progressive action—the intervening years show no indication that use of the term is diminishing within Christian vocabularies. Repentance appears as a key term in efforts to push white Christians beyond largely cosmetic responses and milquetoast multiculturalism (more on this point in relationship to rhetorics of reconciliation in chapter 4). Progressive Christian scholars and public intellectuals likewise refuse to give up the ghost on repentance. New Testament and historical Jesus scholar Marcus Borg argues that Christianity is ultimately about personal and social change, which provides a framework for biblical meanings of forgiveness and repentance. Borg, an Episcopalian, asserts that traditional Christian theology and many liturgical worship practices embody the idea that God accepts, loves, and forgives without condition. Taking just the right actions or holding just the right beliefs is not the central concern of faith. This knowledge relieves practitioners of the need to be "secure by measuring up."[15] In this space of acceptance, a person is paradoxically freed to take risks—like the turning required by repentance—that may result in a new vision. Borg reports that biblical repentance was not bound up with feeling guilt or shame. Rather, it involved making a turn (i.e., redirecting one's life and choices back toward the divine) and "going beyond the mind we have."[16] He argues that socialization within a particular place and time inculcates in practitioners ideas that lead them away from this ongoing transformation-oriented religiosity. Getting wrapped up in being a "good Christian," a "godly man," or a "biblical woman" actually impedes Christian living (as did the monk's separatism in Bonhoeffer's reading). Repentance is not, then, about feeling bad but about taking steps to rededicate oneself to core values.

While evangelicals are unlikely to encounter this idea through Borg's work, Kate Bowler observes that similar sentiments from social work researcher Brené Brown appear ubiquitous at evangelical women's conferences, including the Jen Hatmaker–headlining 2016 "IF:Gathering."[17] An Episcopalian like Borg, Brown labels her core framework for thinking about how individuals develop the capacity to live well with vulnerability the "Wholehearted Way," citing as inspiration a line from the modern language confession in the Episcopal Church's *Book of Common Prayer*: "We have not loved you with our whole heart."[18] Brown's insight about confession (a prelude to repentance) as a moral self-accounting in the context of relational vulnerability with God and others illuminates Borg's definition of repentance as a shift in mind or life direction. Both Borg and Brown speak to the problem of trying to earn love and belonging by enacting certain roles or performing particular identities understood as valuable within a social group, and they associate potential remedies to this problem with Christian traditions of confession and repentance.

Cheap grace, according to Bonhoeffer, resists confession and repentance: "Let [the Christian] be comforted and rest assured in his possession of this grace—for grace alone does everything. Instead of following Christ, let the Christian enjoy the consolations of his grace! That is what we mean by cheap grace, the grace which amounts to the justification of sin without the justification of the repentant sinner."[19] In contrast to cheap grace, Bonhoeffer advocates for "costly grace" that requires judgement for sin and repentance of the sinner.[20] Costly grace makes demands of the Christian, requiring constant turning.[21] Such grace is costly because it may necessitate literally dying for the cause or a metaphorical dying to familiar habits and attitudes: "When Christ calls a man, he bids him come and die."[22] And, as L. Gregory Jones notes, "the goal of repentance, as with grace, is to lead people into community."[23] Divinely sponsored transformation occurs in a community context of mutual vulnerability.

Grace as a source of agency and social transformation emerges as a theme in studies of the literacy and rhetorical activities of women who forge community out of shared traumas. Building on Sylvia Scribner's work, Beth Daniell observes that literacy as grace is often positioned as the culmination of a developmental process that moves from adaptation for everyday purposes, to power for exercising agency, to grace that confers esteemed status. Studying the literacy activities of women in Al-Anon, Daniell argues that this trajectory was reversed among her participants. The grace that the women in Daniell's research received "through informal, vernacular reading and writing" took the form of a personal sense of agency and self-value.[24] "Spiritual awakening" for these women was "a change in understanding or perception."[25] According to Daniell, the women reported that reading and talking about experiences similar to and different from their own increased their options for how to live.[26] She found that the spiritual grace of community-grounded shifts in perception can serve as the basis for literacy understood as daily functions and advancement.[27]

Literacy as grace comes through encounters with and exchanges about differences—significant and small—that enlarge the self's capacity to act and to interpret traumatic experiences. By entering into imaginative worlds through fiction crafted by authors with backgrounds different from their own and into their friends' lives through conversation, the women in

Daniell's study were able to approach their own traumas in transformative ways. For example, the spirituality-informed fiction by Black women (e.g., Alice Walker, Toni Morrison, Ntozake Shange) and the conversations these texts stirred served to present these white women with new perspectives that became the basis for new ways of thinking about boundaries in relationships or the quality of friendships. Likewise, in a rhetorical analysis of the theologies crafted by white and Black women in a domestic violence shelter, Carol L. Winkelmann found that when participants placed the violence done to them into a context of their own design and discussed what they noticed about each other's stories, new theological stances arose that enabled them to act.[28] For example, these women came to "see grace as arising in connection with other people; that is, grace is not simply God's divine power to forgive and transform, but their own relational openness in the context of family . . . and community that redeems."[29] Both Daniell and Winkelmann articulate the grace that is possible through literacy and rhetorical activities for those who have suffered trauma.

These researchers attended to the experiences of women whose literacy and rhetorical activities readied them to receive grace (i.e., a shift in perception accomplished through practices of reading, writing, and talking) within a community context that transformed their relationships to trauma and that created grounds for agency. This expansive sense of self-in-relation-to-others that produces opportunities to encounter a capacious sense of agency resonates with Serene Jones's insights about the "surprising moment" of grace: "In full abundance, this grace strengthens the capacity to act at the very same time it invites you to fuller love of neighbor and ever-deepening love of the God who both frees and holds."[30] By generating rhetorical materials to make such shifts in perception more likely and by reinventing rape culture–enabling proverbs of ashes, faithful deliberators extend a costly rhetorical grace that might change the larger community.

A costly rhetorical grace might urge a turn away from cultural, political, and affective investments in an ideology of purity that promotes victim-blaming and that collaborates with the larger US rape culture. The cost entails potentially sacrificing established means of preserving a strong social order through gender roles, old identities that fail to cohere in light of survivors' stories and reinterpretations of their experiences, and typical ways of feeling and acting. This is the sort of call made by #ChurchToo architects Joy and Paasch and is akin to the calls of #SilenceIsNotSpiritual framers Harper and Bauman. Stories such as those told by the women in Daniell's and Winkelmann's studies help name as sinful those systems that permit violence and trauma-inducing relationships. That naming raises the possibility of community transformation through repentance—not through a guilty feeling but through a turning back to God's plan, a turning from one set of desires and practices to another.[31] Within evangelicalism, a high concern with sexual purity has prevented serious confrontations with rape culture because the community's frameworks allow evangelicals to understand rape as occurring only under certain circumstances.[32] Baptist pastor Kyndall Rae Rothaus likewise argues that churches in her tradition might not understand some instances as assaults because victims "were drinking, or because of what they were wearing, or because they weren't virgins, or because they weren't careful enough, etc."[33] This arrangement of values, which permits only some trauma narratives to register as describing harm and victimization, provides necessary background for understanding comments from several evangelical leaders in the wake of the *Access Hollywood* recording.

CHEAP RHETORICAL GRACE THROUGH PROVERBS OF ASHES

Responses to that recording from many established evangelical leaders relied on three related trauma-minimizing proverbs of ashes. First, they drew on a theology of purity that conflates sexual violence with sexuality generally, configures men as particularly prone to licentiousness, and emphasizes the importance of a strong sense of social order. Such a theology leads these figures to not acknowledge that the central problems with Trump's comments are their abusive nature and their reliance on coercion. For example, Robert Jeffress, pastor of the multi-thousand congregant megachurch First Baptist Dallas, described Trump's comments as "lewd, offensive, and indefensible"; similarly, the founding executive director of the Christian Coalition, Ralph Reed, called the remarks "inappropriate."[34] With an apparent focus on violated etiquette and on procedural concerns about an all-or-nothing approach to sexual purity, one either has purity or not. Whatever else might inform the situation doesn't really matter. Under that rubric, Trump's comments fail to measure up and are unfortunate, but violence, coercion, and questions of consent fail to even register as issues. This lacuna is typical of evangelical narratives about sex. Materials from evangelical organizations and writers rarely acknowledge that stories they narrate depict not sex generally but instances of emotional or physical abuse and coercion. For example, the emotional turmoil following sex within a coercive situation is presented as the natural consequence of sex outside of heterosexual Christian marriage.[35] Purity culture narrates survivors' experiences such that trauma and feelings of shame are among the unfortunate occurrences that befall bad people or people who make bad choices.

Second, this narration directs survivors and their community toward what theologian Pamela Cooper-White calls "an ethic of instant forgiveness."[36] Christians often identify strongly with the call to forgive those who harm them and to be "reconciled" with one another (longer discussions of forgiveness and reconciliation appear in, respectively, chapter 3 and chapter 4). While multiple scriptural references encourage these attitudes, Cooper-White argues that the church's forgiveness often offers a cheap grace to aggressors of violence and faint hope for justice to survivors. Such a failing arises partially from neglecting what Christians call "discipleship." Discipleship involves practices of Christian subject formation that require ongoing emotional, intellectual, and moral transformation.[37] Focusing on survivors forgiving aggressors comes at the expense of urging preparators and enablers to repentance and of pursuing justice. Cooper-White also contends that churches often construct "an atmosphere of niceness" rather than deal with conflict.[38] Recall the emphasis placed on preserving community cohesion among evangelicals and their forebears. Such a rush to unity and conflict-avoidance manifest in Trump supporters' defenses. In his statements, Jeffress went on to say that "the Bible teaches we are all sinners who all need Christ's forgiveness."[39] Likewise, Jerry Falwell Jr. asserted, "We are all sinners, every one of us. We've all done things we wish we hadn't."[40] The impulse toward instant forgiveness appears conditional—not on the nature of the sinner's confession or the quality of his apology but on membership within a preexisting group or on the trust of group members.

A third proverb of ashes that undergirds these responses asserts the high value of in-group trust and a belief in the group's ability to easily identify the right course of action.[41] Anderson recounts the story of a woman harassed and coerced into a sexual relationship by a fellow churchgoer, and when the situation was reported to the pastor, he replied that the aggressor should be trusted "because he's a Christian."[42] Group membership or alliance with the group can, as it were, cover many sins. Reed downplayed news about the *Access Hollywood* recording by highlighting the sense that evangelicals are a monolithic voting bloc with a clear agenda: "A ten-year-old tape of a private conversation with a talk show host ranks low on [evangelicals'] hierarchy of concerns."[43] Eric Metaxas, evangelical author of a popular biography about Bonhoeffer, initially appeared dismissive of Trump's comments when he tweeted, "BREAKING: Trump caught using foul language, combing his hair oddly. Could this be the end of his campaign?"[44] Metaxas later deleted the comment, asserting that he was unaware of the recording's content. He went on to condemn Trump's remarks while also equating them with Hillary Clinton's court-ordered legal defense in a child molestation case where she negotiated a plea for the preparator and with Bill Clinton's sexual history.[45]

From these perspectives, the community and reality itself are viewed as stable and easily understood, and what's important to the group can be readily identified. This maneuver also illustrates the White Christian Strategy, the political-theological alliance that relies on cultural nostalgia and social anxiety. The White Christian Strategy likewise helps explain the strength of evangelicals' endorsement despite Trump's lack of thoroughgoing religiosity. Essentially, Reed, Metaxas, Jeffress, Falwell, and others told their audiences, *We're Christians. Trump's a Christian. We know what's right. Trust us. Believe us.* Other highly visible figures within evangelical circles took these commonplaces (i.e., sex-violence conflation, community-dependent instant forgiveness, and in-group trust) and rearticulated community values through theologically reflective invention in order to promote faithful deliberation.

COSTLY RHETORICAL GRACE THROUGH VALUES ARTICULATION

At the forefront of efforts to reinvent arguments from these commonplaces were some of the leading women in contemporary evangelical cultural production. As Tyler Wigg-Stevenson observed on Twitter, in fall 2016, Moore and Hatmaker each had more followers on that social media platform than various combinations of several longtime evangelical male leaders who vocally supported Trump. Moore and Hatmaker employed values articulation to address the situation. As Ringer argues, values articulation—practicing situational flexibility and leveraging ethos to name new arrangements of shared values—is an important rhetorical strategy for evangelical deliberation.[46] Through social media writing in the wake of the *Access Hollywood* recordings, Moore and Hatmaker enacted a costly rhetorical grace through an articulation of values that sought to reinvent proverbs of ashes.

Beth Moore: Systemic Confrontation

Born in 1957, the Houston-based ministry leader Moore founded the highly influential Living Proof Ministries in 1994. Moore works as an evangelical teacher, author, and ministry leader. As a woman who regularly contributes to Christian media venues and speaks to multi-thousand person gatherings about matters of faith and devotion, Moore does not fit easily within the ostensibly rigid boundaries of the SBC, a Protestant denomination that restricts ordination to men. By framing her activity as teaching (rather than preaching), Moore sidesteps some potential controversy within conservative evangelicalism.[47] Emily Cope argues that Moore "masterfully obscures the very fact of her preaching, a genre that excludes women from the role of rhetor. . . . Importantly, in the rhetorical space that she creates for herself, Moore offers a feminized evangelical message that revises the prevailing evangelical preaching tradition."[48] Through the creation of this rhetorical space, Moore achieves a high level of success within evangelicalism, especially among women. Moore's books are among the most popular items sold by LifeWay, an SBC-affiliated outlet for Christian cultural materials. A prolific writer, Moore uses her texts to convey personal experiences, explore theological issues, and lead readers through highly accessible studies of scriptures. She has authored numerous Bible studies and devotionals.

For Moore, ministry—her writing, speaking, and organizational work—is informed by her status as a survivor of childhood sexual abuse. Moore describes how that abuse influenced her: "My natural tendency to speak out was suddenly stifled when I became a victim of sexual abuse before the age of five by someone close to my family. This experience had a devastating effect on my personality. . . . The effects of abuse wove its way into the fiber of everything I did, including the relationships I formed."[49] When #MeToo appeared widely in social media on October 15, 2017, Moore used the expression in a tweet that day. Moore went on to write, "A [well-meaning] mentor told me at 25 that people couldn't handle hearing about sexual abuse and it would sink my ministry. It didn't."

One year before the mainstreaming of #MeToo, over the course of an hour and a half on October 9, 2016, Moore posted four tweets after the *Access Hollywood* revelations. The series began with the demand that serves as the epigraph for this chapter: "Wake up, Sleepers, to what women have dealt with all along in environments of gross entitlement & power. Are we sickened? Yes. Surprised? NO."[51] In this first tweet, Moore mobilized a costly rhetorical grace that encouraged spiritually grounded shifts in perception, shifts that would necessitate her audience taking action to confront the pervasiveness of rape culture. She addressed those who might be surprised by Trump's comments as "Sleepers," thus directly confronting readers who fail to consider issues of sexual violence or who, perhaps, disbelieve reports of gender-based violence, assault, and harassment. Naming this group "Sleepers" alludes to the Bible: "This is why it is said: Wake up, sleeper, rise from the dead, and Christ will shine on you."[52] Through this reference to scripture, Moore demonstrated her Christian literacy and appealed to the ethos she has crafted over more than thirty years in ministry work focused on women, work within a denomination that subscribes to complementarianism.[53] This allusion implies that becoming aware of sexual trauma's widespread nature and acting to reduce its frequency is like the light of Christ resurrecting the dead. By answering the demand Moore makes, repentance—a turning from inadequate realities and identities toward different ones—becomes possible. The grace—that is, the expansive agency emerging from a new perspective within a community grappling with members' traumatic experiences—that Moore extended here is costly because it links work to address sexual violence with a life spent dying and rising in Christ, that is, with the work of Christian subject formation (i.e., discipleship).

After establishing her identity as a Christian who grounds public discourse in scripture, Moore leveraged her community membership to encourage a rededication to evangelical values. Moore defined rape culture, sexual violence, and ignorance about these conditions as a terrain of sin that leads to spiritual death. She elevated concern about violence above the strong evangelical focus on purity. While evangelicals have produced voluminous commentaries about sexuality (e.g., the moral conduct of heterosexual intimacy, LGBTQ+ sexuality, abortion, gender roles and identity), this attention to personal sexual morality has not often made violence and rape central to those conversations. As Rothaus argues, "Without doubt the primary sexual sin of our time is assault"; however, congregations "seldom, if ever, hear about rape from the pulpit."[54] Moore and Rothaus worked to refocus the mission of the church around sexual sin, interrogate systems that trivialize survivors' experiences, and center survivors' voices.

The costly rhetorical grace Moore practiced contrasts with the cheap rhetorical grace extended by several other prominent evangelical leaders analyzed in the previous section. In an elegant instance of confronting without explicitly naming leaders who dismissed or downplayed the importance of challenging sexually violent language and actions, Moore further called into question the established ranking of community values: "Try to absorb how acceptable the disesteem and objectifying of women has been when some Christian leaders don't think it's that big a deal."[55] Recall how Anderson notes that appealing to the Christian identity of an accused aggressor diminishes the force of the accusation among evangelicals and encourages the victim to doubt her own account.[56] By taking to task high-esteem figures within her own community without specifically naming them, Moore rejected ingroup identity and political affinity as bases for lenient treatment of a person who commits acts of, or mobilizes discourses of, sexual violence. In other words, she was uninterested in grace as niceness or as conflict avoidance. Community cohesion was not paramount.

This rhetoric consequently opened space for others to distance themselves from stances and sentiments held by some vocal evangelical leaders. "Try[ing] to absorb" the feelings of survivors who have dealt with violence involves asking new questions for the purpose of cultural analysis. Asking such questions implies a rejection of previous answers about established values. When asking readers to identify with the experiences of others, Moore promoted empathy with survivors in order to produce new understandings within the community at large. Like the participants in Daniell's research who sought out others' experiences through reading and conversation and who found these experiences a source of perceptual change that fostered a sense of agency, Moore's readers were called to a changed perception that might create the opportunity for a recommitment to core values: repentance-as-a-change-of-life over forgiveness-as-a-niceness-for-getting-along; and solidarity with survivors by addressing violence over in-group identity alliances and gendered purity.

Moore drew on the authority carried by her experience as a survivor of childhood sexual violence and of violent threats to build and extend grounds for identification and community: "I'm one among many women sexually abused, misused, stared down, heckled, talked naughty to. Like we liked it. We didn't. We're tired of it."[57] Moore's discussions of her abuse enable her "to connect interpersonally with others."[58] Invoking those experiences in this comment series connected her with other survivors and, by extension, connected "Sleepers" who hadn't dealt with the reality of rape culture to survivors, their concerns, and their allies. The authority Moore established through her ongoing disclosure also allowed her to identify the problem of violence, to claim her own desires, and to refuse the expectations others might force on her. To name what she did and did not "like" resisted the gendered emotional labor of being expected to anticipate and meet others' desires—sacrificing her own desires and autonomy. She went on to write, "'Keep your mouth shut or something worse will happen.' Yes. I'm familiar with the concept. Sometimes it's terrifyingly true. Still, we speak."[59] By closing this series of related tweets with an example of intimidation tactics and violent threats visited on survivors who might confront abusers, rapists, or harassers, Moore named her and others' commitment to speak even if raising their voices proved personally costly.

Hatmaker: Individual Confrontation

While Moore avoided naming Trump, Jen Hatmaker entered more explicitly into political commentary in a lengthy Facebook post. Hatmaker has written about her life as a Christian woman in several bestselling books that were carried for years by LifeWay (such as *7: An Experimental Mutiny Against Excess*), spoken at many large conferences (such as the IF:Gathering), and hosted a show for the cable channel HGTV. She was a celebrity within evangelical subculture who provided audiences with a glimpse into her daily life and struggles—all with winsome humor. Rhetoric and literacy scholar Bethany Mannon describes Hatmaker's use of personal narrative as mixing "hyperbole, self-deprecation, and references to wine, college football, and popular cultures."[60] As Mannon observes, Hatmaker also fits within a category called "Xvangelical"—a constituency that comes out of evangelicalism, taking its theology seriously while also inviting reevaluations of its conservativism. This label seems particularly true following the social media incident described in this chapter. Graduates of Oklahoma Baptist University, Hatmaker and her husband, after several years of service at an established church, founded Austin New Church in 2008 as a response to their growing concern for economic justice and relationship-oriented ministry with the poor. Like Moore, Hatmaker would be one of the initial signatories of the #SilenceIsNotSpiritual statement in 2017.

On the morning of October 11, 2016, Hatmaker posted to her Facebook page a response to the Trump tapes.[61] Through several interconnected rhetorical choices, Hatmaker established her audiences, appealed to an ethos these communities would recognize as virtuous, and leveraged that ethos to assert evangelical values about family and relationships. Like Moore, Hatmaker located the primary problem with comments like Trump's not in their generally sexual nature but in their description of violence and coercion. By directly confronting Trump, she sought to indict the candidate for his language and actions. Her concern rested not on the use of taboo terms but on the "terrifying, habitual, sexually abusive behavior toward women" that the then-candidate's comments captured. When Hatmaker rejected labels such as "funny, cute, harmless, or normal" or "guy banter," she insisted on naming the harm this discourse accomplished—both to the women its circulation might have re-traumatized and to all women through its acceptance of rape culture's assumptions about women's status as sexual commodities. The costly rhetorical grace she demonstrated demanded a community-level perceptual shift within evangelicalism to re-center its vision on violence instead of purity. It also required her readers to engage with survivors' experiences of assault, which might move them to revise their explanatory stories about sexual violence. New understandings might lead to new actions. In this way, Hatmaker confronts purity and rape cultures, which both minimize sexual trauma and blame victims instead of holding aggressors and their enablers to account. Specifically, acting differently might mean voting differently. In short, Hatmaker argued that no political alliance is worth cheapening the Christian message—a message with the life- and community-transforming power of grace at its center.

The costly rhetorical grace for which Hatmaker argued also involved rejecting instant forgiveness in favor of repentance as a process of identity and behavior reformation (i.e., discipleship). This stance developed through claims that leveraged emotion in order to petition for some measure of justice. Hatmaker opened her post with compassion toward those who've experienced the acts Trump described and with "fury" that a figure who enthusiastically described violence as "locker room talk" would be a presidential nominee. Hatmaker clearly found Trump's explanation inadequate. In her refusal to accept the assault-normalizing label, Hatmaker insisted on what Bonhoeffer called the "justification of the sinner"—the need for confession and a change of life that attend the grace experience.[62] By portraying his language in terms that made it seem ordinary, Trump offered a non-apology and, thus, a lack of repentance.[63] Addressing Trump directly, Hatmaker told him that he "cannot kiss, grope, grab, and move on women without their permission."[64] In short, forgiving the speaker was not her concern. Changed behavior and language were the heart of her message.

Along with her focus on identity and change, Hatmaker leveraged relational categories and her Christian ethos to advocate for an expansive sense of agency that would enable her audience to confront cultural and religious commonplaces that authorize violence. To confront the behavioral model Trump provided in his comments, Hatmaker held up her male relations as examples: her sons, husband, father, father-in-law, and friends. Thereby, she also established her identity as mother, wife, daughter, daughter-in-law, and friend. Such relational categories carry significant cultural cache generally and within evangelicalism. After reminding her audience of these esteemed positions, she made direct appeals to her audience along gendered lines. Through these remarks directed toward "women" and "men," Hatmaker challenged some concepts that underlie rape and purity culture. Reminding women that they "are not just a sexual object," she disrupted the assumptions that lead to a host of evangelical injunctions about how women are to behave, which are based in developing appropriate modes of femininity that at best *might* protect them from sexual violence. Likewise, in her address to men, she chipped away at purity culture's all-or-nothing perspective on sexuality. By naming the actions Trump describes as "deviant," Hatmaker reinforced her earlier focus on the problem as violence and abuse of power, not sexuality itself. By repeating the phrase, "Don't believe it. Don't listen," to open these two sets of remarks, Hatmaker urged readers to not accept identities grounded in sexual objectification or violence. Combined with injunctions of "you are not," these statements subtly echo Jesus's use of antithesis to introduce both commonsense wisdom and ideas from sacred texts (i.e., "You have heard it said") and then to revise them (i.e., "but I say to you"). While not explicitly invoking religious language, she relied on relational categories, faith-informed sensibilities, and a scripturally reminiscent argumentative structure to advocate for values different from those expressed by leaders such as Reed and Jeffress.

Religious sensibilities regarding reconciliation as an orientation toward right relations within a community context were also mobilized when Hatmaker challenged commonplace assumptions about trust. Like the participants in Roxanne Mountford's study of women's approaches to preaching, Hatmaker and Moore, in this instance, "focus not on the regeneration of *individual* souls but rather on the regeneration of *communities*."[65] The regeneration Hatmaker sought would come from shifting the locus of trust: from trust in traditional evangelical leadership, as well as in the claims of privileged men, toward trust in survivors who share their stories of assault. This shift would promote the Christian goal of reconciliation: a restoration of right relationships after ruptures within a community and a "corporate transformation—a turning toward those who have been 'othered,' a restoring . . . of the whole society."[66] To capture the rupture caused by sexual violence and discourses that promote it, Hatmaker quoted Trump's claim that "when you're a star, they let you do it. You can do anything." Countering this sentiment, Hatmaker invoked "the millions of women [who] have been victimized then laughed off."[67] Here, three issues of ethos and trust are at work. First, when accusations of violence are levied against a person of privilege and power, it is important to not automatically trust the individual in a secure position and rather to believe (that is, to consider) the account of the victimized. Second, being aware that patterns of violence and silencing work to disempower women on a significant scale means working to place survivors' stories at the center of the religious community's circle of concern. Third, all of this implies the need to not simply trust the endorsements of established evangelical leaders who claimed a values hierarchy that privileged traditional political alliances over the problem of rape culture.

CONFRONTING THE CHRISTIAN MACHINE

As the legacy of the Trump presidency continues to inform the argumentative landscape, attending to moments during his candidacy that had socially invigorating potential may point toward feminist interventions for the future. Looking at anti-violence resistance within the evangelical community immediately prior to the election and prior to the mainstreaming of the #MeToo movement may allow us to imagine political coalitions, community realignments, and rhetorical practices in later moments. Theorizing and learning from the rhetoric employed by religious women prominent in a constituency that voted so overwhelmingly for Trump may point toward models for confronting rape culture and leveraging religious resources as part of that undertaking.

Given that 81 percent of voting white evangelicals cast ballots for Trump,[68] perhaps not much had changed in the decade after Sharon Crowley lamented the limited paths for invention that she, as a liberal, secular academic, had generated to rhetorically engage with fundamentalist and conservative evangelical Christians. However, even if it appears limited in immediate outcomes, I see rhetorical grace urging community transformation and forging new pathways. A focus on grace may risk individualizing and spiritualizing in escapist ways experiences of trauma with systematic factors. Indeed, within Christian communities, and evangelicalism in particular, the social implications of grace are frequently downplayed against the importance of a personal encounter with God's forgiveness. However, Moore and Hatmaker relied on an understanding that, as Christians, they were liberated to engage in labor that might be difficult or uncomfortable. Recalling evangelical resistance to out-group relationships, these two certainly took personal, costly risks given the political conservatism of much of their audience.

Ultimately, calls for costly grace in this instance appear to have had limited impact on the specific question of supporting a political candidate who unapologetically employed sexually coercive language. On one level, the exit poll numbers would suggest this failure. On another level, the extent of the backlash Hatmaker experienced also speaks to the rejection of this costly grace. Shortly after her Facebook post, Hatmaker gave an October 2016 interview in which she discussed her views about Trump, endorsed marriage equality, and expressed sympathy for the Black Lives Matter movement.[69] These positions landed Hatmaker outside current evangelical consensus. Consequently, she faced vocal backlash, demonstrating the risks involved in questioning the community-preserving functions of white supremacy and heteronormativity. Following that interview, a number of leading evangelicals criticized her apparent departure from orthodox theology, and LifeWay announced that they would no longer carry Hatmaker's books. The amount of media attention the situation generated led to *Texas Monthly* publishing an article that called October 2016 to October 2017 "The Year of Jen Hatmaker."[70] In a 2017 Good Friday blog post, Hatmaker reflects on the aftermath of the controversy she faced: "I became painfully aware of the machine, the Christian Machine. I saw with clear eyes the systems and alliances and coded language and brand protection. . . . I saw how it all works, not as an insider where I've enjoyed protection and favor for two decades, but from the outside where I was no longer welcome. The burn of mob mentality scorched my heart into ashes, and it is still struggling to function."[71] Articulating evangelical culture as a "machine" echoes Bonhoeffer's insight about cheap grace being "grace as a doctrine, a principle, a system," and "a general truth" rather than as a phenomenon uniquely responsive to different situations.[72] Here, the system-machine resisted efforts to dislodge the White Christian Strategy's tight articulation of partisan politics, normative sexuality within purity and rape cultures, and evangelical identity. Moore replied to Hatmaker's post with an expression of sorrow over the situation and a prayer to Jesus for collective solace and direction. Public displays of the friendship between these figures as means of supporting faithful deliberation appear again in chapter 5.

This chapter has explored rhetorical invention that reworks proverbs of ashes so that enclave deliberation can enable costly rhetorical grace to prevail over cheap rhetorical grace. While any strategy for reshaping community deliberations may not yield immediate change, some changes may come from esteemed members repeatedly raising concerns in terms readily intelligible to the in-group. As the following chapters indicate, it may well be that Moore, Hatmaker, and others planted seeds that later began bearing fruit. The next chapter considers a moment that occurred more than a year after the *Access Hollywood* tapes emerged and not quite four months after the October 2017 popularization of the #MeToo movement. As this movement re-constellated conditions within the dominant US public, it also contributed to changes within evangelical enclaves, enabling and amplifying new opportunities for theologically reflective deliberation.

3

More Than Platitudes

Casuistically Tightening Forgiveness

The only reason I am able to have the support of these leaders now is because I am speaking out against an organization not within their community.

—**Rachael Denhollander**

But do all sexual sins call for the same response? Are we meant by God to respond to the sexually abusive the same way we respond to the sexually immoral?

—**Beth Moore**

Just as the preceding chapter identified ethos-dependent values articulation as a means to reinvent cheap grace-yielding proverbs of ashes, this chapter examines inventive work intended to move evangelicals from a platitude-laden notion of forgiveness toward a robust forgiveness. I analyze this work through the lens of casuistry, a case-based approach to generating practical ethics. My analysis focuses on statements produced following the 2017 and 2018 criminal sentencings of Larry Nassar, formerly a well-regarded sports medicine doctor at Michigan State University and a physician with USA Gymnastics. He was sentenced on federal child pornography charges and multiple state sexual assault charges involving minors. Although Nassar's abuse occurred in secular contexts, religious discourse surfaced in his response and his supporters' responses to allegations against him. A 2018 episode of the NPR podcast series dedicated to the Nassar saga, *Believed*, includes an interview with a survivor who noted these reactions. After rumors of a complaint by a victim circulated within the Michigan gymnastics community that trusted Nassar, a woman he'd long-exploited who did not yet realize his actions toward her constituted abuse wrote him a note of concern for his wellbeing. Nassar apparently replied that all he needed for support was "prayers." Between public allegations in August 2016 and Nassar's arrest in November, individuals and groups prayed with Nassar and for his ultimate vindication.[1] At the end of a January 2018 week dedicated to 156 victim impact statements describing the toll of Nassar's abuse, Rachael Denhollander, the first of Nassar's victims to publicly accuse him and the last to offer a statement in court, turned to religion during her remarks.

A self-identified evangelical, Denhollander put her beliefs on display in her victim impact statement, beliefs matching those historically associated with that stream of Christian tradition: biblicism, activism, conversionism, and crucicentrism.[2] Denhollander demonstrated these beliefs as she addressed the importance of the Bible in her theology, argued that forgiveness comes from "genuine repentance," quoted popular Christian writer C. S. Lewis, asserted that a divine "final judgment" bringing "God's wrath" on aggressors will come, and claimed that the "gospel of Christ . . . extends grace" even to Nassar.[3] Mainstream and Christian media outlets highlighted her invocation of faith.[4] Given the centrality of faith in her life, audience members of any or no religious background would surely understand an additional pain Denhollander went on to note in her statement and in a *New York Times* column that followed: that her efforts on behalf of abuse survivors led to the loss of her local church community.[5]

Denhollander, born in 1984, first experienced sexual abuse at age seven, perpetrated by a church member. The experience taught her to remain silent when she later encountered further abuse.[6] Denhollander started gymnastics at twelve. She sought treatment for back pain from Nassar, who began abusing her when she was fifteen. At nineteen, she rstarted remote law school at Oak Brook, a Christian institution in California. While studying law, Denhollander blogged about the conservative theological framework of "Christian worldview" and met her husband through correspondence about their shared theological interests. An activist-writer for conservative causes, Denhollander penned pieces for the pro-life group Live Action and the anti-evolution group Creation Ministries International.[7] Denhollander wrote a *New York Times* column following Nassar's sentencing that detailed her efforts to document the abuse she experienced as well as the personal costs of going public and of becoming an advocate for survivors abused by fellow evangelicals.

On January 31, 2018, *Christianity Today* published online an interview with Denhollander in which she elaborated on her loss of a church community. She situated her experience within the difficulty evangelical communities face when developing adequate responses to sexual violence—responses directed toward survivors generally and toward aggressors connected with their own churches and associations. Denhollander described her advocacy on behalf of survivors who made abuse allegations against figures associated with the influential evangelical network of congregations Sovereign Grace Churches (SGC). In October 2012, several former members filed a lawsuit alleging child molestation and an ensuing cover-up dating to the 1980s and 1990s when C. J. Mahaney was the lead pastor. Just a few months later, former SGC volunteer Nathaniel Morales was indicted on child sexual abuse charges dating to roughly the same period. While the lawsuit was ultimately dismissed in 2014 for technical reasons related to timing and jurisdiction, that same year, Morales was convicted of the charges he faced. Denhollander began in 2012 her own investigation of the issues surrounding these SGC scandals, promoting transparency and accountability within Christian institutions. Indeed, her work eventually convinced Al Mohler—longtime Southern Baptist Theological Seminary president and Mahaney defender who had joked in public about the SGC controversy in dismissive ways—to change his mind and walk back his support of Mahaney in 2019.

This advocacy led to tensions between her and leaders at Immanuel Baptist Church (IBC) in Louisville, which her family attended. When her church invited leaders from the SGC network to preach at IBC, Denhollander challenged that decision. Church elders pushed back in a variety of ways, leaving her with a sense that they thought her "judgment was too clouded" as an abuse victim. She and her family eventually left that congregation.[8] Though evangelical leaders might champion her court testimony against a figure working within secular institutions (i.e., Nassar) and condemn sexual violence outside of their enclave, she asserted that they would not respond assertively when believers of their sort are accused of sexual violence: "The extent that one is willing to speak out against their own community is the bright line test for how much they care and how much they understand."[9] A "poor theology and a poor understanding of grace," according to Denhollander, informed this strong defense of in-group members.[10] Throughout this interview, Denhollander critiqued the limits of her community's ability to identify with survivors, locating those limitations in evangelical theology.

The same day Denhollander's interview was posted, Moore published on her blog a commentary responding to Denhollander's impact statement and her column. The Religion News Service also reposted this commentary. Moore urged her largely evangelical audience members to reflect on their silence surrounding sexual violence, a silence that involves failing to report abusers when accusations come to light and refraining from preaching on the issue. Denhollander's *Christianity Today* interview dovetails in remarkable ways with Moore's commentary given their same-day publication. Noting the remarkable convergence, Moore herself declares that the interview "must not be missed." She went on to say, "Had no idea this [interview] would come out on the same day I published this" blog post.[11] Through these materials, two faithful deliberators invited a rethinking of sin, grace, and forgiveness as they relate to evangelical responses to sexual violence. While Denhollander and Moore focused their attention on in-group members, the abuses they call their community to better contend with may have taken place in any context. They urged strong identification with survivors regardless of where or by whom they were assaulted. Both evangelicals promoted increased accountability for aggressors in their midst no matter whom they attacked or the context of that assault.

Their call places them in a long tradition of Christian and secular practitioners who critique common understandings of forgiveness, especially in the context of sexual assault, because of the way these understandings retraumatize survivors and contribute to a lack of accountability for aggressors. While Denhollander expressed forgiveness toward Nassar in court, she admitted to being "apprehensive" about saying so publicly, an apprehensiveness stemming from her concern that other evangelicals' theology of forgiveness allows many sexually violent aggressors to go unapprehended.[12] As Marie Fortune asserted in 1983, "Forgiveness is a word which has become more and more meaningless."[13] In its vacuous form, forgiveness operates as a vehicle filled with ideological baggage. Judith Herman describes the "fantasy of forgiveness" that sometimes captures survivors' desires: attempts at self-empowerment through appeals to transcendent love without processing trauma.[14] Seminary professor David Augsburger likewise refers to forgiveness of this sort as "a magical fantasy."[15] This magical forgiveness operates as a force that excuses, absolves, and spiritualizes abuse.[16] Like magic, this forgiveness happens as if in a flash. Recall that Pamela Cooper-White characterizes such counsel as an "ethic of instant forgiveness."[17] In contrast to proverbs of ashes that frame forgiveness as instant magic, Denhollander and Moore promote forgiveness as an act of personal, group, and divine healing that involves remembering trauma, restoring justice, and experiencing a kind of wholeness that releases survivors from the lasting hold aggressors might have over them. This revitalized forgiveness enables robust and faithful deliberation about how faith communities should respond to aggressors and survivors in light of specific responsibilities to both figures.

Promoting deliberation within a religious enclave that often defines divine grace and human forgiveness in ways that further harm survivors, Denhollander and Moore hope to fashion an evangelicalism that stops harboring Christian aggressors and retraumatizing survivors. This situation involves a theological problem and a resulting rhetorical task. The theological problem is an implicit-yet-operational antinomianism in evangelical responses to sexual violence. Recalling the discussion of antinomianism in chapter 1, this position severs the link between grace and moral behavior within Christian communities, absolving group members of responsibility for performing works of religious law, such as correcting injustice or seeking solidarity with those who are oppressed.[18] The antinomian problem of in-group privilege in the context of faithful deliberation regarding sexual violence creates a twofold rhetorical task: (1) distinguishing sexual immorality generally from sexually violent immorality when the community flattens such distinctions among its group members and (2) differentiating divine grace from human forgiveness. When conflated with group membership, grace becomes license. When mistaken for cheap grace, forgiveness becomes platitudinous proverbs of ashes that discourage appropriate action.

Denhollander and Moore urge their communities to move away from proverbs of ashes about forgiveness. In doing so, they echo L. Gregory Jones's critique of US Christianity's "trivialization of forgiveness," whereby religious practitioners empty forgiveness of its historic theological content in favor of individualized and interiorized versions of forgiveness that are grafted onto theological concepts and scripture.[19] This blending process and this outcome resemble what Kenneth Burke calls "casuistic stretching" and "demoralization." A particularly promising practice for encouraging deliberation across diverse constituencies, casuistic stretching is the rhetorical act of "introduc[ing] new principles while theoretically remaining faithful to old principles," but "the devices for ostensibly retaining allegiance to an 'original principle' by casuistic stretching eventually lead to demoralization, which can only be stopped by a new start."[20] Denhollander and Moore offer this "new start" through an informal mode of contextual theological analysis and rhetorical invention that I term "casuistic tightening," a kind of rhetorical movement that attempts to reinvigorate earlier principles for the purpose of enclave deliberation. Specifically, they question how stretching *divine grace* in instances of general sexual immorality to include *human forgiveness* in instances of predatory sexual immorality fails to promote appropriate modes of thought and action when addressing sexual assault aggressors within their in-group or when addressing assault survivors in general. They urge fellow evangelicals to take the broad ontological category of *sinner* as it relates to sexual violence and tighten their focus such that the constituent figures of *victim* and *aggressor*—as well as the community's attendant responsibilities to both figures—come into view. Framing Denhollander's and Moore's rhetoric as a revision of casuistic practice highlights how they reinvent platitudes about forgiveness and how they facilitate enclave deliberation.

CASUISTIC PRACTICE AND ETHICAL DELIBERATION

Seeking to stimulate enclave deliberation, Denhollander and Moore stand in what Albert R. Jonsen and Stephen Toulmin characterize as Christianity's casuistic tradition, which works to resolve "conflict[s] of basic obligations."[21] While casuistry fell into disrepute following Blaise Pascal's 1656 attack on its practice among Jesuits, Jonsen and Toulmin attempted to rehabilitate casuistry's reputation in 1988. They present casuistry as a case-based method for generating a practical ethics applicable to given situations; by considering present cases in light of previous, roughly similar cases, a rhetor employing casuistry may discern fitting responses or resolutions.[22] The rabbinic Judaism into which Jesus was born included a vibrant tradition of casuistry aimed at determining proper applications of religious law; this tradition informed Jesus's own rhetorical practice as he established paradigms for argument and action.[23] Through this method, early developers of Christian theology and church practice articulated various options for ethical Christian living.[24] During and following the sixth century, penitential books appeared that provided lists of sins and ranked their seriousness.[25] In this vein of developing a practical ethics grounded in questions of harm and consequences, some contemporary faithful deliberators articulate a reinvigorated understanding of grace and forgiveness in their community's response to sexual violence.

Examining Denhollander's and Moore's rhetorical activity as a repurposing of casuistic practice helps explain how they productively revise theological abstractions—platitudes about forgiveness—that stymie robust deliberation. Paul Lynch argues that casuistry is particularly well-suited to the work of determining ethical options while adopting a stance open to both present situations and precedents.[26] This rhetorical ethics resists the impulse Burke observes: hierarchically ordering absolute values, which can lead to inflexibility and suffering.[27] Building on this insight, Lynch notes the human "tendency to look upward toward abstraction (rather than around us in situation) for our ethics," suggesting that this tendency makes more theoretical, absolutizing ethical models attractive.[28] Despite the pull of absolutism and abstraction, casuistry offers opportunities to revisit commonly agreed upon values.

Scholars of rhetoric view what Burke calls "casuistic stretching" as particularly promising for deliberative purposes. The logic of casuistic stretching works by taking different concepts or positions and finding a broader third term or proposition around which discussion partners with divergent perspectives may reach agreement. For an everyday example, imagine two bargoers who strike up a conversation: One loves beer, while the other drinks only craft cocktails. Both are quite knowledgeable about their own indulgences, but neither enjoys what the other finds pleasurable. Rather than discuss their particular preferences, these conversation partners might discuss what they appreciate about the setting, about going out, or about the experience of imbibing. In short, they appeal to broader terms for the purpose of conversation. While not a deliberative example, this innocuous, expressive instance indicates the ordinariness of the process. For a deliberative example of how casuistic stretching works within religious discourse, Jonsen and Toulmin summarize the Apostle Paul's advice to Christians in Corinth regarding meat used in cultic rituals. Values were in potential conflict: practicality (i.e., purchasing meat from the market) and purity (i.e., abstaining from eating religiously impure substances). Paul invokes scripture to establish the broader value of God's sovereignty over all creation. Thus, even meat used in non-Christian ceremonies may be eaten.[29] Casuistic stretching works to generate a range of ethical responses for particular situations.

Casuistic stretching can enable evangelical deliberation about ethical problems. Jeffrey Ringer identifies the promise and peril of evangelical casuistic stretching for identification across lines of difference. Arguing that casuistic stretching may serve deliberative purposes by facilitating meaningful encounters with others' perspectives and undermining the dualistic thinking that leads to false dichotomies, Ringer emphasizes this point with regard to evangelicals' characterizations of in-groups and out-groups (e.g., assuming virtue as the province of one's own enclave).[30] Indeed, casuistic stretching opens possibilities for engagement outside of the evangelical community and promotes identification for cross-cultural purposes, calling audiences to acknowledge, and act with, those they perceive as different from themselves.

If casuistic stretching yields cross-cultural deliberation with audiences that do not share evangelical assumptions, then what I call "casuistic tightening" may aid enclave deliberation. Whereas casuistic stretching moves from the particular to the broad, Moore and Denhollander journey with their audiences from an already generalized value to a more specific understanding of that value, revitalized through an engagement with Christian tradition. They take their readers from assertions broadly shared within the enclave to related-but-narrower assertions for the purpose of promoting targeted identification and action. Specifically, they reflect theologically in order to move from *sin* to its component elements of *sexual sin* and *sexually violent sin*, from *sinner* to *victims* and *aggressors*, from forgiveness as synonymous with cheap grace and instant forgetting to forgiveness as connected with contextually informed repentance and justice. In so doing, they also move from a cheap, antinomian grace and a demoralized forgiveness toward a new start for evangelical forgiveness.

FORGIVENESS AS DEMORALIZED PLATITUDES AND ANTINOMIAN GRACE

By reflecting theologically on grace and forgiveness, Denhollander and Moore reinvent proverbs of ashes that silence sexual assault survivors' trauma stories, obstruct aggressor accountability, and stall institutional change. Even as the exact relationship between moral behavior (or "good works" or "obedience" to divine law) and divine grace consistently recurs as a contested issue within Christian history, there exists a general understanding that God's forgiving and saving divine grace should provoke the sinner to gratitude. That gratitude should generate a desire to obey divinely sanctioned moral injunctions, including commands to stand with those who suffer and who experience injustice. Denhollander and Moore appeal explicitly and implicitly to such commands as they critique their enclave's demoralized forgiveness that neglects practices of remembering trauma, restoring justice, and releasing emotional entanglements.

In the materials examined here, Denhollander in her statements and Moore in her blog post commentary establish themselves as members of a conservative evangelical community that addresses other members of that community. As insiders speaking to insiders, they affirm a focus on individual sin, assuming that a wide array of actions and thoughts count as "sinful" (that is, as demonstrative of the general enmity that exists between humans and their creator). Moreover, they articulate their evangelicalism through their biblicism, the high authority they ascribe to the Bible. In Denhollander's impact statement, she recalls memories of Nassar holding a Bible during court proceedings and of him saying that he had prayed for forgiveness. Directly addressing Nassar, Denhollander uses the conditional "if" with regard to Nassar actually having read the sacred text. Denhollander employs the phrase "the Bible you carry" three times and "the Bible you speak" once.[31] This framing asserts the importance of sacred texts to her and confronts any superficial appropriation of religious artifacts and terms by abusers. Scripture is often leveraged by abusers to justify their actions or by religious figures to diminish the harm abusers cause.[32] Survivors sometimes recall abuse happening as aggressors quote Bible verses to them.[33] Moore also relies heavily on scripture. She cites the Bible twice: once from the Gospel of Matthew and once from the Gospel of John. In the first instance, Jesus addresses divine wrath and judgment; in the second, Jesus embodies "the way of grace."[34] Both Denhollander and Moore navigate this relationship between justice/judgment and forgiveness/grace within their community's response to sexual violence, finding the former oft-neglected and versions of the latter privileged.

Denhollander and Moore confront a primary response of evangelicalism to sexual abuse: platitudes and silence informed by notions of forgiveness and grace that were demoralized through overstretching. Addressing one example of what this demoralized overstretching looks like in response to the first *Christianity Today* interview question, which inquired about the impact of abuse on her faith, Denhollander replied, "One of the areas where Christians don't do well is in acknowledging the devastation of the wound. We can tend to gloss over the devastation of any kind of suffering but especially sexual assault, with Christian platitudes like "God works all things together for good" or "God is sovereign." Those are very good and glorious biblical truths, but when they are misapplied in a way to dampen the horror of evil, they ultimately dampen the goodness of God."[35] The key terms here are "gloss over" and "misapplied." Belief in the sentiments expressed is not in question. Recall that one insidious element of proverbs of ashes is that a survivor may well believe deeply in a statement that another believer uses in a damaging way. Denhollander acknowledges her belief in enclave-shared assertions derived from scripture about God's ultimate benevolence, all-controlling power, and ability to repurpose evil for good. But when generally true statements are stretched to apply to specific circumstances, they may justify a harmful course of action (i.e., dampening the horror, failing to acknowledge the wounds). These glossed and misapplied truths work in tandem with the rape culture-enabling just-world hypothesis, which suggests since Christians assume the world and God are just, they may end up blaming victims and minimizing their trauma. Denhollander makes a similar assessment: "More often than not, particularly in the case of sexual assault," biblical truths are "really used to mitigate and to minimize—almost as if the victim handles it 'properly,' if the victim just forgives, all of the feelings are going to go away. That's not true and that's not what Scripture teaches."[36] This application of theological abstractions to particular circumstances of trauma demoralizes forgiveness, constructing it as a private, primarily emotional phenomenon defined by the dissolution of negative emotions.

When church communities present scripture verses as proof texts that self-evidently apply to a situation, they contribute to the demoralization of forgiveness. Proof texting may facilitate casuistic stretching by accommodating religious commonplaces to cultural norms—all while obscuring the very acts of interpretation such citations entail. This obscuring accounts for Denhollander's insistence about what scripture does and does not say about forgiveness, which is, of course, itself an act of interpretation. Survivors may hear, and speakers may employ, scriptural injunctions about forgiveness (e.g., "turn the other check," "forgive seven times seventy times," or avoid "throwing the first stone") as shame-inducing and silencing proclamations—that is, as proverbs of ashes.[37] In the comments above, Denhollander critiques how Christians direct notions of divine power and forgiveness toward abuse survivors in ways that frequently truncate whatever forms of healing they might pursue, avoid questions about aggressor accountability, and interiorize forgiveness—transforming it into an individualized, emotional experience separate from the larger context in which harm and healing occur.[38]

Christian forgiveness is also demoralized when understood as an individual act of instant forgetting (e.g., "forgive and forget"), rather than as a process of remembering and naming—that is, the work of "acknowledging the devastation."[39] Herman agrees on the importance of memory, identifying "remembering and mourning" as an important phase in the development of a survivor identity, which includes putting traumatic memories into language and integrating them into a coherent life narrative.[40] As Shari Stenberg notes, given that this trauma is so often "privatized," survivors' "need for grieving is not recognized."[41] If a demoralized forgiveness privileges forgetting, then memory work is important to a revitalized forgiveness. Some theologians emphasize remembering as part of Christian forgiveness in sexual abuse situations, because—while harm cannot be undone—when survivors locate violence and trauma within a moral framework, they enhance their ability to decide how they will respond.[42] In short, if the fact and extent of wrongdoing is named and acknowledged, the possibility of justice for survivors increases. This naming and this possibility, Denhollander suggests, are interrupted when community appropriations of scripture construct an ideal or "proper" victim on whom rests the burden to perform the tremendous, privatized emotional labor of forgiveness.

Just as Denhollander worries about the use of platitudes to silence survivors, Moore worries about the literal silence of many church members and leaders. The demoralization of forgiveness and the practices of "cheap grace" contribute to ethical inaction. Of Denhollander, Moore asserts how "proud" she and other Christians were "to stand with her in the public square" when she testified to her experience of sexual violence and to her identity as a believer. Alluding to (without detailing) Christians' work as "activists in numerous" areas, Moore wonders why this social mobilization falters when it comes to sexual violence, especially against children, when Jesus consistently advocated for the most vulnerable within society.

She frames the problem as one of "the church's silence."[43] Indeed, 64 percent of Protestant lead pastors hardly ever address domestic or sexual violence from the pulpit.[44] While Moore directs her comments to evangelicals broadly, she calls on church leaders in particular to respond in new ways: "We need pastors and teachers who are willing to address these realities often enough to alter the silence culture."[45] To explain this "silence culture," Moore repeatedly mobilizes language that points to feelings and behaviors around sexuality that her readers possibly share: discomfort, guilt, shame. The divine forgiveness (i.e., grace) evangelicals hope to receive for their own general sexual immorality—immoral from their theological orientation that generally locates heteronormative marriage as the only acceptable expression of sexuality (a position that Denhollander and Moore share)—contributes to a lack of proper action when confronted with instances of sexual assault.

Recalling the discussion in chapter 2, scholars of literacy and rhetoric likewise hold an interest in grace as a phenomenon with personal and social consequences.[46] Researchers argue that some groups of women working through painful situations experience grace as a relationally grounded agential capacity.[47] Building on these insights and using Dietrich Bonhoeffer's framework of "cheap grace" (which allows a life to go unchanged) and "costly grace" (which requires ongoing transformation), I identified argumentative commonplaces that extend a cheap grace, which minimizes the harm of sexual violence and abusive language: failing to distinguish sexual violence from sexuality, forgiving quickly, and leveraging in-group trust. I also identified inventive work that extends a grace costly to the dominant political ideology and cultural identity within predominantly white evangelicalism, a grace that places survivors' experiences at its center and orients believers toward personal and social transformation instead of group preservation.

To reinvent trauma-minimizing and community-preserving proverbs of ashes within their enclave, Denhollander and Moore call for theological reflection about divine grace and human forgiveness. Through their reflective work, they confront a permutation of antinomianism that followed from an overly stretched divine grace that results in different standards for in-group and out-group members and that contributes to a demoralized forgiveness. This issue of the in-group's presumed virtue surfaces when Denhollander observes, "The ultimate reality that I live with is that if my abuser had been Nathaniel Morales [an SGC youth group leader] instead of Larry Nassar, if my enabler had been [an SGC pastor] instead of [MSU gymnastics coach] Kathie Klages, if the organization I was speaking out against was Sovereign Grace under the leadership of [C. J. Mahaney] instead of MSU under the leadership of Lou Anna Simon, I would not only not have evangelical support, I would be actively vilified and lied about by every single evangelical leader out there. The only reason I am able to have the support of these leaders now is because I am speaking out against an organization not within their community."[48] Denhollander names here the antinomian problem: a magical instant forgiveness for in-group members and a higher standard of accountability for out-group members.[49] Group membership yields a cheap grace that fails to reach out-group members whose wrongdoing is amplified, that covers a multitude of sins for evangelical aggressors, and that turns forgiveness into one of many bludgeons used to silence survivors. In these ways, this antinomian position demoralizes forgiveness.

While Denhollander and Moore resist assigning bad intentions to their fellow evangelicals who encourage survivors to practice a demoralized forgiveness and who extend a cheap, antinomian grace to aggressors, they work to combat any presumption that community membership establishes right belief and action. Evangelicals' central problem, as they understand it, is not that a majority would allow sexual abuse of children to persist out of "simple institutional protectionism"[50] or the "preservation of the 'greater good.'"[51] Moore, noting that these excuses "have been discussed and cussed," soundly rejects them as deserving of any serious consideration; most Christians would not succumb to such "absurdity."[52] Rather, they view other evangelicals as collaborators able to deliberate about how the confused slippage between divine grace and human forgiveness contributes to a lack of productive compassion for survivors generally and genuine accountability for aggressors within their ranks specifically.

A NEW START: CASUISTIC TIGHTENING

Assuming the best of her audience and arguing from enclave-shared assumptions about the Bible's authority, in her Living Proof Ministry blog, which was also reposted as a commentary in the specialized Religion News Service, Moore casuistically tightens human forgiveness by reclaiming a text used to demoralize it: a scripture about divine grace in an instance of general sexual immorality that was overstretched when applied to sexually violent immorality. John 7:53–8:11, also called the *Pericope Adulterae*, a traditional name that works to highlight the sexual sin of the woman at the center of the episode, recounts a story about Jesus being presented with a woman accused of adultery and being asked for a judgment on the case. When Moore draws on this story, she cites Jesus as a model for resisting the temptation to make judgments about others' sexual impropriety, a model Christians hope would be applied to themselves if their sexual sins ever came to light:

> Even if our sexual sins belong to our pasts and our lives bear fruit of true repentance, we may still have an enormous reluctance to bring sexual misconduct to light.
>
> And for good reason. Take John 8, for instance, and the woman caught in the act of adultery dragged into the temple courts and Christ's response to whether or not she should be stoned. "Let him who is without sin among you be the first to throw a stone at her." Every accuser fell silent to the thuds of rocks dropping at their feet. Which of us has the right to throw a stone? None, of course. That's the way of Jesus. That's the way of grace.
>
> The thought that it could be our own sins shamefully exposed is so horrifying that we've ripped off a piece of duct tape and slapped it across our mouths.[53]

Establishing that a pervasive hermeneutic has stretched grace and forgiveness too far, Moore argues that evangelicals overlook and stay silent—taping their mouths shut—about sexual violence because of shame over their own sexual thoughts or actions. In this case, Moore fears that her audience members take their own hope that others will exercise "the way of grace" toward their nonviolent "sexual sins" that deviate from community standards, overgeneralize (or overstretch) that hope, and misapply that overstretched hope as a standard for human forgiveness in response to sexual assault. This overstretching, which results in a conflation of sexual immorality and sexually violent immorality under the broad category of sin, arises in part from an antinomian hermeneutic that likewise confuses divine grace with human forgiveness. Consequently, the community's use of scripture and theological categories must be tightened.

While the *Pericope Adulterae* historically provoked among theologians some anxiety about antinomianism, Moore rearticulates that concern to focus on particular harms that occur when *immoral/predatory* and *survivor/aggressor* are collapsed into the larger, universal categories of *sin* and *sinner*.[54] Historically, interpretive apprehensiveness around the antinomian potential in this passage centered around how it might undermine legal and social arrangements, including patriarchal control of women's sexuality.[55] For example, John Calvin insisted that Jesus in no way overturns the death penalty for adultery or any other legal consequence for recognized crimes.[56] In contrast to a concern about general immorality, Moore asks questions that focus on consequences and harm, which requires closely examining particular situations, considering specific roles, and discerning different obligations. Her directive to examine sin from an ethical standpoint of harm builds to her asking questions that name cases her audience would understand as general sexual immorality and cases of specific sexual violence: "But do all sexual sins call for the same response? Are we meant by God to respond to the sexually abusive the same way we respond to the sexually immoral? To be sure, all sexual sins have negative repercussions, but all sexual sins don't cause the *same level* of repercussions. Likewise, all predators are immoral but not all immorality is predatory. Do we walk away from an unrepentant rapist because we've all sinned sexually in one way or another or do we apprehend him? Do we ignore a church leader's sexual harassment because we slept with people in college?"[57] These questions from Moore disrupt and reverse what she understands as a misapplication of the *Pericope Adulterae*, a source of first principles as a biblical text vested with authority. Here, Moore casuistically tightens the categories of *sin* and *sinner* to bring into focus the sexually abusive sinner and sexually predatory sin.

To go to the lengths that Moore does to distinguish rape and harassment from casual sex may seem to some readers an unnecessary definitional project, because harassment and rape are categorically different from noncoercive sexuality (we do not, for example, refer to robbery as coercive gift-taking or forced donating). However, drawing such distinctions is necessary when the conflation of sex and violence is so common and when a religious community understands grace as a force that places all sin on a supposedly level field. When interpreted as a text about divine grace in regards to sexual sin generally and then applied to sexually predatory sin specifically, readings of this passage from John 8 result in a practice of human forgiveness as platitudes that promote silence. Moore notes neither contemporary survivor-centered hermeneutics about this passage nor the specific way violence against a woman is disrupted within the story.[58] However, by helping her audience ask potentially new questions in direct ways that work to reassert the centrality of scripture as a source of values, Moore encourages the community to reject theological platitudes that have equated proper action in response to sexual violence with a demoralized forgiveness that relies on instant forgetting and magical healing.

As Moore illustrates, establishing a paradigm for a reinvigorated evangelical forgiveness involves turning to the Bible, the primary source of highly valued principles for this enclave. If the principle of not casting the first stone has been overstretched, going back to the story may help believers revise their understanding of human forgiveness in relationship to divine grace. In addition to John, Moore quotes another Gospel text, Matthew

18:6–7, in which Jesus says of anyone who causes a child "to stumble, it would be better for them to have a large millstone hung around their neck and to be drowned in the depth of the sea."[59] Denhollander likewise quotes this passage as she directly confronts Nassar in court,[60] turning the Bible, a text that the aggressor physically held in earlier court proceedings, into a standard by which to judge his actions. In this regard, both faithful deliberators focus on speakers' practices and effects (i.e., how they prevent, cause, or contribute to childhood sexual abuse) rather than intentions, thus avoiding the trap of assigning good intentions to those with whom they agree and bad intentions to those with whom they disagree.

Given that these well-versed faithful deliberators believe that they address fellow Christians who act in good faith, they seek a new start for grace and forgiveness in their community's response to survivors and aggressors. By quoting texts that address divine wrath and final judgment, they do not simply reject forgiveness and grace, nor do they appeal to a fantasy of vengeance. Rather, they work to tighten the community's understanding of forgiveness and grace such that they are reinvigorated by religious notions of divine justice's ultimate arrival, a justice that finally restores all beings, substances, and relationships to their proper order. In this cosmic accounting and restoration, sinners face the distance they put between themselves and God, as well as the harm they caused others.

This new start for forgiveness, which considers questions of justice, depends upon casuistic tightening of the general category of sinner so that the component roles of victim and aggressor come into focus; outside of these relational categories contained by the broader term, the practice of forgiveness becomes demoralized from its status as a religious practice with specific theological and moral obligations. Attending to these constituent figures results in particular community responsibilities. Given how "forgiveness can really be misapplied," Denhollander tries "to couple forgiveness and justice. . . . Both of those are biblical concepts. Both of those represent Christ. We do not do well when we focus on only one of them."[61] Tightening human forgiveness so as to move it away from a generalized, vacuous, privatized emotional project that is solely the province of the survivor involves restoring a sense of justice for survivors, which may take several forms: persuading aggressors to repent, pursuing legal remedies, advocating for survivors, and enabling survivors to tell their stories. Moore promotes all these options. For example, Moore writes, "So, what can we do? We address [sexual violence] head-on. We start making it well known . . . that the church is henceforth an unsafe hiding place for predators. It's a great place for them to go forward and repent and turn themselves in, casting themselves on the grace of God with the rest of us but it must cease to be a safe harbor where they can hide and perpetuate their crimes."[62] Placing the mysterious work of grace in God's hands, the relational work of repentance in the aggressor's, and the social work of responsible action in the larger community's, Moore demonstrates that promoting forgiveness as a solitary survivor's imperative should not be the Alpha and the Omega of church members' responses.

Moore asserts that the proper response when a church leader learns of an instance of sexual violence is to call the police.[63] While survivors may avail themselves of the legal system, many choose not to pursue (or are not served well by) legal avenues for justice because of their adversarial and often retraumatizing nature.[64] Survivors may gain a sense of justice by recounting their experience of violence in the context of affirming relationships or in a physically safe confrontation with the aggressor.[65] Even if survivors never witness repentance by or legal accountability of aggressors, they may derive a feeling of justice by participating in efforts to counsel, aid, and champion other assault survivors. Addressing injustice through service, advocacy, or education may work to restore order and right relationships.[66] Indeed, Denhollander pursued all these available options by reporting Nassar, offering her victim impact statement, engaging with other survivors, and addressing what she perceives as her own community's problems.

After encouraging her audience to envision justice as bound up with a reinvigorated forgiveness, Denhollander identifies one central link between the two: repentance. While Christians assert that all people are sinners called to repentance, when specific roles come into focus, the community must teach assault aggressors to repent not just for their universal immorality but for their violent immorality. Denhollander defines repentance as "a full and complete acknowledgment of the depravity of what someone has done in comparison with God's holy standard. And I do believe that entails an acknowledgment of that, and a going in the opposite direction. It means you have repented to those you have harmed and seek to restore those you have hurt."[67] This definition involves both intention (i.e., "acknowledgment") and impact (i.e., "going" and "seek[ing] to restore")—commitment to change and accountability for implementing change.[68] While true offender repentance with accountability is a rarity, Denhollander asserts the need for consistent standards among evangelicals whether an aggressor or alleged aggressor shares their religious identity or not. She takes issue with the notion that because grace absolves the believing and repentant sinner, what forgiveness entails must be readily apparent and must resemble widespread current practice. In short, urging survivors to forgiveness without a simultaneous conversation about aggressor repentance relinquishes fundamental community responsibilities and theological commitments.

Denhollander and Moore address how reinvigorating original principles acknowledges the affective dimensions of survivors' healing without reducing forgiveness to prescriptions that survivors should feel any particular way, without turning forgiveness into a magical panacea, and without requiring forgiveness from survivors before the church community provides a compassionate space for survivors and a space for aggressors' repentance. Moore describes how Rick Warren and Kay Warren, cofounders of the highly regarded Saddleback Church, could influence "churches all over the world because they were audacious enough . . . to address the topic of sexual abuse and assault from the platform in all their services. Kay courageously, shamelessly, told her story [about childhood sexual abuse], shared ramifications of the abuse and the road to healing and Rick preached on the themes from Scripture. . . . He also invited abusers to repentance. . . . It was not the abused that left church frightened that day. It was the unrepentant abusers and make no mistake."[69] Moore's description of Kay Warren's testimony helps evangelicals imagine a church that honors survivors' public voice and that preaches no constrained notion of forgiveness. Abuse carries long-term consequences, and healing is a "road" traveled over time, not instant magic performed by a theologically demoralized forgiveness. Denhollander notes how forgiveness may include a movement toward emotional wholeness and a sense of release from an aggressor's hold. When describing her forgiveness of Nassar, Denhollander comments, "It means that I trust in God's justice and I release bitterness and anger and a desire for personal vengeance. It does not mean that I minimize or mitigate or excuse what he has done. It does not mean that I pursue justice on earth any less zealously. It simply means that I release personal vengeance against him, and I trust God's justice, whether he chooses to mete that out purely eternally, or both in heaven and on earth."[70] This stance certainly demonstrates no warm feelings toward Nassar, nor does it suggest that the affective dimensions of forgiveness take a singular, universal form. Nevertheless, Denhollander illustrates how forgiveness as part of a healing process may move survivors away from what Herman calls the "revenge fantasy" in which "the victim imagines that revenge is the only way to restore her own sense of power," but this imagined retaliation "actually increases her torment."[71] In so doing, Denhollander also avoids an "expressive justice" in which the emotional work surrounding sexual and domestic violence narrows the range of feelings about trauma, requiring expressions of a limited range of appropriate feelings.[72] A theologically robust forgiveness that remembers and restores may also release survivors from the fantasy of revenge and sponsor a range of emotional responses.

Neither Denhollander's forgiving stance nor her recognition that grace is available to Nassar expresses the escapism of a demoralized forgiveness or the cheap grace of antinomianism. Rather, this stance and recognition express her anticipation of God's ultimate reign on earth, which brings divine justice and restoration. By sharing her account with authorities, testifying at Nassar's sentencing, writing a column about her efforts to hold Nassar accountable, and talking about her experiences in diverse venues, Denhollander offers a new beginning. She demonstrates forgiveness in a way that remembers trauma, that is, by refusing to "minimize or mitigate or excuse." Such remembering increases the likelihood that some kind of justice might be restored; that is, she reminds us to "trust in God's justice" and "pursue justice on earth . . . zealously." This combination of memory and justice work cultivates Denhollander's ability to release herself from emotional entanglements with the aggressor (i.e., "release bitterness and anger").[73] Despite her affection for church communities, Denhollander claims that they fail victims by providing harmful advice that neglects this theological vision of forgiveness as linked with justice and repentance. Again, Denhollander's concern for the harm that comes when forgiveness, justice, and repentance are severed from each other in favor of a cheap grace is informed by her insistence (like Moore's) that the community return to the source of its first principles—to scripture. For Denhollander, God's divine grace works across domains, from the simply immoral to the deliberately predatory. Such grace is related to, yet different from, a forgiveness that actively remembers, restores, and releases. Within an evangelical biblicist framework that views scripture as authoritative, proper action must be grounded in Jesus's words and actions. Faithful deliberators consider the particulars of a given situation populated with sinners who take different roles (aggressors, survivors, and community members), each with differing responsibilities.

THE FRUITS OF FAITHFUL DELIBERATION

After Denhollander's victim impact statement, the pastors at her former church recognized themselves in her lament about losing her religious community. In a statement titled "We Were Rachael's Church," Immanuel Baptist Church (IBC) pastors describe how that comment from Denhollander led them to "enter a season of deep self-examination," which included broad reading, dialogue with many constituencies, advice from other church leaders, conversation with Denhollander and her husband, and a congregational meeting. When the Denhollanders objected to IBC inviting leaders from

Sovereign Grace Churches (SGC) to preach, IBC pastors viewed the couple as "divisive." As noted earlier, leaders in this church network have been accused of inadequately responding to instances of child abuse and sexual assault. IBC pastors held feelings toward, and shared sentiments about, the Denhollanders that they came to "regret" and to understand as "sin." The pastors assert that at the time of the conflict they "simply did not have the categories to fully discern" the survivor-sensitive concerns the Denhollanders shared with them; however, they consequently chose "to discontinue inviting" SGC leaders.[74] IBC pastors came to view their failure to hear survivors' voices as harmful and ended a partnership with a church network. While casuistic tightening alone certainly didn't achieve these results, such rhetorical invention by insiders who could appeal to highly esteemed values and the enclave deliberation that followed surely helped bring into focus the categories involved in specific instances of assault and in community responses to sexual violence.

Forgiveness, *grace*, and *sin* contain complex bundles of meaning within evangelicalism. Through casuistic tightening, faithful deliberators can examine these concepts in light of the particular categories of survivors and aggressors, creating opportunities to distinguish between demoralized, survivor-harming versions of forgiveness, on the one hand, and revitalized, survivor-affirming versions of forgiveness, on the other. Such tightening may have implications beyond that evangelical enclave, including promoting acts of solidarity with survivors outside the community; this outcome becomes more likely if evangelicals reject understandings of grace and forgiveness that flatten differences among in-group members while amplifying the problems of out-group members. The following chapter offers a case study of a campaign for in-group accountability shaped by #MeToo, #ChurchToo, and #SilenceIsNotSpiritual. It was an #SBCToo moment.

4

Letters to Their Brothers

Southern Baptist Women and a Rhetoric of Reconciliation

I learned early to show constant pronounced deference—not just proper respect which I was glad to show—to male leaders and, when placed in situations to serve alongside them, to do so apologetically.

—Beth Moore

The world is watching us all, brothers.

—"Letter to SWBTS Board of Trustees"

In 1967, two men sat in New Orleans's historic Café du Monde, ate beignets, and imagined a plan referred to variously as the Conservative Resurgence or the Fundamentalist Takeover. This ultimately successful campaign involved electing figures to the SBC presidency who drew hard lines around acceptable theological positions within the denomination, filling agency boards with majorities sympathetic to the presidents' theological agendas, and clearing seminaries of theologically moderate or liberal faculty. Those two men were Paige Patterson and Paul Pressler. Several decades later, in the spring and summer of 2018, Patterson was the longtime president of Southwestern Baptist Theological Seminary (SWBTS), a past SBC president, and a past president of Southeastern Baptist Theological Seminary (SEBTS). By that point, Pressler was a retired Texas state judge, an influential figure in conservative political circles, and a plaintiff facing lawsuits related to allegations that he had sexually abused minors decades ago (one settled in 2004 for $450,000 and more recent lawsuits were dismissed in 2018 and 2019). In February 2021, a Texas appelatte court ruled that a dismissed lawsuit could move forward.

Given Patterson's influence within the SBC and his well-established record of handling clergy misconduct cases in ways that survivor-advocates deemed inadequate, it seemed unlikely that he would experience any significant backlash when some previous comments captured public attention in 2018. For example, one of Patterson's former mentees and a once-rising star within the SBC, Darrell Gilyard, was dismissed from multiple churches for multiple instance of clergy sexual misconduct with congregants and was eventually convicted of exchanging sexual text messages with one minor and the molestation of another. Patterson eventually disavowed Gilyard in the early 1990s. However, in 1987, after Gilyard was fired from a church following allegations of sexual misconduct from more than twenty women, Patterson reportedly told the lead pastor that if he had come to him, he would have found a way to quietly resolve the situation. Even though Patterson viewed Gilyard as a victim of people acting in bad faith, additional firings for similar reasons had followed by 1991. In January 2008, as news broke that Gilyard would face criminal charges related to sexual contact with minors, the Survivors Network of those Abused by Priests (SNAP) sent a letter to the board of SWBTS, asking them to suspend and investigate Patterson over his involvement in incidents pertaining to Gilyard's employment over the years. For more than a year prior to that letter, SNAP had advocated for the SBC to conduct independent reviews of clergy abuse allegations.[1] Responding to an abuse survivor's email, Patterson called SNAP "evil-doers" and labeled them "just as reprehensible as sex criminals."[2] While SNAP is generally associated with accountability campaigns within the Catholic Church (as featured in the movie *Spotlight*), Christa Brown, a survivor of Baptist clergy sexual abuse, was then the director of SNAP's reform efforts aimed at Baptist groups and was a signatory to the SNAP SWBTS letter.

When a troubling recording from summer 2000 resurfaced in spring 2018, Patterson's stance toward survivors' and advocates' calls for transparent and rigorous accountability had long been part of the public record. In this recording, Patterson explained that his advice to domestic violence survivors never included permission to divorce and that he was "happy" when a woman showed up to church with two black eyes, because her suffering that abuse apparently led to the husband's conversion.[3] This 2018 uptake was at least the fourth time the recording had received some attention. The transcript had previously circulated in 2008 on the (now-defunct) *SBC Outpost* and the site of pseudonymous blogger Danni Moss,[4] in 2009 on the *Wartburg Watch* blog,[5] and in 2016 as the opening epigraph to Ruth A. Tucker's memoir of abuse and complementarian theology, *Black and White Bible, Black and Blue Wife*.[6] However, evangelical deliberations were changing in light of #MeToo, #ChurchToo, #SilenceIsNotSpiritual, and related developments.

Eventually, Patterson was terminated from SWBTS; additional comments in which Patterson referred to a sixteen-year-old girl as "built" during a sermon had resurfaced, his handling of rape allegations that occurred while he was president of SEBTS and SWBTS had come to public light for the first time, and pressure built. Patterson's comments constitute proverbs of ashes that set the focus on doctrinal correctness over concern for survivors. I attend to the rhetorical efforts of some of the theologically conservative Southern Baptist women who participated in this controversy, negotiating authority and power within their denomination for the purpose of effecting both short-term and more far-reaching change. Specifically, I examine the contributions to faithful deliberations offered in Beth Moore's blog post "A Letter to My Brothers" and in a collaboratively authored open letter titled "Letter to SWBTS Board of Trustees," designed as an expression of SBC women's concerns over Patterson's comments. These texts articulate a strong case for in-group accountability. By way of contrast, I also briefly examine Al Mohler's response, "The Humiliation of the Southern Baptist Convention." Despite ostensibly identifying the downfall of Patterson (without naming him) as a moment of SBC reckoning, Mohler spends significant space reinforcing his in-group's ultimate righteousness, ascribing to its members good motives and pointing to the faults of other groups. He practices a rhetoric of reiterating doctrine over a reconciling rhetoric.

How religious leaders and communities respond to domestic violence is important, because they may either help create opportunities for abuse survivors' healing work or further harm survivors—or both. While the SBC took many positions on gender-related issues prior to 2018 and a few on the protection of children from sexual abuse, few resolutions adopted by the SBC in the years prior to the Patterson controversy focused on domestic violence. Leaders' and communities' statements matter to many abuse victims, because religion may well "play a vital role in integrating experiences and granting those experiences meaning and motivational force, particularly to those who find themselves with few . . . allies except, in their view, the most powerful of all"—the divine.[7] Researchers, theologians, and counselors find that religious figures and discourse can actually encourage some survivors to accept abuse and reunite with abusive partners.[8] These results may be especially true for religiously conservative women for whom individual and social identity are closely bound up with church.[9] Given this tightly woven sense of personal and communal identity, such survivors face particular difficulties when coping with abuse, and a survivor "who has deep religious convictions needs assistance, not only with ending the abuse . . . but also with addressing the religious issues that are involved."[10] Attending to the way advice like Patterson's ultimately received widespread pushback within the SBC after the mainstreaming of the #MeToo movement presents scholars of rhetoric with an opportunity to understand how changes in the dominant public sphere contribute to changes within enclaves.

While the specific campaign goals that petition signatories and Moore established (i.e., holding men in positions of power accountable and confronting misogyny) fit within the general interests of feminist rhetorical inquiry, these women located themselves within a broad rubric of conservative, complementarian religion. As I exercise an ethics of hope and care toward Southern Baptist women's responses to the 2018 Patterson controversy, I argue that they employed a robust *rhetoric of reconciliation* that involves accountability for individuals and social change for the purpose of confronting violence-enabling discourses. This argument builds on scholarship that examines the rhetoric Christian women use to promote and maintain religious communities. However, while practicing a reconciling rhetoric, these SBC faithful deliberators, as in chapters 2 and 3, expressed no interest in uncomplicated group cohesion. Rather, they operated from theologically conservative commitments: to individual conversion, to community repentance grounded in consistent moral standards, and to the relative freedom that comes from fulfilling divinely ordained gender norms in potentially unexpected ways. Even though Moore announced her departure from the SBC just short of three years after these events took place and months after *Faithful Deliberation* entered the production process, the faithful deliberations examined here still provide insight into in-group arguments.

BAPTIST FREEDOMS, SOCIAL CHRISTIANITY, AND GENDER RESTRICTIONS

Evangelical enclave deliberation is shaped by historical narratives that value democratic participation or sensibilities as part of denominational self-narration. For example, Pentecostalism emphasizes the Holy Spirit's dynamic movement, which created space early on for women's leadership and for interracial engagement, and the SBC (along with Baptists generally) claims a democratic history with an aversion to authoritarianism.[11] Contemporary Southern Baptist women's rhetorical efforts exist within a denominationally informed history of religious engagement for social reformation as well as a contested denominational history of expanding and contracting freedoms. Attention to these histories helps bring out the nuances of situated practices that emerge when employing a feminist rhetorical ethics of hope and care. Such ethics seek to avoid "construct[ing] a narrative . . . that suggests a firmer ideology than the messiness of reality."[12] One distinction that helps bring into focus some of the messiness of today and historically is the one John Storey, historian of Texas Baptists, makes between the "Social Gospel" and "social Christianity." The more radically progressive Social Gospel (a social theology often associated with liberal Christianity) was articulated by figures like Walter Rauschenbusch, but a more moderate "social Christianity" runs throughout the history of some groups within theologically conservative Southern Baptist life.[13] The former orients the believer toward sweeping social transformation, and the latter orients the believer toward individual spiritual regeneration as the basis for addressing social problems.

Despite depictions of evangelical Christians as theologically, politically, and socially conservative, they have often embodied many ideological positions. For example, some Southern Baptists once objected so strongly to blending religion and political efforts, even with regard to Prohibition, that a husband took his wife to church in Hillsboro, Texas, and then sat outside reading the newspaper during an electoral primary season when the pastor endorsed a Prohibitionist as the Democratic candidate for governor.[14] At the same time, other Southern Baptists became involved with the Prohibition movement and found it a gateway into religiously motivated activism on many issues, including economics and poverty. Mattingly makes a similar point: Highly religious temperance women often held wide-ranging political interests, including property ownership, domestic violence, divorce, and voting rights. Storey's distinctions among differing theological motivations for activism are instructive in examining more contemporary efforts.

Just as lived messiness would complicate easy assumptions about the basis for—or avoidance of—religion-motivated social engagement, messiness also manifests in the ways Baptists try to live out their distinctive commitments to freedom. Walter B. Shurden argues that "four fragile freedoms" are defining characteristics of Baptist religion: Bible freedom, soul freedom, church freedom, and religious freedom.[15] These concepts mean, respectively, the individual freedom to interpret scripture, the individual exercise of conscience free from coercion, the autonomy of local congregations, and the opportunity for all religious communities to operate without unwarranted interference from civil authorities. Fisher Humphreys likewise identifies an additional range of freedom-privileging principles as historically central to Baptist life: democratic deliberation within congregations that check the power of pastors, church-state separation, and descriptive confessional statements over prescriptive creedal statements.[16] This Baptist excitement over freedom has contributed to general American attitudes toward religion. Indeed, Martin E. Marty describes "Baptistification" as a historical trend within the United States toward identifying individual autonomy and conscience as markers of authentic religion.[17] Despite the value traditionally placed on freedom, Shurden and Humphreys both express concern that the relatively new conservative hegemony within the SBC would diminish and endanger these traditional Southern Baptist commitments.

The campaign Patterson helped to lead had mixed political and theological motives; arguments about gender norms were central to both sets of motives. In their estimation, Carl L. Kell and L. Raymond Camp view the conservative campaign's rhetoric as defined by themes of exclusion with highly circumscribed parameters for argument.[18] Susan Shaw demonstrates how gender served as a defining issue that shaped those parameters; between 1979 and 1993, the SBC passed numerous resolutions proclaiming an ideology that narrows the scope of what women should do with their bodies, sexuality, autonomy, family life, and vocations.[19] Shaw also documents Southern Baptist women's historical reluctance to embrace positions that depart from traditional roles, as well as contemporary Southern Baptist women's conflicted relationship to feminism.[20] First adopted in 1925, *The Baptist Faith and Message* of the SBC, a confessional statement listing various points of agreement among its churches, was amended in 2000 to solidify complementarianism, limit the pastorate to men, and define marriage as heteronormative. While the SBC disapproves of women's ordination based on complementarian theology, the Convention has endorsed a range of other ministry-related roles for women.[21] Within this context, Emily M. Cope takes the highly successful Beth Moore as a case study and argues that it was still possible for women to negotiate increasingly rigid gender boundaries in order to carve out space for ministry purposes by embodying a feminized style of evangelical preaching—even as Cope wonders about the longevity of such spaces.[22] This background serves to illustrate the relative-yet-much-regulated freedom afforded women within this evangelical tradition. By leveraging their gender identity and the concerns they share with other Southern Baptists in ways that recognized denominational norms, Moore and the SBC women's collective enacted a rhetoric of reconciliation.

A RHETORIC OF RECONCILIATION

As a way to understand the rhetorical performances historically available to women who were both thoroughly religious and oriented toward preserving their community traditions, Adams-Roberts, Eves, and Rohan distinguish the "apostolic" from the "prophetic." They examine epistolary, sermonic, and public discourse by eighteenth- and nineteenth-century religious women, locating the ways they "used an apostolic rhetoric to speak authoritatively and simultaneously to foster a sense of community within their religious groups."[23] Distinguishing prophetic from apostolic rhetoric, they argue that the "call to repentance" in the latter involves a rhetor who "speaks as a community insider" with "injunctions for pragmatic action."[24] Women practicing apostolic rhetoric seek "to call into being particular ideals of community," and they are "shaping, creating, and maintaining communities."[25] Moreover, particular religious and denominational contexts shape women's enactments of apostolic rhetoric.[26] This rhetoric operates in open letters by Moore and the SBC women's collective.

While the functions performed in contemporary SBC women's rhetoric match those fulfilled by apostolic rhetoric, the women's denominational specificity and theological orientation suggest the need for an alternative term. Baptists tend to resist labels like "apostle" or "apostolic" for multiple reasons. First, Baptist groups differ from ordination traditions that subscribe to a notion of "Apostolic Succession," like Roman Catholicism and Anglicanism, which trace the lineage of church leadership back through a line of connection to Jesus and the Apostle Peter. Second, within US Baptist history, strong conflicts arose over a controversial mid-nineteenth-century movement known as Landmarkism, which attempted to locate Baptist modes of ecclesiology in a continuous tradition dating to the apostolic era of early Christianity. Third, apostolic as a titular term holds close associations for many Southern Baptists with Pentecostal denominations. Using the "apostolic" label would not adequately embody ethical care for the community and individuals whose efforts I examine.

In addition to the apostolic rhetorical functions that appear in the statements considered below, these letters also perform work that the religious notion of *reconciliation* names theologically and politically. Within rhetorical studies, Brian Fehler draws on fictional, historical, and theological examples of suffering and doubt to articulate a rhetoric of reconciliation as a dialogic genre that enables believers to develop new understandings of God in light of painful experiences and that promotes the dynamic development of theology as a discipline.[27] While this reconciling rhetoric's attention to pain and transformation resonates with the concerns of SBC women, it is not the kind they enact. A concept from Christian tradition valued across diverse groups, reconciliation appears explicitly in St. Paul's letters. As received from Paul, reconciliation involves a sense of fundamental change grounded in the divine's own effort to restore right relationships between humanity and God. The Greek terms Paul employs for this concept in his second letter to the Christian community in Corinth are *katallage* and *katallasso* (i.e., "reconciliation" and "to reconcile"). He writes, "Therefore, if anyone is in Christ, the new creation has come: The old has gone, the new is here! All this is from God, who reconciled us to himself through Christ and gave us the ministry of reconciliation: that God was reconciling the world to himself in Christ, not counting people's sins against them. And he has committed to us the message of reconciliation. We are therefore Christ's ambassadors, as though God were making his appeal through us."[28] The primary agent in this configuration is the divine; believers serve as representatives of the re-creation God accomplished through Christ. In this regard, as reconciliation takes shape in human communities, it involves more than simply getting along—more than a forced or false unity. Reconciliation extends beyond, and rests not primarily on, warm interpersonal feelings between individuals in unique and isolated situations. This reconciliation language is a primary way Christians talk about the work of bringing the self and community back into a rightly ordered relationship with the divine, including conflict resolution efforts such as the South African Truth and Reconciliation Commission under the direction of Archbishop Desmond Tutu and similar efforts among various ecumenical communities and political groups in Northern Ireland.

Among Southern Baptists and evangelicals more generally, reconciliation serves as the dominant language for political engagement around racial justice issues. For example, one of the strongest SBC statements that embraces responsibility, and apologizes, for racism within the denomination and the broader US culture came in June 1995: *Resolution on Racial Reconciliation on the 150th Anniversary of the Southern Baptist Convention.*[29] Likewise, twenty years later, a two-day seminar on "The Gospel and Racial Reconciliation" took place under the leadership of Russell Moore, director of the Ethics and Religious Liberty Committee (ERLC), the SBC's policy advocacy agency. Although the racial reconciliation model clearly leads to corporate statements and action, it frequently operates within an individualist theological framework that traces social problems to the sinful nature of human beings and honors the freedom of each soul to change course or not. This approach aligns with the overview provided earlier of Baptists' social Christianity and notions of freedom.

Acknowledging "the powerful hold 'reconciliation' has on the white Christian imagination," Jennifer Harvey critiques this model because its assumptions generally fail to take into account historically enduring and still-current structural inequities.[30] Reconciliation generates urgency around the desire for healed relationships while jumping over the work required to address "the actual situation" and "an unacknowledged history" of racism, all of which "may do more harm than good."[31] Similarly, Robert P. Jones argues that Christian campaigns to address racial injustices have largely been based on reconciliation models that focus on individuals, truncate history, and neglect structural legacies of injustice.[32] Jones instead calls for an understanding of "reconciliation as a result of a journey—rather than as a destination that can be reached directly."[33] To that end, he turns to language of *repentance,* which is about establishing relationships, accounting for differences in power, and "resist[ing] the urge to ask for forgiveness before meaningful action has been taken."[34] While concerns about reconciliation as a model are justified, a social Christianity understanding of reconciliation helps situate contemporary SBC women's rhetorical practices within generally available social and theological options as faithful deliberators push denominational leaders to confront abuse-enabling discourse.

Beyond its ubiquity as a theologically grounding framework for evangelicals' social and political action to confront racism, reconciliation also offers a broadly Christian motivating vision for confronting violence against women. While Pamela Cooper-White acknowledges that "reconciliation is often misunderstood in the church to mean an atmosphere of niceness and the suppression of conflict," she also maintains that reconciliation provides a religious resource for understanding that "violence against women is not only an abuse of an individual person, but a violation of trust and rupturing of right relation with the entire community."[35] Even as Robert McAfee Brown observes how this concept can involve reconciling those with less power to hegemonic arrangements,[36] Cooper-White lifts up Paul's vision of diverse groups joining together in peace to argue that reconciliation's "sign would not be the oppressed forgiving their oppressors but, rather, the hearts of the oppressors recognizing the full dignity and humanity of those whom they had objectified, and entering into true repentance."[37] From this perspective, reconciliation in the context of domestic violence is not about an abuse survivor going back to an abusive situation; it is about addressing both personal and systemic factors that make abuse more or less likely.

BETH MOORE: A SINGULAR INSIDER

While Moore posts almost daily to her more than 950,000 Twitter followers, she occasionally uses her Living Proof Ministry blog for longer pieces. In her May 3, 2018, "A Letter to My Brothers," Moore responded to the then-unfolding Patterson saga, even though she never directly addresses Patterson by name or situation. As noted in chapter 2, Moore often confronts without directly naming figures who are either prominent within evangelicalism or admired among evangelicals. Several factors make it clear that Moore is dealing with the Patterson situation. First, she opens with a humorous-yet-biting anecdote involving former LifeWay Research Executive Director Ed Stetzer (recall that LifeWay is the SBC-affiliated company that distributes Moore's books). Two days earlier, Stetzer had published a piece with *Christianity Today* calling for Patterson to not speak at the forthcoming SBC annual gathering in June and to retire from SWBTS.[38] Second, Moore describes her Southern Baptist heritage, locating her conversion and ministerial calling experiences in SBC churches. While Southern Baptists are highly "denominationalized,"[39] Moore's ministry is interdenominational and broad in scope. A search of the *LPM Blog* reveals only two earlier entries by Moore containing either "Southern Baptist" or "SBC." Consequently, to invoke her denominational identity and personal history at this moment locates her comments within the controversy that the SBC faced. Third, Moore mentions her time taking classes at a SWBTS branch campus in Houston. Fourth, her piece details, without naming individuals involved, some of her encounters with misogyny within evangelicalism. Taken together, these elements make clear that her writing is responding to the Patterson situation, but she also seeks a larger-scale transformation within evangelicalism: a reconciliation of Christians' actions with standards of right behavior that she understands as biblical in nature.

Moore's reconciling rhetoric begins by appealing to an ethos that enables her to situate herself denominationally and theologically:

> A few years ago I told my friend, Ed Stetzer, that, whenever he hears the news that I'm on my deathbed, he's to elbow his way through my family members to interview me about what it's been like to be a female leader in the conservative Evangelical world. He responded, "Why can't we do it before then?"
>
> "Because you know good and well what will happen," I answered. "I'll get fried like a chicken." After recent events following on the heels of a harrowing eighteen months, I've decided fried chicken doesn't sound so bad.
>
> I have been a professing Evangelical for decades and, at least in my sliver of that world, a conservative one. I was a cradle role Southern Baptist by denomination with an interdenominational ministry. I walked the aisle to receive Christ as my Savior at 9 years old in an SBC church and exactly nine years later walked the aisle in another SBC church to surrender to a vocational calling. Being a woman called to leadership within and simultaneously beyond those walls was complicated to say the least but I worked within the system. After all, I had no personal aspirations to preach nor was it my aim to teach men. . . . My unwavering passion was to teach and to serve women.[40]

After humorously noting the risk she takes in going public with her experiences, Moore claims and establishes her identity as a "conservative Evangelical" who believes in the importance of a personal conversion encounter with God. In a brief section dedicated to her religious conversion and initial ministerial commitment, Moore employs typically evangelical language: "professing," "receive Christ," "surrender," "vocational calling." Within this theological and denominational context, she also subtly but directly addresses how she accepted the gender restrictions established by the SBC; she states that she "worked within the system," dissuades readers of the idea that she might have wanted to preach or hold authority over men, and emphasizes her dedication to working on behalf of women.[41] At first, Moore appears to depart from the conventions of conversion and vocational narratives; she does not assess her own sinfulness, as often occurs in such narratives, but instead goes on to describe misogyny, critiquing its regulatory functions, which constrained her choices and belittled her personhood. By the end of her letter, Moore frames her complicity with these actions as a personal failure that requires forgiveness from others harmed by her participation in this system. Such framing locates her within orthodox evangelical thinking about the personal nature of sin, conservative theology's individualist focus, and Baptist social Christianity's pursuit of social change through personal salvation.

Even as Moore details personal encounters with misogyny within her religious community and among its leaders, as well as her begrudging acceptance of it for decades, the reconciling rhetoric she practices aims not primarily at forgiveness within any given interpersonal relationship but rather at repair of harms that extend beyond isolated incidents. Describing how she employed gendered acts of accommodation to men's supposed authority, Moore provides a litany of discursive and embodied actions that diminished herself and elevated men: "I learned early to show constant pronounced deference—not just proper respect which I was glad to show—to male leaders and, when placed in situations to serve alongside them, to do so apologetically. I issued disclaimers ad nauseam. I wore flats instead of heels when I knew I'd be serving alongside a man of shorter stature so I wouldn't be taller than he. I've ridden elevators in hotels packed with fellow leaders who were serving at the same event and not been spoken to and, even more awkwardly, in the same vehicles where I was never acknowledged. I've been in team meetings where I was either ignored or made fun of, the latter of which I was expected to understand was all in good fun."[42] While acknowledging differences between her experiences in church contexts and the experiences of those subjected to sexual violence at the hands of religious leaders or fellow churchgoers, Moore argues that they have a common source, "growing from the same dangerously malignant root."[43] Positioning her decision to only now publicly critique the misogynistic treatment she received over the decades as an altruistic act to improve conditions for other women and the whole religious community, Moore strikes a reflective tone: "This is where I cry foul and not for my own sake. Most of my life is behind me."[44] A sense of purpose that comes from facing her own mortality orients Moore toward building a different kind of community through reconciliation, which requires that she both critique practices that harm women and acknowledge her own participation in shoring up such practices within her enclave.

Repenting of her error (i.e., indulging misogyny for so long), Moore creates space for divine agency to restore human relationships and models reconciliation for her broader audience. Early on, Moore understood her actions as accommodation to a particular theology: "I accepted the peculiarities accompanying female leadership in a conservative Christian world because I chose to believe that, whether or not some of the actions and attitudes seemed godly to me, they were rooted in deep convictions based on passages from 1 Timothy 2 and 1 Corinthians 14."[45] However, following male evangelical leaders' handling of the Donald Trump–Billy Bush *Access Hollywood* interview, Moore came to understand the rationale behind that treatment as human sinfulness rather than as fidelity to theological tenets or scriptural interpretation. Moore acknowledges, "My acquiescence and silence made me complicit in perpetuating an atmosphere in which a damaging relational dynamic has flourished."[46] She repents of her complicity with Christian misogyny, comes to understand misogynistic actions as sin disguised as theology, and seeks forgiveness from her coreligionists. A standard topos for New Testament figures, speakers admit failings and flaws as a prelude to claiming that the divine works through them to accomplish good.[47] If reconciliation meant accommodation to the standard mode of operations, that would mean continuing to support patterns of belittling and controlling practices. Moore expresses no interest in that prospect. Rather, she names individual and community deficiencies, which connects this rhetoric of reconciliation with historical and scriptural precedents. Finding precedents in sacred texts is paramount for much evangelical argumentation.

As an evangelical addressing an evangelical audience, Moore acknowledges issues of biblical interpretation pertaining to questions of women's status in religious communities. She articulates tensions that exist within scripture and between various church emphases. Moving within a biblically oriented worldview requires skill and attention, because the text is not transparent in how it should be applied. To highlight the diversity of relevant biblical references and the frequently inadequate translation of contemporary conservative hermeneutics into ecclesial practice, Moore employs antithesis: "Many churches quick to teach submission are often slow to point out that women were also among the followers of Christ (Luke 8), that the first recorded word out of His resurrected mouth was 'woman' (John 20:15) and that same woman was the first evangelist. Many churches wholly devoted to teaching the household codes are slow to also point out the numerous women with whom the Apostle Paul served and for whom he possessed obvious esteem."[48] She juxtaposes positions from churches that emphasize women's submission with texts that show women as disciples[49] and that show the importance of women in the post-resurrection moment.[50] Likewise, Moore contrasts the privilege some contemporary churches ascribe to domesticity codes that promote narrowly circumscribed gender roles with the high regard Paul held for certain women working on behalf of the early church, a move in the tradition of Margaret Fell, Phoebe Palmer, Frances Willard, and many others who made similar arguments throughout the history of rhetoric. She seeks an evangelicalism that maintains elevated esteem for scripture but that reorients its interpretive approach so that a wider array of positions become available regarding how to establish biblical standards for women and men.

Moore also enacts a reconciling rhetoric through her genre choice, framing this blog post as an open letter. Epistolary forms hold an esteemed place in Christian history. The Apostle Paul used letters to perform community maintenance when he received news from early churches. He addressed practical problems that emerged from their life together, and he asserted theological positions.[51] In like manner, Moore addresses problems within her community and situates those problems within a theological context. She attempts to repair the harm caused by misogyny and her accommodation to it; this social transformation work follows Paul's articulation of reconciliation as bringing about a new sense of identity and a new set of relationships. Beyond the generally Christian function of this genre choice, the form and its tone also carry a denominational dimension. As noted earlier, Baptist spirituality puts a premium on individual conscience and Baptist polity privileges institutional autonomy. Given these atomizing features, Baptists consequently seek ways to cooperate with each other on points of agreement—most frequently, evangelizing goals as well as areas of social concern.

"CONCERNED SOUTHERN BAPTIST WOMEN": A COLLECTIVE EXPRESSION

Like Moore, the SBC women participating in the "Letter to SWBTS Board of Trustees" begin by setting forth their Southern Baptist credentials. Thirty women contributed to the authorship of this letter.[52] More decisively and directly than Moore, they assert their current belief in theologically conservative complementarianism as defined by the SBC. Posted on May 6, 2018, the text declares that its authors and signers "are concerned Southern Baptist women who affirm the Baptist Faith and Message 2000, including its statements on the roles of men and women in the family and in the church."

They establish right away that they share an identity, theology, and broader ideology with the letter's recipients.

While the document's authorship remains mostly anonymous, one member of the collaborative has spoken about the group's work and aims. Several media accounts name longtime Liberty University English professor and lifelong Baptist Karen Swallow Prior as one of the writers.[53] A conservative evangelical university, Liberty was founded by Southern Baptist pastor and Moral Majority cofounder Jerry Falwell. It was until quite recently run by his son Jerry Falwell Jr. Prior attended Thomas Road Baptist Church, the congregation Jerry Falwell pastored for decades, which is now led by his son Jonathan Falwell. Clearly, Prior has worked, worshipped, and lived as an evangelical insider—one deeply committed to its values, hermeneutics, practices, and long-term maintenance. She explains, "Because this is a grassroots effort designed to reflect many SBC women, we prefer not to focus on the writers, but the signers," noting also that the writers solicited much feedback before publishing the piece.[54] Ed Stetzer tweeted the same day the letter was published that it was "a big deal" for "theologically conservative women leaders to call for [Patterson's] resignation." In 2020, Prior moved to SEBTS, an institution once headed by Patterson, where her new title is "Research Professor of English and Christianity and Culture."

Enacting Southern Baptist ideals, the authors employ a reconciling rhetoric that embraces confrontation for the purpose of accountability within a community context. These SBC women would clearly reject any simplistic unity that elevates institutional preservation or personal prestige over their understanding of what constitutes divinely ordained gender norms or of the respect those norms confer on women. While their beliefs may include women's submission to husbands in marriage and abstention from ordained ministry as pastors, they reject women's subservience. In their effort to obey the will of God as they understand it, the writers enumerate Patterson's comments and repeatedly note his failure to denounce his remarks: "We are shocked by the video that has surfaced showing Dr. Paige Patterson objectify a teenage girl and then suggest this as behavior that is biblical. We are further grieved by the dangerous and unwise counsel given by Dr. Patterson to women in abusive situations. His recent remarks of clarification do not repudiate his unwise counsel in the past; nor has he offered explanation or repentance for inappropriate comments regarding a teenage girl, the unbiblical teaching he offered on the biblical meaning of womanhood in that objectification, and the inappropriate nature of his own observations of her body."[55] Framing his comments as repentance-worthy, the authors and signatories deem them reckless, even sinful, and not in keeping with the reconciled divine order. Reconciling rhetoric aims to name and repair the harm caused not solely between individuals in personal situations but within simultaneously personal, spiritual, and social contexts.

Just as Moore establishes generally Christian and specifically Baptist goals by composing an open letter to evangelical men, these letter writers perform similar work. First, these women more directly than Moore follow in the Pauline tradition in that they direct their piece to a quite specific audience. Both the title and salutation indicate the intended recipients. When Paul sent letters to specific Christian communities, he provided guidance and counsel on particular problems that arose in his absence. These SBC women likewise address a targeted audience and focus on a particular problem within their community: Patterson's "unbiblical teaching regarding womanhood, sexuality, and domestic violence."[56] Practicing issue-specific address, they seek reconciliation of the present situation with what they understand as a biblical standard. Such a reconciliation proceeds through appeals to the community's structures (i.e., boards of trustees, churches) and defining documents (i.e., Baptist Faith and Message 2000) for the purpose of maintaining, repairing, and expanding the community.

Second, this letter, like Moore's, enacts a Baptist vision of invitational cooperation that respects a free conscience, viewing cooperation and discernment as preferable to the coercion of imperative demands. Through the salutation and opening, the writers recognize the hierarchy within the institution they seek to influence: "Dear Pastor Ueckert and Board of Trustees." They address the president of the board (i.e., Ueckert) and other members of that governing authority. In their opening paragraph, the authors write, "We urge you to exercise the authority you have been given by the churches of the Southern Baptist Convention."[57] While the writers clearly imply that the trustees should dismiss Patterson, they never explicitly state that as a goal. Rather, they urge those in authority to uphold what they view as a consistent moral standard derived from scripture: "This pattern of [Patterson's] discourse is unbefitting the sober, wise, and sound character required of an elder, pastor, and leader. It fails in the call to protect the helpless, the call of Christ to love our neighbor as ourselves, and the biblical standard of sexual purity. These comments are damaging, sinful, and necessitate a decisive response. It seems inevitable, for instance, that a youth pastor in any of our churches would be removed from his position if he made the comments that Dr. Patterson made."[58] They note that a youth pastor making sexualized remarks about a teen would be fired. Making their evaluation of the situation clear and grounding it in religious terms—Christ's call, human sinfulness, biblical standards—these faithful deliberators call on those vested with authority to exercise their institutional power as denominational leaders, a group that should not continue to include someone with Patterson's record. The letter goes on: "The Southern Baptist Convention cannot allow the biblical view of leadership to be misused in such a way that a leader with an unbiblical view of authority, womanhood, and sexuality be allowed to continue in leadership."[59] Through these gestures, the writers and signatories observe men's leadership, recognize established channels of authority, and encourage the exercise of authority in ways that honor Baptist traditions of individual conscience and free cooperation toward agreed upon goals. All these goals they accomplish while negotiating gender boundaries and maintaining community bonds. Indeed, they claim that Patterson's statements placed him outside recognized Southern Baptist thinking "and, more importantly, the Bible's elevated view of womanhood."[60] Consequently, while professing denominational identity in connection with the Baptist Faith and Mission, they simultaneously appeal to biblical foundationalism, in keeping with the confessional nature of Baptists' traditional contention that the Bible is their only creed.

Even as these SBC women establish that sexualized discourse and dangerous advice to abuse victims are anathema to their religious sensibilities, they also articulate a primary interest among Southern Baptists as central to the work of reconciliation: the importance of evangelism, that is, sharing with others their knowledge of Jesus. Expressing a broad sense of potential audience members, they address the board: "The world is watching us all, brothers. They wonder how we could possibly be part of a denomination that counts Dr. Patterson as a leader. They wonder if all Southern Baptist men believe that the biblical view of a sixteen-year-old girl is that she is 'built' and 'fine'—an object to be viewed sexually. They wonder if all Southern Baptist pastors believe it is acceptable to counsel an abused woman in the way that Dr. Patterson has done in the past. They wonder if the Jesus of the Bible is like such men. We declare that Jesus is nothing like this and that our first duty as Southern Baptists is to present a true picture of Jesus to the world."[61] Like Moore, they cultivate an intimate sense of community bonds through familial language (i.e., "brothers") and signal that they work toward goals they all hold in common. Specifically, Southern Baptists hold in common the goal of evangelism, bringing others into the fold. These SBC women attend to evangelism by writing "the world is watching us" and by repeating "they wonder" in the next four sentences to capture the questions outsiders might ask regarding the SBC handling of the Patterson situation. As ambassadors who represent Christ's reconciliation to those outside their group's boundaries and who anticipate potential concerns among those outside the SBC, these faithful deliberators remind group members of their charge to likewise declare this message beyond the Convention's current membership. Indeed, while a central goal among Southern Baptists has historically been evangelism for effecting conversions to Christianity, conversion and evangelistic revival have also historically served as their main paths to resolving social problems. Consequently, invoking the difficulties that continued support for Patterson might bring with regard to conversions indicates neither a crass market sense of religious competition nor an accommodation of a conservative religious community to standards set by the broader culture. Rather, raising the question of conversions stands in the Southern Baptist social Christianity tradition that urges believers to accept responsibility for engaging with worldly problems and that holds genuine conversion to Jesus's lordship as the ultimate answer to those problems. In this way, their rhetoric emerges from enclave commonplaces, directs its claims toward enclave members, and forwards values shared by those members. This relatively high insularity that also considers outsiders' perspectives enables faithful deliberation.

EVANGELICAL HUMILIATION OR DOCTRINAL REITERATION?

Sixteen days after the petition launched, the *Washington Post* covered newly disclosed information on Patterson's 2003 handling as SEBTS president of a student's report that she was raped: He reportedly solicited many details about the attack and urged the student to forgive her attacker. The survivor was also subject to disciplinary probation as a student for unknown reasons, but likely for being alone with the man who attacked her. That same day, May 22, 2018, the SWBTS board of trustees was already scheduled to meet and decide on Patterson's future. At the conclusion of that thirteen-hour meeting, they asked Patterson to retire as president and accept an appointment as president emeritus that included a substantial compensation and an on-campus residence.[62]

By way of contrast to the earlier, more enclave-directed indictments of the letters oriented toward reconciliation, Albert Mohler, longtime president of Southern Baptist Theological Seminary, released a statement on May 23, "The Humiliation of the Southern Baptist Convention," which aimed more to reiterate recent SBC orthodoxy. The piece implies without directly stating that the removal of Patterson (whom he does not name) was appropriate: "At one of our seminaries, controversy has centered on a president (now former president). . . . The issues only grew more urgent with the sense that the dated statements represented ongoing advice and counsel."[63] Despite its ostensibly contrition-oriented title, Mohler's piece ultimately seems more oriented toward defending the Conservative Resurgence's theological agenda, reaffirming the SBC view that Roman Catholic celibacy in the priesthood is "unbiblical," and equating theological and political liberalization among former SBC groups with the "morally compromised" status of the SBC. Writing in the collective voice ("we thought"), Mohler claims ignorance regarding the existence of abusive and dismissive practices within his denomination. Indeed, that this moment entailed humiliation and judgment seemed premised on the notion that Mohler and others in the SBC previously lacked knowledge about the extent of abusive behavior or of the license that widespread practices within the denomination provided for such behavior. However, survivor-advocates and their allies within the SBC had brought forward accounts of abuse many times; furthermore, for more than a decade, the SBC has been arguing over accountability mechanisms within the denomination, including church-to-church information sharing about credibly accused and convicted abuse aggressors as well as independent investigations of abuse allegations.[64] Humiliation here might surely be limited to the sense of becoming a public spectacle. However, that term could exceed its everyday definition and include a technical meaning derived from an important figure in American evangelical theology.

Great Awakening revivalist Jonathan Edwards wrote that "evangelical humiliation" is the "sense that a Christian has his own utter insufficiency, despicableness, and odiousness, with an answerable frame of heart."[65] This species of humiliation engenders such humility, that beyond honoring those outside their community's bounds, Christians must respect even those they understand to be explicitly engaged in evil and theological falsehood to the extent they practice something praiseworthy: "That same spirit will dispose a Christian to honor all men. . . . A humble Christian is not only disposed to honor the saints in his behavior; but others also, in all those ways that do not imply a visible approbation of their sins. . . . Not only will Christian humility dispose persons to honor those wicked men that are out of the visible church, but also false brethren and persecutors."[66] Admittedly, this Calvinist guidance on inter- and intrareligious dealings surely would not result in any endorsement of Roman Catholics or progressive Baptists whom Southern Baptists perceive as doctrinally incorrect. However, this review of humiliation suggests that the account would focus on the faults of one's own group (as Moore and the SBC women's collective did) or highlight that which is honorable in other groups as it pertains to the sinfulness under discussion. Instead, Mohler begins with certainty that the theological conservatism he champions is right, that the current Southern Baptist understanding of gender is divinely ordained, and that the way conservatives gained denominational power was motivated by good intentions—all while throwing rhetorical barbs at other groups. Hardly an evangelical humiliation or a reconciliation of current sinfulness with a biblical standard of justice for community members that might also serve the goal of evangelizing to those outside the community. Rather than humiliation or reconciliation, this response from an SBC leader acknowledged the changing context forged by the #MeToo movement, all while primarily serving as a reiteration of proverbs of ashes unaltered by this changing context.

TOWARD RESURRECTION

After Mohler's piece, new information came to light on May 30 that reportedly contradicted Patterson's statements to the full seminary board. The executive committee of the board of trustees met and unanimously voted to terminate Patterson from all continuing benefits and recognitions.[67] Board President Ueckert shares that, in an email discussing a 2015 rape report by a SWBTS student, Patterson wanted to meet one-on-one with the victim in order to "break her down."[68] Clearly referencing these revelations, Moore quotes this expression, attributing it to "Mortal Man," which she juxtaposes with a reference to the gospel passage Mark 5:41 in which Jesus raises a little girl from the dead: "'Raise her up.'—Son of God."[69] As we saw in the discussion of Hatmaker and Moore in chapter 2, Moore called Christians who are oblivious to the abuse-enabling culture in churches "sleepers." In a move reminiscent of this earlier gesture, this tweet continued the theme of linking sexual abuse survivors' experiences—and, in the context of this larger SBC controversy, the experiences of domestic violence survivors—to the resurrection power of the God who brings new life out of death and who transforms proverbs of ashes into life-giving spiritual insights that become sources of agency.

In contrast to the lack of immediately apparent outcomes in that earlier episode, Moore's letter and the SBC women's letter surely helped claim attention and keep pressure on the SWBTS board and the broader Convention. While many religious survivors of abuse may not listen to Moore or read online petitions, some do; others see news coverage about them, and these rhetorical engagements may become resources in survivors' efforts to locate their trauma within a narrative that enables them to make sense of the experience. Moreover, such efforts undermine positions and advice that, perhaps unintentionally, permit violence. Following Patterson's departure from SWBTS and his decision to not preach at the 2018 denominational gathering, the SBC faced further scrutiny regarding how its churches and institutions address sexual assault and abuse within the denomination. A social media thread Moore launched in response to this denominational abuse scandal is the focus of the next chapter.

5

A Fellowship of Survivors

Archiving Abuse, Inviting Healing, and Drawing Lines

Grieving with you.
—Rachael Denhollander

And I with you. And I stand with you.
—Beth Moore

From May 2018 to March 2019, hardly a week seemed to go by without news about sexual abuse and assault investigations involving several denominations. As recounted in the preceding chapter, May and June 2018 saw the fall of the SBC's Paige Patterson because of his "handling of an allegation of sexual abuse against a student during [his] presidency at another institution and resulting issues connected with statements" he made.[1] While the decades-long clerical abuse of children and the ensuing cover-ups within the Roman Catholic Church has received widespread coverage since the 2002 Spotlight series by the *Boston Globe*, documented extensively in the book *Betrayal* and dramatized in the 2015 Oscar-winning film *Spotlight*, new developments in the summer of 2018 put that institution under the spotlight once again. In July, after law enforcement and news investigations documented credible abuse allegations against Cardinal Theodore McCarrick, McCarrick resigned his ecclesiastical leadership post. The next month, a Pennsylvania grand jury released an almost nine-hundred-page report, detailing decades of abuse allegations against more than three hundred priests. As August came to a close, Pope Francis held mass on one side of Dublin, Ireland; on the city's other side, a group calling for increased accountability for clerical abuse gathered and sang the Black freedom song "We Shall Overcome." December's final days saw the *Fort Worth Star-Telegram* publish a report documenting 412 alleged instances of abuse involving 187 churches and institutions connected to the independent fundamental Baptist (IFB) community. This separatist religious movement of loosely connected churches emerged in the 1940s in opposition to moves by evangelicals such as Billy Graham, who engaged with the broader culture and with other Christians who held beliefs different from their own (i.e., who practiced ecumenism).

At the time news broke about the extent of abuse within IFB churches, the executive vice president of ERLC (the SBC's advocacy group) Philip Betancourt expressed that he would be unsurprised if a similar investigation about the SBC weren't forthcoming. In fact, it was. February 2019 witnessed the *Houston Chronicle* and the *San Antonio Express-News* publishing the first in a multipart "Abuse of Faith" series, which documented twenty years of sexual abuse involving seven hundred victims and 380 SBC-affiliated pastors, leaders, and volunteers.[2] In a Twitter thread on February 16, Robert Downen described the origin of the report. Almost a year earlier, Downen had found settlement documents related to the first sexual assault lawsuit against SBC leader Paul Pressler. Downen consulted with activists, who asserted that the situation was larger than an isolated case. Consequently, Downen studied court records and public accounts describing abuse that occurred within SBC churches, which led to the devastating investigating report. In June 2019, the SBC released a report to help congregations understand abuse, care for survivors, and prevent future abuse. These issues received intense discussion at the denominational gathering that month, including an ERLC-sponsored panel, which included Russell Moore, Beth Moore, Rachael Denhollander, and others. While the voting attendees at that same convention ultimately passed a resolution tentatively affirming (with several caveats) the usefulness of critical race theory and intersectionality (CRT/I) as "analytical tools," this development was a response to an effort to define these theoretical frameworks as anti-Christian "worldviews." Advocates for this anti-CRT/I campaign also took aim at Moore because of her perceived softening on complementarian norms within the SBC.

This chapter focuses on two rhetorical situations (one more bounded, the other more diffuse) within this SBC time line, situations that brought into focus the question of religious community boundaries in relationship to survivor-advocates. First, I examine Beth Moore's social Christianity–informed rhetoric that expressed solidarity with survivors, enlarged her community's circle of concern, and maintained religiously conservative doctrinal stances. I examine this faithful deliberation as it appeared in a particular social media thread largely composed of posts from survivors of childhood sexual abuse. These posts came in response to Moore's engagement with the "Abuse of Faith" investigative series. After posting a link to the first article in the series on February 10, 2019, Moore shared a follow-up tweet, which included a childhood photograph of herself and a comment directed at church leaders, "We understand how you feel. We didn't want to know about sexual abuse either."[3] In reply, dozens of survivors—mostly women and a few men—posted about the abuse they experienced in family and church contexts. Following Moore's lead, along with disclosures about abuse, many replies included photographs of the survivors (often pictures from childhood) or objects important in their healing journeys. Analysis of this thread illustrates traditional and alternative rules for evangelical discourse: that a woman asserting the full measure of her agency within accepted gender norms obtains relative freedom and that centering survivors' voices entails creating space for emotions within deliberations.

Second, I attend to efforts that took place from May through June 2019 aimed at policing the boundaries of Southern Baptist community, questioning the theological orthodoxy of Moore and other abuse survivor advocates, and mobilizing ideological anxiety around questions of gender, sexuality, and race. Moore's critics took aim at her addressing a Southern Baptist congregation from the pulpit on Mother's Day morning and at her removing a discussion regarding the sinfulness of LGBTQ+ sexuality in later editions of a book she first published in 2000. Similarly, footage of Rachael Denhollander speaking on the ERLC panel about sexual abuse was used in (and later removed from) a trailer for a documentary intended to critique the encroachment of intersectionality, critical race theory, and secular social justice frameworks within the SBC. These episodes illustrate the traditional discursive rules that community preservation is paramount and that this preservation and gendered freedom rely on avoiding fundamental questions about race and sexuality. More broadly, they also illustrate the risk of perceived contamination that building connections outside the enclave entails.

At work in both situations is an understanding of the theological notion of *fellowship*. Drawing on strands of Baptist theology about the Lord's Supper (sometimes called communion), interdisciplinary feminist insights about practices of sharing, and Moore's thinking about fellowship, intimacy, and community-building, I articulate how a Twitter thread Moore initiated came to function as a widening fellowship of survivors established through an archive of abuse and healing. These acts of writing and assembling served to generate rhetorical materials that could further evangelical deliberations about institutional responses to abuse. In contrast, constituencies critical of Moore pursued a narrowing fellowship of believers through doctrinal line-drawing, policing vigorously the forms of evangelical deliberation and reinforcing reactionary arguments about gender and sexuality.

LITERACY COMMUNIONS AND ARCHIVING EXPERIENCE

The fellowship-generating-and-reinforcing rhetoric within the social media activity examined in this chapter resembles the "communion of friendship" described by Daniell and participants in her Al-Anon study. When articulating the phenomenon of a spiritual-but-not-necessarily-religious communion, Daniell articulates experiences and practices of sharing that become grounds for reinterpreting trauma in community-generating and agency-rousing ways. One participant, Lilly, linked "communion" and "friendship" in the comment that became the title of Daniell's book[4] and that Daniell records within a chapter examining the kinds of life- and reading-related sharing that occurred among participants. Reading and conversation were not for the purpose of "correct" interpretation; rather, "sharing . . . is arguably the most significant aspect of the reading," as the participants' talk is "embedded in ongoing conversations" that "explore, translate, clarify, and articulate their feelings and beliefs on any number of issues."[5] Lilly explained that discussing books is more than an individual, expressive disclosure; reading-based discussion results in an expanding and deepening of the self in relation to others. Reading also serves as a form of invention because it can "touch feelings, and then I have to find words for the feelings."[6] A communion of friendship, then, involves inventing personal and rhetorical resources through literacy-shaped conversations where thoughtful listening occurs.

The mutual exchange of experiences and feelings in an empathetic way may produce relationships that become resources for agency. Social interaction appears as central in scenes of literate activity outside the academy that are both historical[7] and contemporary,[8] in the deeply collaborative nature of modern workplace writing,[9] in the general history of advanced writing within the university,[10] and in accounts of women's participation in writing study and work.[11] Literacy studies and feminist psychology explore the agential possibilities of listening and sharing within groups.[12] Listening empathetically provides both speakers and listeners with a sense of their own power to serve as positive presences in the lives of others: "Recognizing someone else's feelings, feeling *with* the other person, empowers not only the speaker, who is taken seriously, acknowledged, and therefore affirmed, but also the hearer, who in taking seriously, acknowledging, and affirming another, has an effect on the speaker."[13] Embedded in ongoing literacy and rhetorical encounters that allow individuals to examine and recontextualize traumatic experiences, these mutual exchanges of recognition create opportunities for—and are evidence of—intimate communities. While the kinds of tightly woven, local communities that Daniell observes are not the same as the sort in Beth Moore's Twitter feed, there are elements of overlap. The February 2019 thread became a survivor-generated archive interlaced with individual memories, prior encounters among participants, personal artifacts, and community literacy practices.

Archives privileging experiences not well-represented in the dominant public sphere nor readily understood within an enclave may help create conditions for forms of healing that acknowledge emotion, promote critique of conditions that inequitably distribute harm, and enable action. Archives authorize rhetorical invention.[14] Discussing the inventive power of lesbian archives, Jean Bessette finds that those who engage with them may "transform their feelings of guilt, fear, and isolation into self-acceptance" while also finding themselves encouraged "to find more local community."[15] In addition to these affect-transforming and community-forming functions, archives may help those who encounter them understand "personal trauma not as a result of individual pathology but rather as a world hostile to" an aspect of their identity or experience.[16] Archives focusing on sexual violence survivors' experiences likewise create opportunities to critically reflect, establish relationships, and confront violence-enabling discourses.[17] Even as archives may assemble the important disclosures that survivors are willing and able to share, archives can also bring into view how trauma, affect, and rhetoric intersect not only in texts and "narrative[,] but in material artifacts," such as "photographs" and "objects whose relation to trauma might seem arbitrary," except for the affective charges they carry.[18] Expanding on the idea that reading and conversation create the opportunity to name experiences, Lilly noted, "Sometimes . . . they will give me the situation, a picture. The picture helps. It begins to make the feelings clearer until I find the words," and the words develop through interactions with others.[19] In light of these insights into group experience- and object-sharing that mutually affirm reader and writer, as well as archives' capacities to achieve positive social and individual outcomes, I understand Moore's social media effort as generating an archive that documents survivor accounts of abuse in ways that link personal healing and enclave deliberation.

CHRISTIAN FELLOWSHIP AND BETH MOORE

For reasons similar to those explained in chapter 4 regarding the label "apostolic" in reference to SBC women, I refrain from using the term "communion" to describe the kind of sharing, mutual recognition, and memory work that emerges in Moore's thread. Evangelicals and Baptists vary widely from congregation to congregation in their observance of and terminology for communion or the Lord's Supper. Region as well as denominational affiliation generally function as determining factors, but other contributing factors influencing what term is used include congregational worship style, theological influences of previous and present ministers, and ecumenical and associational connections. Race and location may also be factors. The language used within the Southern Baptist confessional statement "Baptist Faith and Message 2000" is that of the Lord's Supper. Perhaps a more appropriate, community-employed term to aid analysis—a term that is recognizable within Baptist communities and that carries both religious and community functions—is "fellowship." Fellowship serves many uses within Christian discourse. It may signal an everyday sense of community shared over a meal, a particular church ("fellowship" sometimes appears in congregation names), the bounds of denominational affiliation (indeed, "disfellowshipped" is a term used to name the process of removing a church from a denominational or ministerial association), or the mystical relationship that binds all Christians together in unity with God.

During the month of July 2019, Beth Moore's Living Proof Live program on Trinity Broadcasting Network, a Christian television network, dealt with the concept of fellowship among Christians. This sequence of five episodes dealt with many of the issues Moore faced throughout and before 2019: the charge of being a "false teacher," the problem of evangelical-insider language that fails to connect with out-group members, the difficulties social media can present to thoughtful discussion, and the divisions community insiders draw to maintain the exclusive and privileged status of a group. In characteristic style, Moore addresses these issues without naming particular people or specific circumstances. Titled Staying Afloat on the Fellow Ship, this series explores the notion of fellowship as seeking a relational engagement with other Christians (i.e., "insiders") and non-Christians (i.e., "outsiders"). She urges insiders to meet outsiders in a context of situational awareness and care. Fellowship requires actual others—not just an idea or notion of community—and it is predicated on insiders relating with outsiders in ways that are "intentionally relational."

Relational fellowship leads to encounters with difference, which promotes listening and deliberation within the in-group and with the out-group. To illustrate the importance of listening and the deliberative aspects of fellowship within the community, Moore urges restraint regarding charges that some are "false teachers" promoting "heresy" (something she herself has experienced). She invokes the story of an unnamed woman who had been criticized for preaching prosperity gospel theology, changed her position on that theological understanding of material success as a sign of divine favor, and continued to receive criticism despite having changed her thinking. Critical of what she refers to as "insider-outsiding," Moore voices concern about Christian insiders constructing narrow community boundaries that are rigidly enforced in ways that reduce variation within the religious community and expel even those who may hold the same beliefs yet express them differently. Instead of relationships with other Christians being grounds for practicing faith and sources of strength for the task of sharing faith with others in intentionally relational ways, those relationships become signs of community dysfunction. This dysfunction, according to Moore, potentially preempts evangelism (a defining preoccupation of evangelical Christianity), dissuading non-Christians from joining the community.

As seen in the discussion of reconciliation in chapter 4, deliberative engagement to reshape the parameters of Christian community may be motivated by the religious commitment to share one's faith with others (i.e., to evangelize). These are precisely the terms in which Moore articulates the need for fellowship. Evangelism in this fellowship framework would look less like shouting on street corners and more like conversations conducted with mutual respect while listening for difference, less like guarding a border and more like setting a table. From this standpoint, which seeks encounters with difference and understands how difference can occur within an enclave, Moore addresses how much she has learned from reading work by Christians of color and by celibate Christians who experience "same-sex attraction." When she urges her audience to not be "scandalized" at this reading program, Moore recognizes that promoting this kind of engagement might seem unusual to her audience. This request to delay judgment anticipates and attempts to preempt concerns about moral contamination. She argues that Jesus provides a model of engagement in which Christians should not be concerned about contamination from contact with outsiders or insiders whose beliefs are different from other evangelical Christians' beliefs. Consequently, fellowship and evangelism work in tandem to dismantle a firm sense of in-group identity established through more narrowly drawn boundaries and to facilitate listening across lines of difference without anxiety about moral contamination through conversation and reading.

A FELLOWSHIP OF SURVIVORS CREATING AN ARCHIVE OF ABUSE AND HEALING

The Twitter thread Moore created following the first publication in the "Abuse of Faith" journalism series generated a kind of fellowship among participants as they created an archive of abuse and healing. Keeping in mind the moderation Haskins urges when making claims about the archival and memory work of digital spaces,[20] the archive these participants produced preserved memories, fostered a sense of community history, and served as a deliberative resource. While feminist researchers affirm the popular assumption that digital spaces, and Twitter in particular, are generally unwelcoming toward women's full participation because of the ease with which attacks are made,[21] others have examined how activists, advocates, and survivors engage digital environments to represent and characterize experiences of sexual violence.[22] Viewed as a kind of digital rhetorical activism, Moore's social media activity involves a relational challenge to a culture that licenses sexual violence. While such communications are public, many contributors might not want their posts studied in this way or circulated further. Given the sensitive nature of the information shared in this Twitter thread, examining this material carries ethical implications. After consulting studies of #NotOkay[23] and #WhyIStayed[24] and recommendations from the Association of Internet Researchers, I focus on comments from public figures who have discussed their stories elsewhere. In these cases, I identify them by name. When a contributor had fewer than one thousand followers or no link to an additional online media presence, I did not use their names and I paraphrased their posts, quoting no more than a word or short phrase.

Thinking of posts and disclosures in Moore's Twitter thread as an archive fits the framing in Moore's original post, which speaks to the question of personal knowledge coming up against dominant and institutional unknowing: "We understand how you feel. We didn't want to know about sexual abuse either."[25] In several of the replies, participants repeated or riffed on this knowledge/desire comment, turning it into a conversational trope. Frequently, replies repeated some aspect of the opening prompt: "I didn't want to know either." The word "either" often appeared, signaling both repetition of and agreement with Moore's initial position. Intensifiers, such as "so," "really," or "certainly," sometimes marked the strong emotion writers wished to convey. A few respondents used similar language but shifted perspective to talk about themselves in the third person. For example, along with a picture of herself as a small child, one participant wrote, "She didn't either" and ended the post with a broken heart emoji. Moore addressed the respondent by name, provoking a reply that expresses gratitude for this moment of recognition and acknowledgment. The respondent shifted to the first person, "You saw me!" Using the third person, some respondents posted pictures of themselves as children, referring to themselves as "this little girl" or "this little lady." Noting the difficulty of posting a picture of herself as a child, Hannah Bunker observed, "I had a hard time sharing this and looking at this little girl and remembering what she was going through."[26] As they acknowledged past trauma, contributors found different ways to name and document aspects of their abuse. Like the discussion of Rachael Denhollander's connection between remembering and forgiving in chapter 3, the participants building this Twitter archive insisted on remembering. The language of God "redeeming" experiences of abuse recurs—that is, God makes some new use of past trauma. Situating the present in light of the past may help explain current difficulties; remembering the past may also serve survivors as they pursue a better future for themselves and others.

The fellowship that emerged in this Twitter thread both expressed and reinforced bonds of affection. Throughout their interactions, Moore and the other contributors repeatedly used words signaling affection and emotion: "precious," "favorite," "sorry," "tears," "sweetest," "magical," "beautiful," "broken," "heart," "sorry," "friend." Such terms indicate a sensitivity to the situation in which these interactions unfolded, the existence or emergence of caring relationships, and a kind of community that acknowledges trauma, places it in a relational context, and narrativizes pain within the identity framework of a capable survivor. One participant, in response to a comment from a friend unaware of her story of abuse, replied that she does not generally discuss it but that a brief disclosure of her experience along with sharing an image functioned in a healing way: as acts of naming.

These expressions of care were sometimes grounded in ongoing conversations and relationships. For example, Jen Hatmaker replied to Moore's post with a tweet that conveyed her sorrow and anger: endless sobbing and "rage forever into the void. Sweet little Beth. All the young innocents. And then to be blamed or disbelieved. You know Jesus will have the last word here."[27] After Hatmaker established the mix of emotions that dominate her response to the abuse Moore experienced, she used a term of endearment (i.e., "sweet little Beth") to address the child Moore was at the time of the abuse. Hatmaker connected that story with all those individuals whose abuse was reported on in the *Houston Chronicle* (i.e., "all the young innocents") and those still unacknowledged publicly. Moore picked up on Hatmaker's final comment about the ultimate authority and justice of Jesus and affirmed a sense of abiding trust in God. Moore went on to summarize how many who suffered similar traumas drew on that experience to help others in meaningful ways; she prayed that "God will do the same for each one. He plays no favorites."[28] Riffing on Moore's last line, Hatmaker replied: "He plays all favorites. You told me at a very, very crucial moment that you didn't wear this and Jesus was faithful and not to be afraid. . . . But I sure would love it if He could get some help from his church leaders."[29] Moore affirmed this memory and comment. In the context of this digital archive and the conversation surrounding it, these moments spent reflecting on previous encounters among participants assert a sense of agency as they support survivors and urge church leaders to pursue more robust programs of abuse prevention and aggressor accountability.

Other contributors likewise situated their posts within the context of previous encounters or discussions with Moore. One respondent expressed gratitude for Moore's acknowledgment and kindness toward her. She recalled an event Moore conducted at a Southern Baptist seminary where the two of them had interacted as the beginning of her movement toward her own recovery from abuse. Concluding with gratitude and a reiteration of an action-oriented plan that came out of their in-person conversation, she stated her intention to begin "breaking free" as she had "promised" Moore she would. In another instance of these fellowship-forming and archive-generating exchanges occurring within ongoing relationships, a different participant shared a photograph of a cassette tape from a 2002 Babbie Mason Music Seminar. Mason is a gospel singer and songwriter who often performs at events for Christian women, including those featuring Moore. The Music Seminar is a conference for singers and songwriters, which includes worship components. Along with a picture of a cassette tape from one of these seminars, the respondent asked Moore if she recalled speaking at one of these gatherings. After confirming that Moore remembered the occasion, the respondent noted she would never forget Moore's remarks on the biblical story of Ezekiel preaching to a valley of the dry bones. This blending of photos, memories, scriptures, and everyday objects illustrate the ongoing relational work that generates healing opportunities.

Some contributions also incorporated the voices of SBC survivor-advocates in ways that recognized them as part of a wide fellowship and that situated the documented abuse, along with this particular social media thread, within a longer history of denominational deliberation. Rachael Denhollander wrote, "Grieving with you."[30] Moore replied, "And I with you. And I stand with you."[31] These interactions suggest a reciprocity of feeling and sentiment, but they also bespeak a commitment to solidarity and action. Denhollander then expressed gratitude for the community of survivor-advocates of which she is a part, tagging and naming Jules Woodson, Megan Lively, and Tiffany Thigpen. Woodson came forward shortly after the popularization of #MeToo and the advent of #ChurchToo with sexual misconduct allegations against her former youth pastor from twenty years prior; he had gone on to a leadership position within a megachurch. Lively identified herself as a rape survivor and seminary student at SEBTS whom Paige Patterson advised to not report her assault. Thigpen alleged sexual harassment against Darrell Gilyard, whose history I discussed in the previous chapter as it related to Patterson, and she proactively collected accounts from other women who also alleged harassment by Gilyard. By tagging these women and bringing them into the conversation, Denhollander added others' advocacy to the archive. In doing so, she expressed, reinforced, and widened the fellowship of survivors and advocates, which also provided a lens through which to interpret the February 2019 news account about abuse in the SBC and the stories shared in the Twitter thread. That is, Denhollander linked this conversation with #ChurchToo developments within the SBC, the Patterson controversy, and the longer history of survivor self-advocacy within the denomination. Such a link connects these largely narrative, descriptive, and expressive posts to ongoing deliberations within the SBC and evangelicalism.

Interpretation—reading scripture and reading life in light of scripture—appears in many posts, constituting a shared literacy that generated a sense of intimate community, of fellowship. Indeed, biblical literacy is effortlessly woven into the conversation, often without citation because some commonplace expressions are so readily accessible. For example, one commenter responding to another used the phrase "beauty for ashes"[32] to describe the work God performs through the survivor in the wake of abuse, taking the pain and using it toward some ultimate good. A few participants name abuse and its accompanying trauma as the work of "the enemy," which could have several meanings but most likely refers to the Devil or Satan, who is called "the enemy" in scripture as well as in public discourse and everyday conversations among evangelicals. This biblical literacy, the theology it implies, and the healing it suggests mirror the rhetorical practices studied throughout this book—taking proverbs of ashes and reinvigorating them through rhetorical invention.

Beyond citing and interpreting scripture, participants further demonstrated how building an archive of abuse and healing can work to generate fellowship by documenting how scripture functioned as proverbs of ashes when used to justify or minimize abuse and by enabling scriptural reinterpretation. One participant shared how she disclosed abuse by her father to the pastor at the Assemblies of God church where her father served in a leadership position. The pastor told her, "Touch not God's anointed!" Moore replied, "One of the most abused scriptures in the entire canon."[33] Moore clearly recognized this injunction as a biblical passage. Passages that source this commonplace expression describe occasions when David could have killed King Saul—and others even exhorted him to—yet refused.[34] Similar passages appear to apply a comparable level of divinely sanctioned protection to ordinary believers.[35] Given how abusers often appeal to scripture to justify their behavior and how church authorities also use it to minimize trauma and to victim-blame, survivors with religious backgrounds frequently must revise interpretations of scripture promoted within their communities.[36] Such uses of scripture recall the antinomian problem of in-group privileging and out-group policing discussed in chapter 3 and the commonplace use of shared religious identity to leverage others' trust described in chapter 2. When this survivor posted a picture of herself as a child, when she disclosed publicly her abuse, when she quoted the biblical words used by a pastor to protect an aggressor, and when Moore in reply repudiated ubiquitous misappropriations of this scripture for silencing purposes, they both created space for inventively reinterpreting scripture and renegotiating religious identity in the wake of sexual and spiritual trauma.

Contributors also blended the invocation of biblical stories with photographs, material objects, and personal memories, further establishing the thread's archival function as it enabled relational and emotional exchanges. For example, Bunker attached to her post an image of herself as a child in a costume that included a white beaded garland and a flowing dress covered with dark purple sequins. Moore employed the term "magical" to name the child in the picture and the adult she became: "No one has taken that from you. I still see it."[37] Bunker used bodily language to characterize the feelings and went on to provide background regarding the costume: "Those words pierce deep into my heart, Beth. Only the Lord knows how deep they go. Knot in my throat. Thank you. I thought you might get a kick out of knowing that is me dressed as Esther for Bible character day at school. My granny sewed the costume for me."[38] Remembering and conveying the details behind that costume offers access to a powerful and capable identity grounded in a sense of loving community and of connection to an important biblical character who was a woman. Family here creates beauty and passes on shared traditions. Additionally, Bunker's comment places this moment in an ongoing conversation with Moore's work, including her 2008 publication *Esther: It's Tough Being a Woman.*

A FELLOWSHIP OF BELIEVERS AND DOCTRINAL LINE-DRAWING

In using their evangelicalism and Southern Baptists platforms to confront sexual violence, Moore and others have faced increasing scrutiny on other issues that are considered doctrinal and identity litmus tests, particularly their adherence to complementarianism, resistance to LGBTQ+ affirmation, and opposition to CRT/I. Recall the division within evangelical feminism and the eventual breakaway of many EWC members described in chapter 1 in response to perceptions that hermeneutics within EWC had veered away from a strict biblicism as some members grew more accepting of pro-LGBTQ+ civil rights stances. In that instance, divisions arose in response to a vote the organization made that affirmed lesbian and gay civil rights, a perceived departure from conservative orthodoxy. In the summer of 2019, certain constituencies made statements or asked questions that implied that Moore had moved outside acceptable bounds for Southern Baptist thinking, because she had asserted that a woman can speak from the pulpit on a Sunday morning; because she has apparently softened her language regarding LGBTQ+ issues, not singling them out for particular attention in discussions about sinfulness; and because she associated with and has been admired by some theological liberals, LGBTQ+ Christians (such as Jonathan Merritt), and LGBTQ+-affirming Christians (such as Hatmaker). At the same time, she continued to maintain that her beliefs regarding human sexuality and Christian ethics had not changed, which she went on to explicitly articulate in an easily summarized statement: Marriage is between a man and a woman, and sex before marriage is sinful.[39] Not about a fundamental difference in doctrinal belief or ethical practice, line-drawing in this situation enforced expectations that evangelicals must address a particular issue and convey their position in a specific manner. If an expressive justice within the dominant public sphere limited survivors' acceptable range of emotions, then an expressive evangelicalism works here to patrol evangelical speech.

Responding to a prompt asking Twitter followers to imagine work they might perform along with their current vocations, Moore, noting that she was "in a tad of a mischievous mood," posted that she had deleted an additional item from her list: "Teaching a men's Sunday School class at a church full of Calvinists just to get everybody going."[40] In the thread that followed, one respondent mentioned that she would be preaching on Mother's Day 2019, playfully asking that Moore not share that information. Moore replied, "I'm doing Mother's Day too! Vicki, let's please don't tell anyone this."[41] Of course, they understand the public nature of the forum in which their exchange occurred, and they leveraged that publicness to humorous effect. However, some Southern Baptists didn't see the humor in the suggestion that women could preach on Sunday morning to a mixed-gender audience. Owen Strachan, a Southern Baptist seminary professor, tweeted that, while complementarians hold diverse views, they agree that "women do not preach on Sunday to the church. . . . We will not capitulate here."[42] Southern Baptist women's preaching persisted as a Twitter topic, with Moore posting, and then deleting, a link to a 1984 pamphlet by Roy Honeycutt, a former Southern Baptist seminary president, titled "Affirming Women in Ministry." While Moore intended to illustrate historical diversity in Southern Baptist thinking on this topic, the post resulted in tweets expressing high levels of concern from Al Mohler and other SBC leaders, framing the sharing of such material as an affront of historic proportions.[43] Given that Moore herself is a complementarian, the issue was less about shared belief than it was about how to interpret that doctrine and about current perceptions of allies Moore cited. In other words, doctrinal purity and the desire to avoid moral contamination were at stake.

Just as Moore encountered questions regarding her adherence to complementarianism, between June and August 2019, she likewise encountered persistent, publicly circulated inquiries about her position on LGBTQ+ identities and sexualities. On June 18, "An Open Letter to Beth Moore," originally signed by six "female Bible teachers," asked Moore to explain her current position on "homosexuality," "the homosexual lifestyle," and "same sex attraction" in relationship to sinfulness, Christian living, the afterlife, and nature. The authors grounded their questions in her positive and friendly associations with Jen Hatmaker and Jonathan Merritt, as well as her recent lack of public comment on these topics. The letter gained 498 additional signatures.

Over the next two weeks, the original signatories circulated the letter online and others tweeted questions to Moore that echoed this letter. During that time, while not addressing her thinking about LGBTQ+ affirmation, nor specifically responding to the letter, Moore posted on social media comments critical of (1) "Bible beaters void of the Holy Spirit" who fail to demonstrate "the love of God,"[44] (2) those who promote "shunning" behaviors because they seem to have "figure[d] out who Jesus doesn't love,"[45] and (3) "hunters" and "trappers" whose "hobby is discrediting fellow" Christians by posing questions that lack "good faith."[46] That final tweet was in reference to one of the original signatories of the open letter. These rule-enforcing and boundary-drawing conversations resulted in scrutiny that led some of Moore's readers to identify a revision she had made in recent digital editions of a popular devotional text first published in 2000. The 2009 hard copy edition of *Praying God's Word* declares "homosexuality . . . a deadly sexual assault of the evil one [the devil]" and a "sin" that divine intervention can "deliver" a person from if "forgiveness" is sought; Moore writes that "transformation . . . is possible . . . because God's Word says so" and that she has met "plenty of believers who have been set free from" same-sex desire.[47] These and additional words related to LGBTQ+ sexuality were removed from the Kindle version at some point prior to 2019. Upon being asked about the recently noticed changes, Moore explained that after "test[ing] the fruit, it became clear to me that my words in this section, words that exceeded Scripture, were stopping many from God's words which follow."[48] In a blog post titled "Why I Removed Some of My Commentary from a Chapter of *Praying God's Word*," she repeats this language about having "exceeded Scripture" in singling out nonheteronormative sexuality as especially sinful. Such a move reflects her biblicism and her approach to fellowship as seeking out—rather than avoiding—difference. The modification and its justification also echo the SBC women's collective's concerns in the preceding chapter: that persisting in a status quo course of action would diminish opportunities for evangelism.

In July 2019, Founders Ministries released a trailer for a then-forthcoming documentary arguing that CRT/I diminish the centrality of scripture and cultivate a potentially unbiblical social justice program within the SBC. Founders, led by Tom Ascol, was created to support the goals of the Conservative Resurgence discussed in chapter 4. This trailer for *By What Standard?* included imagery of Rachael Denhollander speaking at ERLC's panel on sexual abuse at the 2019 SBC denominational gathering (Beth Moore and Russell Moore were also panelists). That imagery was juxtaposed with comments that drew on biblical language about evil powers. Denhollander's primary focus in public life since the Nassar trial had been preventing sexual abuse and holding aggressors accountable; using imagery of her speaking about that topic to an SBC audience, thus, associated abuse survivor-advocates with, specifically, biblical language about the influence of evil in the world and, generally, with concerns about secular social justice frameworks displacing the authoritative nature of scripture. The trailer provoked significant controversy and the footage of Denhollander was removed. When released, the full film narrated a story of the SBC's moral and theological drift away from biblicism and complementarianism. Evidence for this drift includes Beth Moore's influence, Russell Moore's racial reconciliation agenda (discussed in chapter 4), and the SBC's 2019 adoption of resolutions describing CRT/I as potentially useful analytical tools. Such a list bears a resemblance to the list of contamination concerns that run throughout the history of White Christian America.

The organization that produced a documentary investigating a possible SBC liberalization, the Bible teachers who inquired about Moore's views on LGBTQ+ sexuality, and the leaders who worried about a possible softening of complementarianism did not necessarily oppose Beth Moore's and others' specific stances on behalf of abuse survivors. However, for Moore, leveraging her long-standing prominence and platform to voice concerns about sexual abuse, domestic violence, and their relationship to misogyny while exercising her full freedom as a woman in ministry within the SBC strictures has certainly provoked increased scrutiny regarding her place within

Southern Baptist fellowship. Drawing doctrinal lines guards the believing fellowship's boundaries and monitors the expression of shared beliefs in deliberative contexts. Of course, this situation is not new but stands in a long line of rules and responses that exist in dynamic tension: preserving community cohesion and seeking out-group connections, fulfilling gendered expectations in new ways and chancing reprisals, advocating for victims of systemic injustice and risking group purity. Reinventing proverbs of ashes for faithful deliberation occurs in the midst of such tensions.

Conclusion

In the preceding chapters, I have investigated the question of invention for faithful deliberation within evangelicalism in light of the #MeToo movement. As chapter 2 makes apparent, there are sometimes disconnects between the positions of long-recognized representatives for this religious constituency and the faithful deliberation of the women whose rhetoric I studied. Through feminist rhetorical analysis, I have examined how some contemporary evangelical women address the problems of sexual and domestic violence and their community's responses to these issues in contexts related to theological concepts of grace, forgiveness, reconciliation, and fellowship.

Leveraging in-group-dependent ethos, faithful deliberators reinvented trauma-minimizing commonplaces (i.e., conflating sexual assault and general sexuality, promoting instant forgiveness, and appealing to in-group identity and trust), confronting a cheap rhetorical grace with a costly rhetorical grace that requires ongoing community transformation. They casuistically tightened forgiveness, reinvigorating it through theological reflection, to challenge the culture of silence fostered by theologically informed platitudes about forgiveness. The rhetoric of reconciliation as restoration of a just creation that SBC women forwarded stands in contrast to an understanding of reconciliation as primarily the reuniting of survivors and aggressors in cases of domestic violence. A deliberative fellowship of survivors constructed an archive of abuse and healing, widening the community's circle of concern, which contrasted with a narrowing fellowship of believers who drew firmer doctrinal lines.

The faithful deliberators at the center of the study did not withdraw from engagement with a possibly suspicious US public or from deliberation with a potentially confrontational enclave. Rather, they waded into troubled waters and walked into the discomfort of hard moments for the sake of moving their own communities toward compassion for survivors and accountability for aggressors and their enablers. In what follows, I consider what inventional possibilities arise from understanding faithful deliberation and how rhetorical studies might benefit from understanding those possibilities.

By attending to the work of women committed to deep engagement with changing dynamics within evangelicalism and the larger public sphere, I add to rhetorical studies' knowledge about how theologically informed rhetorical invention may aid deliberation.

CENTERING SURVIVORS' VOICES AND ASSERTING ABSOLUTES

At play in each concept examined in the preceding chapters is the pull of, and resistance to, in-group and out-group thinking. For example, costly rhetorical grace confronts patterns that license violence common in both the church and the wider culture. This confrontation requires privileging survivors' stories over proverbs of ashes. Moore and Hatmaker both urged their readers who might not know survivors' stories to learn from them, a task resonant with what Daniell reports about the personal and collective resources white women gained from reading works by Black women. Such encounters with others' stories demand that the writer practice care to avoid an appropriative, cheap rhetorical grace. Cheap encounters would simply make readers feel good for learning about others or provoke a momentary outrage over descriptions of sinful systems. Put simply, a cheap encounter rests on an expressive justice predicated on feelings easily appropriated into a hegemonic project. An encounter with trauma stories needs to be a costly one that leads to community judgment against practices that perpetuate violence, especially routine and everyday practices. Audiences are bid to repent of how things have been and move toward something else; the outcome of a costly encounter remains unpredictable.

A stance that centers survivors' voices is not about deifying and thus accepting others' suffering or reducing complex healing to steps in one, universal sequence, as might occur in a substitutionary atonement-based logology's pursuit of sacrifice for restoring order. However, rhetoricians can center our vision on the stories of those who survive and thrive in the midst of unjust systems that inequitably distribute life's precariousness. That is, deliberation makes the most sense when lessons are drawn from—when we listen to—people and communities who have been marginalized. In the tradition of letters by Sarah Grimké and by Moore, engaging with such accounts helps Christians to identify systems that single out some groups for greater suffering, name these systems as violating the divine order, and free believers to undertake work that would change these systems—to imagine the world differently.

Practicing deliberation shaped by costly grace, casuistically tightened forgiveness, justice-oriented reconciliation, widening fellowships, and archives of abuse and healing may look quite different depending on the circumstances. In some instances, faithful deliberators may employ absolutist assertions to reject old ideas and promote new practices. Michael-John DePalma, Jeffrey Ringer, and Jim Webber argue that rhetors lose powerful resources for argumentation when absolutist discourse is dismissed in favor of liberal proceduralism. They offer a diverse array of sample counterstatements to illustrate the value of absolutist assertions to a robustly deliberative democracy. A small sample of their counterstatements includes: "'Inefficiency is preferable to efficiency'; 'Civil deliberation deserves disruption'; 'Monkey-wrench orderly discursive operations'; 'Conflict beats comity'; 'Disrespect the "respectable" and respect the "disrespectable."'"[1] Rhetorical scholars assert the value of uncivil rhetoric that breaks with standard rules and procedures of decorum, including when these breaks in convention find motivation in religious or spiritual commitments.[2] Consequently, generating and circulating religiously grounded absolutist discourse informed by perspectives that have not received receptive hearings in the past may actually serve deliberative ends. I offer here a few absolutist statements inspired by the practices examined in preceding chapters: *Stop peddling cheap grace. Life over purity. Burn your proverbs of ashes. Speak life into a hurting world. Forgiveness means seeking justice. Trust survivors, not church leaders. Cease silencing survivor stories. Reconcile creation, not just couples. Widen the fellowship.* Uncivil, absolutist rhetoric, rather than shutting down deliberative possibilities, may open rhetorical space for intervening into both mainstream and enclave discourses.

FAITHFUL DELIBERATION AND AN ETHICS OF HOPE AND CARE

My study of evangelical women's faithful deliberation suggests a few potential lessons for employing an ethics of hope and care in future studies of deliberative discourse, particularly when considering contributions from religiously conservative women. First, an ethics of hope and care when naming religious rhetorics may usefully extend existing rhetorical theories. As observed in chapter 4, while "apostolic rhetoric" covers many elements of SBC women's rhetoric responding to the Patterson controversy, a feminist rhetorical ethics enables fruitful elaboration of the related phenomenon of reconciling rhetoric. Similarly, while "communion" may name the intimate rhetorical literacy at work in the Twitter thread examined in chapter 5, denominational distinctions suggested "fellowship" as a more appropriate key term. As some SBC women practice a social Christianity through faithful deliberation, they maintain their theological conservatism by proclaiming the need to repent of individual sinfulness. They uphold their gender complementarianism while also challenging socially harmful expressions of that theological notion. Listening carefully to the differences among religious rhetors, and not collapsing them, may generate new avenues for invention.

Second, taking rhetors' stated motivations and audiences' commitments seriously matters in terms of persuasion. Faithful deliberators write from a sense of religious conviction as the very grounds of their ability to undertake enclave discussion. Indeed, their high level of religiosity enables them to receive a hearing within their community, which is the context of their deliberation. They demonstrate that answers to the problems of misogynistic discourses sanctifying violence within their communities need not rest on appeals to sources outside their tradition. Given the fears Humphreys expressed about the potential decline of robust democratic decision-making and about authoritarian drift within the SBC following the Conservative Resurgence, it might be appropriate to characterize contemporary women's efforts as part of a (to riff on Martin Marty) *re*-Baptistification of the SBC. Their practices embody denominational characteristics that privilege individual conscience, interpretive freedom, institutional autonomy, and the spirit of cooperation. Rather than these developments reflecting a liberalization within the SBC—a fear expressed in relationship to figures like Moore and Denhollander who forward a more assertive evangelical response to sexual abuse than the SBC had traditionally seen—the episodes examined in the preceding chapters depict the power that follows women mobilizing denominational traditions within complementarianism.

Third, faithful deliberation finds its grounding in a conservative variety of Christian hope rather than in progressive political commitments. Moore explains her belief that, if "presented with the facts," right action will follow. She holds that people easily discern truth and that right courses of action readily present themselves. This perspective may sound like a rational, liberal notion of the public sphere and human subjectivity. Alternatively, this stance suggests a remnant of Puritan epistemology: Good people easily find the readily apparent truth of a situation.[3] For the rhetor herself, this notion of political change finds mooring in a transcendent ground of being that beckons to Christians: *Be reconciled.* That there exists an ultimate truth about how the social order should be arranged neither absolves believers of their responsibility to work for an outcome nor holds them ultimately responsible for achieving that outcome.

However, in light of the concerns raised by Paasch and Joy about evangelical visions for social order, these #ChurchToo founders would urge a radical restructuring of evangelical sexual ethics away from a heteronormative purity culture as necessary to address sexual violence. Most of the women whose rhetoric I study appear to accept positions regarding normative sexuality typically held within their socially conservative rhetorical enclave. As Donna Freitas might put it, there seems still no "possibility of yes" to sexual expression outside a heteronormative Christian marriage.[4] When Freitas explored if, how, and under what circumstances college students at Catholic, evangelical, and public institutions perceived their religious and romantic lives as interacting, she found that they do not generally see their religious background as having anything to say to their sexual lives, nothing beyond a more or less stern admonition to abstain. While evangelical students did see a mutually informing relationship between religion and sexuality, the purity culture hermeneutic that guided the interaction produced a significant amount of shame and frustration. Normative evangelical purity expectations may well add to the ethical problems that faithful deliberators face. Indeed, the evangelical conflation of sexual violence with general sexuality is informed by a purity-oriented perspective, which may obstruct conservative Christian communities from teaching the importance of consent. They might find it tricky to say, "Don't have sex outside of marriage, but when you do, make sure to practice and respect consent." At the same time, casuistically tightening forgiveness, as in examined chapter 3, illustrates that it is possible to achieve an explicit ranking of values that puts avoiding harm above preserving purity while still affirming the community accepted need for both.

Fourth, even as faithful deliberation may occur through denominationally specific practices, such as a rhetoric of reconciliation in the SBC, problems that follow a reconciliation framework, as is often the case in evangelical work for racial justice, may well stymie long-term change. Through their responses to Patterson's comments, SBC women reaffirm the SBC's theological conservativism and social Christianity. While the writers and signatories surely understand abuse as "contrary to the will of God," it remains unclear whether they would, with Episcopal priest Susan Thistlethwaite, frame abuse as "an unjust power distribution in society."[5] Such framing does seem possible when Moore addresses misogyny,[6] when Denhollander addresses community preservationism,[7] when the fellowship in Moore's Twitter thread addresses the misuse of scripture, and when the SBC women's collective addresses institutional hierarchies. Some systematic critique is present, and it appears that this critique receives a hearing within the SBC. But it is still possible that any changes taking place may amount to moving furniture around inside the same room—the redecorating of a cheap rhetorical grace, of perfunctory forgiveness, of an individual-oriented reconciliation, of a narrowly drawn fellowship—not the more thoroughgoing renovation predicated on repentance. All the same, paying attention to the work that theologically conservative women accomplish generates a fuller picture of how power, gender, theology, and rhetoric interact within some evangelical enclaves. Faithful deliberation shows that repentance seeks the proliferation of revised practices instead of more shame and requires a vulnerability that finds its grounding in reciprocal relationships of risk. In this way, rhetorical scholars may come to see how repentance productively contributes to religious enclave deliberation rather than simply expresses static positions within a stark binary of good and evil.

ADDRESSING SKEPTICISM

The forms of enclave deliberation investigated here may meet with skepticism from nonevangelicals, who hold these faithful deliberators don't go far enough in their reinventive work, and from fellow evangelicals, who object to perceived departures from orthodoxy. I witnessed the first dynamic when I asked undergraduate writing and rhetoric majors in a women's rhetoric course to read Beth Moore's "What about the Church's Silence?" and "A Letter to My Brothers." Two-thirds of students focused their response writing on "A Letter." They drew connections between the arguments made in Moore's pieces and those of nineteenth-century activists. Several students specifically noted similarities between Moore and the Grimké sisters. At first, students hesitated to see Moore as speaking in as forceful a way as the Grimkés. Students read her tone as conciliatory. As the class examined specific passages where Moore names misogynistic practices as sinful (even if particular people are not named), students acknowledged the productive power of the piece for her audience. These politically astute critical thinkers with generally feminist stances were perhaps reading into Moore's blog post a more accommodating stance given their nonidentification with evangelicalism.

Other contributing factors might involve a pre-discussion framing activity and the commonplace practice of using a claimed identity as a shorthand for a speaker's argument. The class-opening student presentation examined an instance of religious rhetoric from a complementarian pastor. Directed toward his daughter, the pastor's blog post urged her to maintain certain gender norms that embody modesty and submissiveness. The student presenter critiqued this position as circumscribing the daughter's life options, denying her autonomy, and embodying an ideology similar to the cult of true womanhood that many of the women they read throughout the semester reacted against. Since Moore claimed a complementarian identity, perhaps this label and the student presentation primed the class to interpret her piece as more about peacekeeping than reinventing. Even as labels, particularly self-adopted ones, may yield a sense of community and power, they may also limit opportunities for coalition-building and, on a more basic level, for evaluating arguments offered rather than group identities claimed or inferred.

During another teaching moment, as I tried to responsibly create rhetorical space sensitive to trauma where students could make historically informed, deliberative contributions to discussions in the public sphere and within their enclaves, a stumbling block came in the form of history as an account of Great Individuals to the exclusion of People's Movements. This orientation to history feeds into a notion of cultural and social change as predicated on the actions of individuals—or even just one person. As observed in earlier discussions about the relationship between rape culture and purity culture, ideologies operative within the United States generally are intensified within evangelicalism. Individualism is another such generally operative ideology amplified within evangelicalism. The individual and that person's unique relationship to God holds a special place in evangelical thinking. James Davison Hunter identifies pietistic individualism as a key problem within evangelicalism generally and its approach to social change specially.[8] Whether in an enclaved setting or a deliberative situation that involves crossing lines of difference, faithful deliberators and their allies may find it helpful to both acknowledge and reinvent individual-centric historical narratives by placing individual stories within the framework of a familiar movement, a strategy akin to the situating of proverbs of ashes within trauma-informed and survivor-sensitive contexts.

Such a strategy would have been useful during a senior seminar I recently taught on religious rhetoric and spiritual writing when a few students directed skepticism toward the story of civil rights activist Fannie Lou Hamer. Students in the course were unfamiliar with Hamer, a sharecropper turned organizer for the Mississippi Freedom Democratic Party, who experienced physical and sexual assault while in police custody following a voter registration effort. The first occasion when a student questioned the legitimacy of a narrative came after reading a piece that profiled Hamer's life and activism; the student, in this case a white evangelical man, wondered whether Hamer was being represented too favorably. This questioning came even after viewing clips of the "Mississippi: Is This America?" episode of the documentary *Eyes on the Prize*, which presents the atmosphere of terror and violence that Hamer and other Black liberation activists confronted. While the frame of individual, heroic action was familiar to students in the course, understanding this historical figure (i.e., a poor, rural, Black woman) as heroic seemed not in keeping with the established framework for such recognition. In retrospect, perhaps I could have connected Hamer to histories of the saints in the early Christian communities working in the context of empire. This comparison might have given students pause, because it would require imagining the United States as an oppressive state actively opposed to Christian practice; however, such conversation might have yielded productive reflections and helped link Hamer's mission of social transformation to a historical evangelizing context that this evangelical student and others would recognize.

Faithful deliberators who come to voice as theological and social conservatives following the #MeToo and #ChurchToo movements also present challenges to theological, social, *and* political arrangements that reduce arguments to easily identifiable and marketable identities. For example, Denhollander, a religious and political conservative, critiques the in-group protectionism her community exhibited during the Supreme Court confirmation process for Brett Kavanaugh, particularly the maligning and dismissal of Christine Blasey Ford. She points out that this kind of in-group defense is not the province of any particular political constituency or of any specific social institution. At the same time, she argues for consistency in the application of principled standards in response to sexual assault and abuse allegations.[9] Rhetors from any background may similarly encounter moments when exercising their voices within home communities causes trouble or results in a skeptical reaction. Studying the work of faithful deliberators may provide insight into how and why group members confront their own and reinvent the terms of discussion.

A FINAL WORD

One of the book-sharing participants in Daniell's study of Al-Anon women, Lilly, offered a moment of self-reflective evaluation that encouraged change within a relational context by describing her experience of reading Alice Walker's *The Temple of My Familiar*. Characters Fanny and Suwelo exchanged books they found important. The wife would read the books given to her, but the husband accumulated a stack of unread books. Eventually Fanny realized that the unread stack was "a little murder," a concept Lilly found so instructive that she shared the book with others for the purpose of talking about that idea.[10] This image of the stymied sharing that results in little murders—in contrast to the mutual sharing that generates fellowship (i.e., a communion of friendship)—works as a metaphor for the situation faithful deliberation aims to remedy. Recall Paige Patterson labeling as evildoers those survivors of clergy sexual abuse who advocated without ceasing for religious leaders' accountability; recall, too, Al Mohler's and other SBC leaders' long-held opposition to a denominational database of abuse aggressors despite years of survivors' stories indicating the need for a systematic response. Remember the preservation of in-group privilege that turned Christian injunctions to forgive into accountability exemptions; remember, too, the cheap rhetorical grace that maintains community cohesion at the expense of consistent standards for in-group and out-group members.

After hearing stories from survivors for years, several evangelical institutions and leaders have allowed these stories to pile up, like a stack of books politely, procedurally received, but left unread—preventing those voices from informing the enclave's perspective and action. In biblical language, they had eyes but failed to see, ears but failed to hear. It took shifts like #MeToo and #ChurchToo to create a context for hearing these voices in community-transforming ways, for opening up and actually reading the books filled with survivors' experiences. By reinventing commonplace proverbs of ashes from within evangelicalism, Moore, Hatmaker, Denhollander, Prior, and other advocates worked to ensure that the books of survivors' experiences were read and that they led to faithful deliberation. This is a kind of salvation involving both personal and social change. If rhetoric preforms salvific work, it is here and now: a world redeemed and transformed in response to trauma.

NOTES

Preface

1. The Episcopal Church, *The Book of Common Prayer and Administration of the Sacraments and Other Rites and Ceremonies of the Church: Together with the Psalter or Psalms of David According to the Use of the Episcopal Church* (New York: Seabury, 1979), 232.

2. Gregory A. Smith and Jessica Martínez, "How the Faithful Voted:A Preliminary 2016 Analysis." Pew Research Center, November 9, 2016, https://www.pewresearch.org/fact-tank/2016/11/09/how-the-faithful-voted-a-preliminary-2016-analysis/.

3. Jon Huang, Samuel Jacoby, Michael Strickland, and K. K. Rebecca Lai. "Election 2016: Exit Polls," *New York Times*, November 8, 2016, https://www.nytimes.com/interactive/2016/11/08/us/politics/election-exit-polls.html.

4. Michel Foucault, *The History of Sexuality, Vol. I*. Translated by Robert Hurley (New York: Random House, 1990).

5. Tamika L. Carey, *Rhetorical Healing: The Reeducation of Contemporary Black Womanhood* (Albany: SUNY Press), 5–6, emphasis in the original.

6. Beth Daniell, *A Communion of Friendship: Literacy, Spiritual Practice, and Women in Recovery* (Carbondale: Southern Illinois University Press, 2003), 29.

7. Daniell, *A Communion of Friendship*, 122.

8. Daniell, *A Communion of Friendship*, 26–32.

9. Toni Cade Bambara, *The Salt Eaters* (New York: Vintage, 1981), 3.

10. Carey, *Rhetorical Healing*, 29.

11. Beth Moore, "Do You Want to Get Well?" Living Proof Ministries, July 25, 2016. https://subsplash.com/livingproofwithbethmoore/lb/mi/+8efddcb.

12. Ann Cvetkovich, *An Archive of Feelings: Trauma, Sexuality, and Lesbian Public Culture* (Durham, NC: Duke University Press, 2003), 2–3.

13. Cvetkovich, *An Archive of Feelings*, 4.

14. Crowley qtd. in Jeffrey M. Ringer, *Vernacular Christian Rhetoric and Civil Discourse: The Religious Creativity of Evangelical Student Writers* (New York: Routledge, 2016), 2.

15. Carol J. Adams, "Foreword: Diving into the Wreck," in *Women, Religion, Revolution*, ed. Xochitl Alvizo and Gina Messina (Cambridge, MA: Feminist Studies in Religion Books, 2018), xv–xix.

Author's Note

1. Beth Daniell, *A Communion of Friendship: Literacy, Spiritual Practice, and Women in Recovery* (Carbondale: Southern Illinois University Press, 2003), 31–32.

2. Jonathan Spear, Tyrell Jones, and Stephanie Jones, qtd. in Barbie Lelek, "Young Children Have Questions for the President," *Big Spring Herald*, February 1990.

3. T J Geiger II, qtd. in Lelek, "Young Children Have Questions for the President."

4. Anne Ruggles Gere, *Intimate Practices: Literacy and Cultural Work in U.S. Women's Clubs, 1880–1920* (Champaign: University of Illinois Press, 1997).

5. Daniell, *A Communion of Friendship*.

6. Marilynne Robinson, *Gilead* (London: Virago, 2004), 25.

Introduction

1. Job 1, NRSV.

2. Job 2.

3. Job 11.

4. Job 11:16–17.

5. Cathy Caruth, *Trauma: Explorations in Memory* (Baltimore, MD: Johns Hopkins University Press, 1995); Ann Cvetkovich, *An Archive of Feelings: Trauma, Sexuality, and Lesbian Public Culture* (Durham, NC: Duke University Press, 2003), 2–3; Ruth Leys, *Trauma: A Genealogy* (Chicago: University of Chicago Press, 2000).

6. James 5.

7. Job 13–12.

8. Job 13:15, 23:3–4.

9. Job 10:16–18.

10. Job 19:6–8.

11. Job 7:11.

12. Job 4:7, 5:17.

13. Job 42:7–8.

14. Jane Mansbridge, "Using Power/Fighting Power: The Polity," in *Democracy and Difference: Contesting the Boundaries of the Political*, ed. Seyla Benhabib (Princeton, NJ: Princeton University Press, 1996), 57.

15. Dianna Anderson, *Damaged Goods: New Perspectives on Christian Purity* (New York: Jericho, 2015), 150–54; Nicola Gavey, *Just Sex? The Cultural Scaffolding of Rape* (London: Routledge, 2005), 3; Sophie Sills et al., "Rape Culture and Social Media: Young Critics and a Feminist Counterpublic," *Feminist Media Studies* 16, no. 6 (2016): 936.

16. Anderson, *Damaged Goods*; Samantha Field, "How We Teach Purity Culture Isn't the Problem: Purity Culture Itself Is the Problem," *Rewire News*, October 24, 2016, https://rewire.news/article/2016/10/24/teach-purity-culture-isnt-problem-purityculture-problem/.

17. Delores S. Williams, *Sisters in the Wilderness: The Challenge of Womanist God-Talk* (Maryknoll, NY: Orbis, 1993), 143–51.

18. JoAnne M. Terrell, *Power in the Blood? The Cross in the African American Experience* (Eugene, OR: Wipf and Stock, 2005), 43.

19. D. Michael Lindsay, *Faith in the Halls of Power: How Evangelicals Joined the American Elite* (New York: Oxford University Press, 2007), 3–4.

20. Kristy Maddux, "Finding Comedy in Theology: A Hopeful Supplement to Kenneth Burke's Logology," *Philosophy & Rhetoric* 39, no. 2 (2006): 228.

21. Sharon Crowley, *Toward a Civil Discourse: Rhetoric and Fundamentalism* (Pittsburgh, PA: University of Pittsburgh Press, 2006), 52, 201.

22. Peter Simonson, "Reinventing Invention, Again," *Rhetoric Society Quarterly* 44, no. 4 (2014): 313, emphasis in the original.

23. Catherine Matthews Pavia, "The 'My Online Friends' Religious Enclave: Expanding the Definition and Possibilities of Enclaved Discourses," *Rhetoric Review* 39, no. 1 (2020): 89.

24. Gerard A. Hauser, *Vernacular Voices: The Rhetoric of Publics and Public Spheres* (Columbia: University of South Carolina Press, 1999); Mansbridge, "Using Power/Fighting Power"; Cass Sunstein, *Going to Extremes: How Like Minds Unite and Divide* (Oxford: Oxford University Press, 2009).

25. Bob Smietana, "Pastors Seldom Preach About Domestic Violence," LifeWay Research, June 27, 2014, https://lifewayresearch.com/2014/06/27/pastors-seldom-preach-about-domestic-violence/.

26. Andrea Smith, *Native Americans and the Christian Right: The Gendered Politics of Unlikely Alliances* (Durham, NC: Duke University Press, 2008), xxiv.

27. Emily Murphy Cope and Jeffrey M. Ringer, "Coming to (Troubled) Terms: Methodology, Positionality, and the Problem of Defining 'Evangelical Christian,'" in *Mapping Christian Rhetorics: Connecting Conversations, Charting New Territories*, ed. Jeffrey Ringer and Michael-John DePalma (New York: Routledge, 2015), 103–24.

28. David Bebbington, *Evangelicalism in Modern Britain: A History from the 1730s to the 1980s* (London: Unwin Hyman, 1989), 2–19; Mark Noll, *The Scandal of the Evangelical Mind* (Grand Rapids, MI: Eerdmans, 1994), 8.

29. James S. Bielo, *Words upon the Word: An Ethnography of Evangelical Group Bible Study* (New York: New York University Press, 2009), 92.

30. T. M. Luhrmann, *When God Talks Back: Understanding the American Evangelical Relationship with God* (New York: Vintage, 2012).

31. Molly Worthen, *Apostles of Reason: The Crisis of Authority in American Evangelicalism* (New York: Oxford University Press, 2014), 261.

32. Worthen, *Apostles of Reason*, 134; Manya B. Pashman and Jeff Coen, "After Year of Inquiries, Willow Creek Pastor Denies Misconduct Allegations." *Chicago Tribune*, March 23, 2018, https://www.chicagotribune.com/news/breaking/ct-met-willow-creek-pastor-20171220-story.html. Willow Creek Community Church, a "seeker-sensitive" church, is an example in this tradition. Willow Creek founder Bill Hybels faced a series of allegations related to inappropriate comments, groping, long hugs, and invitations to women to stay a bit longer with him in hotel rooms after group meetings. Denying these allegations in 2018, Hybels ultimately accelerated the timing of his scheduled retirement, and his pastoral successors also resigned.

33. Robert P. Jones, *The End of White Christian America* (New York: Simon & Schuster, 2016), 5–44, 79–110.

34. Naomi Clark, "Circulation Across Structural Holes: Reverse Black Boxing the Emergence of Religious Right Networks in the 1970s," in *Circulation, Writing and Rhetoric*, ed. Laurie Gries and Colin Brooke (Louisville: University of Colorado Press, 2018), 152–69.

35. Randall Balmer, *Blessed Assurance: A History of Evangelicalism in America* (Boston: Beacon, 1999), 97, 99; Randall Balmer, *Thy Kingdom Come: How the Religious Right Distorts the Faith and Threatens America; An Evangelical's Lament* (New York: Basic, 2006).

36. Jürgen Habermas, *The Structural Transformation of the Public Sphere: An Inquiry into a Category of Bourgeois Society*, trans. Thomas Burger with Frederick Lawrence (Cambridge, MA: MIT Press, 1989). This work was originally published in Germany in 1962 as *Strukturwandel der Öffentlicheit.*

37. Patricia Roberts-Miller, *Deliberate Conflict: Argument, Political Theory, and Composition Classes* (Carbondale: Southern Illinois University Press, 2004). Indeed, Roberts-Miller overviews six political theories of the public sphere in relation to argument.

38. Michael Warner, *Publics and Counterpublics* (New York: Zone, 2002), 114.

39. Warner, *Publics and Counterpublics*, 113–14.

40. Michael Warner, Jonathan Van Antwerpen, and Craig Calhoun, eds., *Varieties of Secularism in a Secular Age* (Cambridge, MA: Harvard University Press, 2010).

41. Elizabeth Drescher, *Choosing Our Religion: The Spiritual Lives of America's Nones* (New York: Oxford University Press, 2016).

42. Crowley, *Toward a Civil Discourse*; Douglas Downs, "True Believers, Real Scholars, and Real True Believing Scholars: Discourses of Inquiry and Affirmation in the Composition Classroom," in *Negotiating Religious Faith in the Composition Classroom*, ed. Elizabeth Vander Lei and Bonnie Lenore Kyburz, 39–55 (Portsmouth, NH: Heinemann, 2005); Keith Gilyard, *Composition and Cornel West: Notes Toward a Deep Democracy* (Carbondale: Southern Illinois University Press, 2008); Amy Goodburn, "It's a Question of Faith: Discourses of Fundamentalism and Critical Pedagogy in the Writing Classroom." *JAC* 18, no. 2 (1998): 333–53; Priscilla Perkins, "'A Radical Conversion of the Mind': Fundamentalism, Hermeneutics, and the Metanoic Classroom," *College English* 63, no. 5 (2001): 585–611.

43. Jeffrey M. Ringer, *Vernacular Christian Rhetoric and Civil Discourse: The Religious Creativity of Evangelical Student Writers* (New York: Routledge, 2016); Michael-John DePalma, "Reimagining Rhetorical Education: Fostering Writers' Civic Capacities through Engagement with Religious Rhetorics," *College English* 79, no. 3 (2017): 251–75; Michael-John DePalma, Jeffrey Ringer, and Jim Webber, "(Re)Charting the (Dis)Courses of Faith and Politics, or Rhetoric and Democracy in the Burkean Barnyard," *Rhetoric Society Quarterly* 38, no. 3 (2008):

311–34; Heather Thomson-Bunn, "Mediating Discursive Worlds: When Academic Norms and Religious Belief Conflict," *College English* 79, no. 3 (2017): 276–96; Elizabeth Vander Lei, "'Ain't We Having Fun Yet?': Teaching Writing in a Violent World," in *Renovating Rhetoric in Christian Tradition*, ed. Elizabeth Vander Lei et al. (Pittsburgh, PA: University of Pittsburgh Press, 2014), 89–104; Elizabeth Vander Lei et al., *Renovating Rhetoric in Christian Tradition* (Pittsburgh, PA: University of Pittsburgh Press, 2014); Mark Alan Williams, "Transformations: Locating Agency and Difference in Student Accounts of Religious Experience," *College English* 77, no. 4 (2015): 338–63.

44. Roberts-Miller, *Deliberate Conflict*, 190.

45. Nancy Fraser, "Rethinking the Public Sphere: A Contribution to the Critique of Actually Existing Democracy," *Social Text* no. 25/26: 1990.

46. Aristotle, *Rhetoric*, in *The Rhetoric and Poetics of Aristotle*, translated by W. Rhys Roberts, Reprint (New York: Modern Library, 1984); Wayne C. Booth, *The Rhetoric of RHETORIC: The Quest for Effective Communication* (Malden, MA: Blackwell, 2004).

47. Booth, *The Rhetoric of RHETORIC*; Roberts-Miller, *Deliberate Conflict*.

48. Hauser, *Vernacular Voices*.

49. Jane Mansbridge et al., "The Place of Self-Interest and the Role of Power in Deliberative Democracy," *Journal of Political Philosophy* 18, no. 1 (2010): 64–100.

50. Roberts-Miller, *Deliberate Conflict*, 5.

51. Christopher F. Karpowitz, Chad Raphael, and Allen S. Hammond IV, "Deliberative Democracy and Inequality: Two Cheers for Enclave Deliberation Among the Disempowered," *Politics and Society* 37, no. 4 (2009): 582–83.

52. Kimmo Grönlund, Kaisa Herne, and Maija Setälä, "Does Enclave Deliberation Polarize Opinions?" *Political Behavior* 37, no. 4 (2015): 996.

53. Irving L. Janis, *Victims of Groupthink* (New York: Houghton Mifflin, 1972).

54. Sunstein, *Going to Extremes*, 3.

55. Grönlund, Herne, and Setälä, "Does Enclave Deliberation Polarize Opinions?" 1014.

56. Shari J. Stenberg, "Liberation Theology and Liberatory Pedagogies: Renewing the Dialogue," *College English* 68, no. 3 (2006): 288.

57. DePalma, "Reimagining Rhetorical Education."

58. Anderson, *Damaged Goods*, 150–54.

59. Susan Brownmiller, *Against Our Will: Men, Women and Rape* (New York: Ballantine, 1975); Margaret Lazarus and Renner Wunderlich, prods., *Rape Culture*, Cambridge Documentary Films, 1975.

60. Gerd Bohner et al., "Rape Myth Acceptance: Cognitive, Affective, and Behavioural Effects of Beliefs That Blame the Victim and Exonerate the Perpetrator," in *Rape: Challenging Contemporary Thinking*, ed. Miranda Horvath and Jennifer Brown (Cullompton: Willan, 2009), 17–45.

61. Pamela Cooper-White, *The Cry of Tamar: Violence Against Women and the Church's Response*, 2nd ed. (Minneapolis: Fortress, 2012).

62. Adrian Furnham, "Belief in a Just World: Research Progress over the Past Decade," *Personality and Individual Differences* 34, no. 5 (2003): 795–817; Ronnie Janoff-Bulman, Christine Timko, and Linda L. Carli, "Cognitive Biases in Blaming the Victim," *Journal of Experimental Social Psychology* 21, no. 2 (1985): 161–77; Gertrude Summers and Nina S. Feldman, "Blaming the Victim Versus Blaming the Perpetrator: An Attributional Analysis of Spouse Abuse," *Journal of Social and Clinical Psychology* 2, no. 4 (1984): 339–47.

63. Susan J. Brison, "Trauma Narratives and the Remaking of the Self," in *Acts of Memory: Cultural Recall in the Present*, ed. Mieke Bal, Jonathan Crewe, and Leo Spitzer (Hanover, NH: University Press of New England, 1999), 37–54, 42.

64. Christine Shearer-Cremean and Carol Winkelman, eds., *Survivor Rhetoric: Negotiations and Narrativity in Abused Women's Language* (Toronto: University of Toronto Press, 2004), 12.

65. Linda Alcoff and Laura Gray, "Survivor Discourse: Transgression or Recuperation?" *Signs: Journal of Women in Culture and Society* 18, no. 2 (1993): 265–67.

66. Jennifer Patterson, ed., *Queering Sexual Violence: Radical Voices from Within the Anti-violence Movement* (Kindle ed., Riverdale Avenue Books, 2016); Joshua Daniel Phillips and Rachel Alicia Griffin, "Crystal Mangum as Hypervisible Object and Invisible Subject: Black Feminist Thought, Sexual Violence, and the Pedagogical Repercussions of the Duke Lacrosse Rape Case," *Women's Studies in Communication* 38, no. 1 (2015): 36–56.

67. Katherine S. Nelson, "My Justice Is Her Justice: Toward a New Vision of Survivorhood," in *Queering Sexual Violence: Radical Voices from Within the Anti-violence Movement*, ed. Jennifer Patterson (Kindle ed., Riverdale Avenue Books, 2016).

68. Sujata Moorti, *The Color of Rape: Gender and Race in Television's Public Spheres* (Albany: SUNY Press, 2002), 5; Tanya Serisier, "Speaking Out Against Rape: Feminist (Her)Stories and Anti-Rape Politics," *Lilith: A Feminist History Journal*, no. 16 (2007): 85.

69. Allison Crowe and Christine E. Murray, "Stigma from Professional Helpers Toward Survivors of Intimate Partner Violence," *Partner Abuse* 6, no. 2 (2015): 157–79, doi:10.1891/1946–6560.6.2.157.

70. Andrea J. Ritchie, *Invisible No More: Police Violence Against Black Women and Women of Color* (Boston: Beacon, 2017).

71. Elana Newman, "Narrative, Gender, and Recovery from Childhood Sexual Abuse," in *Survivor Rhetoric: Negotiations and Narrativity in Abused Women's Language*, ed. Shearer-Cremean and Winkelman (Toronto: University of Toronto Press, 2004), 26–30.

72. Alcoff and Gray, "Survivor Discourse," 262.

73. Susan M. Shaw, "Gracious Submission: Southern Baptist Fundamentalists and Women," *NWSA Journal* 20, no. 1 (2008): 51–77.

74. Chris Bull and John Gallagher, *Perfect Enemies: The Religious Right, the Gay Movement, and the Politics of the 1990s* (New York: Crown, 1996).

75. Daniel K. Williams, "The Partisan Trajectory of the American Pro-Life Movement: How a Liberal Catholic Campaign Became a Conservative Evangelical Cause," *Religions* 6 (2015): 451–75.

76. Balmer, *Blessed Assurance*, 97, 99.

77. Anderson, *Damaged Goods*, 20.

78. This more recent purity ideology has led theological and political conservatives to interesting, if momentary, alliances. For example, the night before serial killer Ted Bundy was executed in 1989, he gave an interview to James Dobson, founder of Focus on the Family and a major figure within evangelicalism. Dobson and Bundy focused on the dangers of pornography. Similarly, this same issue produced non-deliberative alignments between some right-wing conservatives and some radical feminists (see Roberts-Miller's *Deliberate Conflict* for a discussion of the problems of non-deliberative, peaked-preference political actions).

79. Rachael Denhollander, "My Larry Nassar Testimony Went Viral: But There's More to the Gospel Than Forgiveness," *Christianity Today*, January 31, 2018, https://www.christianitytoday.com/ct/2018/january-web-only/rachael-denhollander-larry-nassar-forgiveness-gospel.html.

80. For the Toast roundtable on Harris: Lyz Lenz, "Recovering from *I Kissed Dating Goodbye*: A Roundtable," The Toast, June 8, 2016, https://the-toast.net/2016/06/08/recovering-from-i-kissed-dating-goodbye-a-roundtable/. For Lavery and Ortberg: Bob Smietana, "Megachurch Pastor John Ortberg Kept a Family Member's Attraction to Children Secret. Then His Son Blew the Whistle," Religion News Service, July 6, 2020, https://religionnews.com/2020/07/06/megachurch-pastor-john-ortberg-family-member-attraction-to-children-secret-menlo-church-daniel-lavery-whistelblower.

81. Cathy Caruth, *Trauma: Explorations in Memory* (Baltimore, MD: Johns Hopkins University Press, 1995); Ann Cvetkovich, *An Archive of Feelings: Trauma, Sexuality, and Lesbian Public Culture* (Durham, NC: Duke University Press, 200); Ruth Leys, *Trauma: A Genealogy* (Chicago: University of Chicago Press, 2000).

82. Judith Herman, *Trauma and Recovery* (New York: Basic, 2015); Leys, *Trauma*.

83. Herman, *Trauma and Recovery*, 28.

84. Cvetkovich, *An Archive of Feelings*, 33.

85. Shane Borrowman, ed., *Trauma and the Teaching of Writing* (Albany: SUNY Press, 2005); Anderson and Marian M. MacCurdy, *Writing and Healing: Toward an Informed Practice* (Urbana, IL: NCTE, 2000).

86. Daphne Desser, "Teaching Writing in Hawai'i after Pearl Harbor and 9/11: How to 'Make Meaning' and 'Heal' Despite National Propaganda," in *Trauma and the Teaching of Writing*, ed. Shane Borrowman (Albany: SUNY Press, 2005), 87.

87. Desser, "Teaching Writing in Hawai'i after Pearl Harbor and 9/11," 96.

88. Cvetkovich, *An Archive of Feelings*, 10.

89. Herman, *Trauma and Recovery*, 189.

90. Sara Ahmed, *The Cultural Politics of Emotion* (Edinburgh: Edinburgh University Press, 2004).

91. Kate Bowler, *The Preacher's Wife: The Precarious Power of Evangelical Women Celebrities* (Oxford: Oxford University Press, 2019), 166–67.

92. Brené Brown, *I Thought It Was Just Me (But It Isn't)* (New York: Avery, 2007), 69.

93. Ellen Bass and Laura Davis, *The Courage to Heal: A Handbook for Healing* (Washington, DC: Child Welfare League of America, 1988), 104–8.

94. Eve Kosofsky Sedgwick and Adam Frank, eds., *Shame and Its Sisters: A Silvan Tompkins Reader* (Durham, NC: Duke University Press, 1995).

95. Elspeth Probyn, *Blush: Faces of Shame* (Minneapolis: University of Minnesota Press, 2005), 148.

96. Shari J. Stenberg, "'Tweet Me Your First Assaults': Writing Shame and the Rhetorical Work of #NotOkay," *Rhetoric Society Quarterly* 48, no. 2 (2018): 124.

97. Jacqueline Jones Royster and Gesa E. Kirsch, *Feminist Rhetorical Practices: New Horizons for Rhetoric, Composition, and Literacy Studies* (Carbondale: Southern Illinois University Press, 2012), 145.

98. Royster and Kirsch, *Feminist Rhetorical Practices*, 145–47.

99. Royster and Kirsch, *Feminist Rhetorical Practices*, 146.

100. Shelly Rambo, *Spirit and Trauma: A Theology of Remaining* (Louisville, KY: Westminster John Knox, 2010), 42.

101. Cathy Caruth, *Unclaimed Experience: Trauma, Narrative, and History* (Baltimore, MD: Johns Hopkins University Press, 1996).

102. Janice Haaken, *Pillar of Salt: Gender, Memory, and the Perils of Looking Back* (New Brunswick, NJ: Rutgers University Press, 1998), 67.

103. Caruth, *Trauma*, 10–11.

104. Robert Schreiter, *Constructing Local Theologies* (Maryknoll, NY: Orbis, 1985), 2–3, emphasis in the original.

105. Hans Waldenfels, "Contextual Theology," in *Dictionary of Mission: Theology, History, Perspectives*, ed. Karl Muller, Theo Sundermeier, Stephen B. Bevans, and Richard H. Bliese (Maryknoll, NY: Orbis, 1985), 82–87.

106. Charlotte Hogg, "Including Conservative Women's Rhetorics in an 'Ethics of Hope and Care,'" *Rhetoric Review* 34, no. 4 (2015): 392.

107. Saba Mahmood, *The Politics of Piety: The Islamic Revival and the Feminist Subject* (Princeton, NJ: Princeton University Press, 2005).

108. M. Jacqui Alexander, *Pedagogies of Crossing: Meditations on Feminism, Sexual Politics, Memory, and the Sacred* (Durham, NC: Duke University Press, 2005).

Chapter 1

1. Patricia Bizzell and Bruce Herzberg, *The Rhetorical Tradition: Readings from Classical Times to the Present* (Boston: Bedford/St. Martin's, 2001), 1046–47.

2. Gerda Lerner, *The Grimké Sisters from South Carolina: Pioneers for Women's Right and Abolition* (New York: Oxford University Press, 1998), 148–49.

3. Dorothy Sterling, *Ahead of Her Time: Abby Kelley and the Politics of Antislavery* (New York: W. W. Norton, 1991), 384.

4. Danielle L. McGuire, *At the Dark End of the Street: Black Women, Rape, and Resistance: A New History of the Civil Rights Movement from Rosa Parks to the Rise of Black Power* (New York: Alfred A. Knopf, 2010).

5. Bizzell and Herzberg, *The Rhetorical Tradition*, 562–63; Roxanne Mountford, *The Gendered Pulpit: Preaching in American Protestant Spaces* (Carbondale: Southern Illinois University Press, 2003), 9–10.

6. Sarah Grimké, *Letters on the Equality of the Sexes, and the Condition of Woman* (Boston: Isaac Knapp, 1838), 24–25.

7. Ann Cvetkovich, *An Archive of Feelings: Trauma, Sexuality, and Lesbian Public Culture* (Durham, NC: Duke University Press, 2003), 117.

8. Caroline Dadas, "Making Sense of #MeToo: Intersectionality and Contemporary Feminism," *Peitho* 22, no. 3 (Spring 2020): http://cfshrc.org/article/making-sense-of-metoo-intersectionality-and-contemporary-feminism/; Kimberlé Crenshaw, "Demarginalizing the Intersection of Race and Sex: A Black Feminist Critique of Antidiscrimination Doctrine, Feminist Theory, and Antiracist Politics," *University of Chicago Legal Forum* 1, Article 8 (1989): 139–67.

9. Hugh Peter qtd. in Susan H. Lindley, *You Have Stept Out of Your Place: A History of Women and Religion in America* (Louisville, KY: Westminster John Knox, 1996), 5.

10. John Winthrop, qtd. in David D. Hall, ed., *The Antinomian Controversy: 1636–1638*, 2nd ed. (Durham, NC: Duke University Press, 1990), 310.

11. Hall, *The Antinomian Controversy*, xii.

12. Patricia Roberts-Miller, *Voices in the Wilderness: Public Discourse and the Paradox of Puritan Rhetoric* (Tuscaloosa: University of Alabama Press, 1999), 21.

13. Michelle Payne, *Bodily Discourses: When Students Write about Abuse and Eating Disorders* (Portsmouth, NH: Boynton/Cook, 2000), 34–36.

14. John D'Emilio and Estelle B. Freedman, *Intimate Matters: A History of Sexuality in America* (New York: Harper & Row, 1988), 31.

15. Sharon Block, *Rape and Sexual Power in Early America* (Chapel Hill: University of North Carolina Press, 2006), 161–62, 167.

16. Richard Godbeer, *Sexual Revolution in Early America* (Baltimore, MD: Johns Hopkins University Press, 2002), 44–50.

17. Lisa Shaver, *Beyond the Pulpit: Women's Rhetorical Roles in the Antebellum Religious Press* (Pittsburgh: University of Pittsburgh Press, 2012), 129.

18. Susan Zaeke, *Signatures of Citizenship: Petitioning, Antislavery, and Women's Political Identity* (Chapel Hill: University of North Carolina Press, 2003), 21–26.

19. Nancy A. Hardesty, *Women Called to Witness: Evangelical Feminism in the Nineteenth Century*, 2nd ed. (Knoxville: University of Tennessee Press, 1999).

20. Lisa Shaver, *Reforming Women: The Rhetorical Tactics of the American Female Moral Reform Society, 1834–1854* (Pittsburgh: University of Pittsburgh Press, 2018), 33–36, 51–52.

21. Shaver, *Reforming Women*, 53.

22. Carol Mattingly, *Well-Tempered Women: Nineteenth-Century Temperance*

Rhetoric (Carbondale: Southern Illinois University Press, 1998).

23. Jane E. Larson, "'Even a Worm Will Turn at Last': Rape Reform in Late Nineteenth-Century America," *Yale Journal of Law and the Humanities* 9, no. 1 (1997): 54–55.

24. Mary E. Odem, *Delinquent Daughters Protecting and Policing Adolescent Female Sexuality in the United States, 1885–1920* (Chapel Hill: University of North Carolina Press, 1995), 26–30.

25. Cynthia Gorney, *Articles of Faith: A Frontline History of the Abortion Wars* (New York: Simon & Schuster, 1998), 89.

26. Susan Schechter, *Women and Male Violence* (Boston: South End, 1982); Kathleen J. Tierney, "The Battered Women Movement and the Creation of the Wife Beating Problem," *Social Problems* 29, no. 3 (1982): 207–20.

27. Maria Bevacqua, *Rape on the Public Agenda: Feminism and the Politics of Sexual Assault* (Boston: Northeastern University Press, 2000); Nancy A. Matthews, *Confronting Rape: The Feminist Anti-rape Movement and the State* (London: Routledge, 1994).

28. Jennifer Patterson, "Introduction," in *Queering Sexual Violence: Radical Voices from Within the Anti-violence Movement*, ed. Jennifer Patterson (Kindle ed., New York: Riverdale Avenue, 2016).

29. INCITE! Women of Color Against Violence, eds., *Color of Violence: The INCITE! Anthology* (Cambridge, MA: South End, 2006); INCITE! Women of Color Against Violence, eds., *The Revolution Will Not Be Funded: Beyond the Non-Profit Industrial Complex* (Durham, NC: Duke University Press, 2007); Patterson, *Queering Sexual Violence*.

30. Susan Brownmiller, *Against Our Will: Men, Women and Rape* (New York: Ballantine, 1975), 55.

31. Andrea Dworkin, *Letters from a War Zone: Writings, 1976–1989* (Chicago: Lawrence Hill, 1993), 170, 171.

32. Kristin Bumiller, *In an Abusive State: How Neoliberalism Appropriated the Feminist Movement Against Sexual Violence* (Durham, NC: Duke University Press, 2008), 55.

33. Angela Y. Davis, *Women, Race and Class* (Toronto: Vintage, 1984), 177–8[illegible], 196–99. Nine Black teenagers known as the Scottsboro Boys were accused in 1931 of raping two white women in Alabama; their case is now commonly recognized as a racially motivated miscarriage of justice. Emmett Till was a Black fourteen-year-old from Chicago who was lynched in 1955 in Mississippi following an alleged instance of flirting with a white woman. bell hooks similarly criticizes Brownmiller's treatment of these topics.

34. Pacifica Radio is a listener-sponsored radio network featuring progressive, radical, and pacifist programming, founded in the wake of World War II. As of 2015, 1,900 Pacifica recordings related to the women's movement are cataloged and available online in the collection *American Women Making History and Culture, 1963–1982*.

35. Davis, *Women, Race and Class*, 190–96.

36. McGuire, *At the Dark End of the Street*, 3–48.

37. McGuire, *At the Dark End of the Street*, 195–200.

38. Becky Thompson, *A Promise and a Way of Life: White Antiracist Activism* (Minneapolis: University of Minnesota Press, 2001), 147.

39. Bumiller, *In an Abusive State*.

40. Matthew Haag, "Thousands of Immigrant Children Said They Were Sexually Abused in U.S. Detention Centers, Report Says," *New York Times*, February 27, 2019, https://www.nytimes.com/2019/02/27/us/immigrant-children-sexual-abuse.html. Haag reports that during a four-year period, detained migrant children made more than 4,500 allegations of sexual abuse while they were in custody; claims escalated markedly during the family separation policy designed to deter migrant families from seeking asylum or otherwise trying to enter the United States.

41. In 2019, Democratic presidential primary candidates made Joseph Biden's central role in authoring the Crime Bill a contentious issue.

42. Elizabeth Swavola, Kristine Riley, and Ram Subramanian, *Overlooked: Women and Jails in an Era of Reform* (New York: Vera Institute of Justice, 2016), 6, 11.

43. Randall Balmer, *Thy Kingdom Come: How the Religious Right Distorts the Faith and Threatens America; An Evangelical's Lament* (New York: Basic, 2006). Throughout the decades-long school desegregation battles, opponents (not just resistant evangelicals) understood this issue as a site of sexualized struggle: the white establishment defending against the perceived moral and sexual contamination that Black students (boys and girls) would bring to white students; see Rachel Devlin, *A Girl Stands at the Door: The Generation of Young Women Who Desegregated America's Schools* (New York: Hachette, 2018).

44. Daniel K. Williams, "The Partisan Trajectory of the American Pro-Life Movement: How a Liberal Catholic Campaign Became a Conservative Evangelical Cause," *Religions* 6 (2015): 451–75.

45. Randall Balmer, *Blessed Assurance: A History of Evangelicalism in America* (Boston: Beacon, 1999), 97, 99.

46. Tim LaHaye is best known as a coauthor of the bestselling *Left Behind* book series—evangelical apocalyptic, dystopian literature.

47. Kendra Weddle and Jann Aldredge-Clanton, *Building Bridges: Letha Dawson Scanzoni and Friends* (Eugene, OR: Cascade, 2018), 57, 62–64. The name of the organization has changed many times over the years.

48. Balmer, *Thy Kingdom Come*; Julie Ingersoll, *Evangelical Christian Women* (New York: New York University Press, 2005), 146.

49. Letha Scanzoni, qtd. in Weddle and Aldredge-Clanton, *Building Bridges*, 19, 60.

50. Smith, *Native Americans and the Christian Right*; Weddle and Aldredge-Clanton, *Building Bridges*; Pamela D. H. Cochran, *Evangelical Feminism: A History*

(New York: New York University Press, 2005). This conversation includes the writing of Letha Scanzoni, Virginia Ramey Mollenkott, Patricia Grundy, Catherine Kroeger, and Nancy Hardesty.

51. Smith, *Native Americans and the Christian Right*, 133–41.

52. Weddle and Aldredge-Clanton, *Building Bridges*, 62, 64.

53. Weddle and Aldredge-Clanton, *Building Bridges*, 71, 134–35.

54. Weddle and Aldredge-Clanton, *Building Bridges*, 5–6.

55. Smith, *Native Americans and the Christian Right*, 167.

56. Ingersoll, *Evangelical Christian Women*, 130.

57. Daphne Desser, "Fraught Literacy: Competing Desires for Connection and Separation in the Writings of American Missionary Women in 19th Century Hawai'i," *College English* 69, no. 5 (2007): 443–69.

58. Smith, *Native Americans and the Christian Right*, 163–64.

59. Robert D. Lupton, *Toxic Charity: How Churches and Charities Hurt Those They Help (and How to Reverse It)* (New York: HarperOne, 2011), 5.

60. Matt Zapotosky, "Judge Strikes Down Trump Administration Effort to Deny Asylum for Migrants Fleeing Gang Violence, Domestic Abuse," *Washington Post*, December 19, 2018; Josh Dawsey, "Trump Derides Protections for Immigrants from 'Shithole' Countries," *Washington Post*, December 19, 2018, https://www.washingtonpost.com/politics/trump-attacks-protections-for-immigrants-from-shithole-countries-in-oval-office-meeting/2018/01/11/bfc0725c-f711–11e7–91af-31ac729add94_story.html.

61. Connie Brewer, *Escaping the Shadows, Seeking the Light: Christians in Recovery from Childhood Sexual Abuse* (San Francisco: Harper, 1991); Joanne Ross Feldmeth and Midge Wallace Finley, *We Weep for Ourselves and Our Children* (San Francisco: Harper, 1990); Thomas Giles, "Coping with Sexual Misconduct in the Church," *Christianity Today*, January 11, 1993, 48–49; Joy Jordan-Lake, "Conduct Unbecoming a Preacher," *Christianity Today*, February 19, 1992, 26–32.

62. For an extensive list, see A. Smith, 154–55.

63. Smith, *Native Americans and the Christian Right*, 181–89.

64. Smith, *Native Americans and the Christian Right*, 189.

65. Tarana Burke, "The Inception," *JustBe*, https://justbeinc.wixsite.com/justbeinc/the-me-too-movement-cmml.

66. Emily Joy, "#ChurchToo," Emily Joy Poet, accessed August 12, 2019, http://emilyjoypoetry.com/churchtoo; Hannah Paasch, "Sexual Abuse Happens In #ChurchToo—We're Living Proof," *HuffPost*, December 4, 2017, https://www.huffpost.com/entry/sexual-abuse-churchtoo_n_5a205b30e4b03350e0b53131.

67. Eliza Griswold, "Silence Is Not Spiritual: The Evangelical #MeToo Movement," *New Yorker*, June 15, 2018, https://www.newyorker.com/news/on-religion/silence-is-not-spiritual-the-evangelical-metoo-movement.

68. "#SilenceIsNotSpiritual," #SilenceIsNotSpiritual, accessed January 15, 2021, https://silenceisnotspiritual.org.

69. Mattingly, *Well-Tempered Women*, 15.

70. Joy appeared on Harper's *Freedom Road* podcast in October 2018, and the exchange was positive. Harper expressed appreciation for the honesty with which Joy addressed the distance she now has from evangelicalism.

Chapter 2

1. Elizabeth Bernstein, "Militarized Humanitarianism Meets Carceral Feminism: The Politics of Sex, Rights, and Freedom in Contemporary Antitrafficking Campaigns," *Signs: Journal of Women in Culture and Society* 36, no. 1 (2010): 45–71.

2. Ruth Bader Ginsberg, *Brief* of the ACLU et al. as Amicus Curiae, Coker v. Georgia, No 75-5444 (1976): 14–16.

3. Laurie Goodstein, "Donald Trump Reveals Evangelical Rifts That Could Shape Politics for Years," *New York Times*, October 17, 2016, https://www.nytimes.com/2016/10/17/us/donald-trump-evangelicals-republican-vote.html.

4. Laura Turner, "How Long Can Evangelical Women Stay Behind Donald Trump?" *Politico*, October 12, 2016, https://www.politico.com/magazine/story/2016/10/donald-trump-evangelical-women-2016-videotape-214346.

5. Ruth Graham, "These Evangelical Women Speaking Out Against Trump Have More Influence Than You Think," *Slate*, October 12, 2016, https://slate.com/human-interest/2016/10/the-evangelical-women-speaking-out-against-trump-have-more-influence-than-you-think.html.

6. Sara Groves, qtd. in Joshua DuBois, "Powerful Evangelical Women Split from Male Church Leaders to Slam Trump," *Daily Beast*, October 10, 2016, https://www.thedailybeast.com/powerful-evangelical-women-split-from-male-church-leaders-to-slam-trump.

7. Katelyn Beaty, "'No More': Evangelical Women Are Done with Donald Trump and His Misogyny," *Washington Post*, October 13, 2016 https://www.washingtonpost.com/news/acts-of-faith/wp/2016/10/13/no-more-evangelical-women-are-done-with-donald-trump-and-his-misogyny/.

8. Charlotte Hogg, "Including Conservative Women's Rhetorics in an 'Ethics of Hope and Care,'" *Rhetoric Review* 34, no. 4 (2015): 392; Saba Mahmood, *The Politics of Piety: The Islamic Revival and the Feminist Subject* (Princeton, NJ: Princeton University Press, 2005); Carol Mattingly, *Well-Tempered Women: Nineteenth-Century Temperance Rhetoric* (Carbondale: Southern Illinois University Press, 1998).

9. Dietrich Bonhoeffer, *The Cost of Discipleship*, trans. R. H. Fuller (New York: Macmillan, 1963), 47.

10. L. Gregory Jones, *Embodying Forgiveness: A Theological Analysis* (Grand Rapids, MI: Eerdmans, 1995), 13.

11. Charles Marsh, *Strange Glory: A Life of Dietrich Bonhoeffer* (New York: Alfred A. Knopf, 2014), 245.

12. Ralph G. Clingan, *Against Cheap Grace in a World Come of Age: An Intellectual Biography of Clayton Powell, 1865–1953* (New York: Peter Lang, 2002), 65.

13. Bonhoeffer, *The Cost of Discipleship*, 46.

14. Bonhoeffer, *The Cost of Discipleship*, 46–48.

15. Marcus J. Borg, *Speaking Christian: Why Christian Words Have Lost Their Meaning and Power—and How They Can Be Restored*. Kindle ed., New York: HarperCollins, 2011.

16. Borg, *Speaking Christian*, 70.

17. Kate Bowler, *The Preacher's Wife: The Precarious Power of Evangelical Women Celebrities* (Oxford: Oxford University Press, 2019), 166–67.

18. *Book of Common Prayer*, 390.

19. Bonhoeffer, *The Cost of Discipleship*, 44.

20. Bonhoeffer, *The Cost of Discipleship*, 47–49, 257–58.

21. Bonhoeffer, *The Cost of Discipleship*, 45.

22. Bonhoeffer, *The Cost of Discipleship*, 99.

23. Jones, *Embodying Forgiveness*, 16.

24. Beth Daniell, *A Communion of Friendship: Literacy, Spiritual Practice, and Women in Recovery* (Carbondale: Southern Illinois University Press, 2003), 130.

25. Daniell, *A Communion of Friendship*, 131.

26. Daniell, *A Communion of Friendship*, 138.

27. Daniell, *A Communion of Friendship*, 143–44.

28. Carol Winkelmann, *The Language of Battered Women: A Rhetorical Analysis of Personal Theologies* (Albany: SUNY Press, 2004), 215.

29. Winkelmann, *The Language of Battered Women*, 212.

30. Serene Jones, *Trauma and Grace: Theology in a Ruptured World* (Louisville, KY: Westminster John Knox, 2009), 161.

31. Borg, *Speaking Christian*.

32. Dianna Anderson, *Damaged Goods: New Perspectives on Christian Purity* (New York: Jericho, 2015).

33. Kyndall R. Rothaus, "Christians Need Consistency in Principles of Inclusion, Compassion," *Waco Tribune-Herald*, December 10, 2016, https://www.wacotrib.com/opinion/columns/guest_columns/kyndall-rae-rothaus-guest-columnist-christians-need-consistency-in-principles/article_f9ca5e87–2990–55f9-b810–099c00cceb24.html.

34. Quoted in Sarah P. Bailey, "'Still the Best Candidate': Some Evangelicals Still Back Trump Despite Lewd Video," *Washington Post*, October 8, 2016, https://www.washingtonpost.com/news/acts-of-faith/wp/2016/10/08/still-the-best-candidate-some-evangelicals-still-back-trump-despite-lewd-video/?utm_term=.93e997ea5a42.

35. Anderson, *Damaged Goods*, 154–57.

36. Pamela Cooper-White, *The Cry of Tamar: Violence Against Women and the Church's Response*, 2nd ed. (Minneapolis: Fortress, 2012), 251.

37. Cooper-White, *The Cry of Tamar*, 255.

38. Cooper-White, *The Cry of Tamar*, 260.

39. Quoted in Michael F. Haverluck, "Jeffress: Trump Still Best Choice

After Lewd Tape," *OneNewsNow*, October 10, 2016, https://onenewsnow.com/politics-govt/2016/10/10/jeffress-trump-still-best-choice-after-lewd-tape.

40. Quoted in Sarah P. Bailey, "'We're All Sinners': Jerry Falwell, Jr. Defends Donald Trump After Video of Lewd Remarks," *Washington Post*, October 10, 2016, https://www.washingtonpost.com/news/acts-of-faith/wp/2016/10/10/jerry-falwell-jr-the-gop-establishment-could-be-behind-donald-trump-video-leak/.

41. Patricia Roberts-Miller, "Dissent as 'Aid and Comfort to the Enemy': The Rhetorical Power of Naïve Realism and Ingroup Identity," *Rhetoric Society Quarterly* 39, no. 2 (2009): 170–88.

42. Anderson, *Damaged Goods*, 153.

43. Quoted in Betsy Woodruff, "Evangelical Leaders Shrug at Donald Trump's Lewd Comments," *Daily Beast*, October 7, 2016, https://www.thedailybeast.com/evangelical-leaders-shrug-at-donald-trumps-lewd-comments.

44. Quoted in Kimberly Winston, "Popular Christian Author Eric Metaxas Stands by Donald Trump," *Religion News Service*, October 12, 2016, https://religionnews.com/2016/10/12/popular-christian-author-eric-metaxas-stands-by-donald-trump/.

45. Winston, "Popular Christian Author Eric Metaxas Stands by Donald Trump."

46. Jeffrey M. Ringer, *Vernacular Christian Rhetoric and Civil Discourse: The Religious Creativity of Evangelical Student Writers* (New York: Routledge, 2016), 47–48.

47. Sarah P. Bailey, "Why Women Want Moore," *Christianity Today* 54, no. 8 (2010): 25.

48. Emily M. Cope, "Learning Not to Preach: Evangelical Speaker Beth Moore and the Rhetoric of Constraint," in *Rhetoric, History, and Women's Oratorical Education: American Women Learn to Speak*, ed. David Gold and Catherine Hobbs (New York: Routledge, 2013), 224. Several books that insightfully explicate gendered dynamics in relationship to Moore, evangelical culture, or complementarian theology appeared after *Faithful Deliberation* was significantly drafted or was in the production process; see Beth Allison Barr, *The Making of Biblical Womanhood: How the Subjugation of Women Became Gospel Truth* (Grand Rapids, MI: Brazos, 2021); Kristin Kobes Du Mez, *Jesus and John Wayne: How White Evangelicals Corrupted a Faith and Fractured a Nation* (New York: W. W. Norton, 2020); Stephanie A. Martin, *Decoding the Digital Church: Evangelical Storytelling and the Election of Donald J. Trump* (Tuscaloosa: University of Alabama Press, 2021).

49. Beth Moore qtd. in Leslie Montgomery, *Were It Not for Grace: Stories from Women After God's Own Heart* (Nashville, TN: B&H, 2005), 97.

50. Moore (@bethmoorelpm), "A well meaning," Twitter, October 15, 2017, 9:04 a.m. https://twitter.com/BethMooreLPM/status/919745870635175937?s=20.

51. Moore (@bethmoorelpm), "Wake up," Twitter, October 9, 2016, 9:07 a.m. https://twitter.com/BethMooreLPM/status/785119502769852418.

52. Ephesians 5:14.

53. Cope, "Learning." Moore's oratorical career took shape within the SBC's rising complementarianism and conservatism, and the rhetorical strategies she uses both establish her role as a leader in women's ministry and define her work as not preaching.

54. Kyndall R. Rothaus, "In the meeting," Facebook, November 15, 2016, https://www.facebook.com/541260186/videos/10157769065520187/. Rothaus's comments came during a November 2016 meeting of the Baptist General Convention of Texas. As debate ensued over the question of whether the association should remain in relationship with Baptist congregations that take LGBTQ+-affirming stances, a procedural motion ended discussion before she could speak as part of the official proceedings. However, a Facebook video recorded the statement she intended to make.

55. Beth Moore (@bethmoorelpm), "Try to absorb," Twitter, October 9, 2016, 9:22 a.m., https://twitter.com/BethMooreLPM/status/785123300636667905?s=20.

56. Anderson, *Damaged Goods*, 153.

57. Beth Moore (@bethmoorelpm), "I'm one," Twitter, October 9, 2016, 9:34 a.m., https://twitter.com/BethMooreLPM/status/785126388776873985?s=20.

58. Clint Bryan and Mohammed Albakry, "A Little Bit Transparent with One Another: Constructing Vulnerability in the Evangelical Discourse of Women Preachers," *Culture and Religion* 16, no. 4 (2015): 402.

59. Beth Moore (@bethmoorelpm), "'Keep your mouth,'" Twitter, October 9, 2016, 10:23 a.m., https://twitter.com/BethMooreLPM/status/785141013085949952?s=20.

60. Bethany Mannon, "Xvangelical: The Rhetorical Work of Personal Narratives in Contemporary Religious Discourse," *Rhetoric Society Quarterly* 49, no. 2 (2019): 143.

61. Jen Hatmaker, "Good Morning." Facebook, October 11, 2016, https://www.facebook.com/jenhatmaker/posts/1066241836808144.

62. Bonhoeffer, *The Cost of Discipleship*, 44.

63. James Dobson, "Dr. James Dobson on Donald Trump's Christian Faith," *Family Talk*, July 21, 2016, http://drjamesdobson.org/news/dr-james-dobson-on-trumps-christian-faith-em. Repentance is a priority for a "baby Christian," as longtime leading evangelical figure James Dobson described Trump following his political endorsement of the candidate. When the young Jesus movement grew after its founder's crucifixion, Peter declared to a large crowd of potential converts: "'Repent, and be baptized'" (Acts 2:36–41).

64. Hatmaker, "Good Morning."

65. Roxanne Mountford, *The Gendered Pulpit: Preaching in American Protestant Spaces* (Carbondale: Southern Illinois University Press, 2003), 149.

66. Cooper-White, *The Cry*, 260.

67. Hatmaker, "Good Morning."

68. Gregory A. Smith and Jessica Martínez, "How the Faithful Voted: A Preliminary 2016 Analysis," Pew Research Center, November 9, 2016,

https://www.pewresearch.org/fact-tank/2016/11/09/how-the-faithful-voted-a-preliminary-2016-analysis/.

69. Jen Hatmaker, "The Politics of Jen Hatmaker: Trump, Black Lives Matter, Gay Marriage and More," interviewed by Jonathan Merritt, RNS,October 25, 2016, https://religionnews.com/2016/10/25/the-politics-of-jen-hatmaker-trump-black-lives-matter-gay-marriage-and-more/.

70. Courtney Runn, "The Year of Jen Hatmaker," *Texas Monthly*, October 4, 2017, https://www.texasmonthly.com/articles/year-jen-hatmaker/

71. Jen Hatmaker, "My Saddest Good Friday in Memory: When Treasured Things Are Dead," Jen Hatmaker, April 14, 2017, http://jenhatmaker.com/blog/2017/04/14/my-saddest-good-friday-in-memory-when-treasured-things-are-dead.

72. Bonhoeffer, *The Cost of Discipleship*, 45.

Chapter 3

1. "What Have You Done?" *Believed*, Episode 7, on Michigan Radio, December 3, 2018, https://believed.michiganradio.org/larry-nassar-what-have-you-done/.

2. David Bebbington, *Evangelicalism in Modern Britain: A History from the 1730s to the 1980s* (London: Unwin Hyman, 1989), 2–19; Mark Noll, *The Scandal of the Evangelical Mind* (Grand Rapids, MI: Eerdmans, 1994), 8.

3. Rachael Denhollander, "Read Rachael Denhollander's Full Victim Impact Statement About Larry Nassar," *CNN*, January 30, 2018, https://www.cnn.com/2018/01/24/us/rachael-denhollander-full-statement/index.html.

4. Ruth Graham, "Larry Nassar's First Accuser Is Taking on Another Big Target—This Time, Within Her Own Evangelical Community," *Slate*, March 9, 2018, https://slate.com/human-interest/2018/03/larry-nassars-first-accuser-rachael-denhollander-is-now-taking-on-a-big-target-within-her-evangelical-community.html; Lori Johnston, "She Helped Bring Down Larry Nassar," *Washington Post*, January 25, 2018, https://www.washingtonpost.com/news/acts-of-faith/wp/2018/01/24/she-helped-bring-down-larry-nassar-at-his-sentencing-for-sex-crimes-she-spoke-about-her-faith/?utm_term=.82cd7f21b6d2; Justin Taylor, "The Incredible Testimony as a Former Gymnast Confronts Her Sexual Abuser in Court," The Gospel Coalition, January 24, 2018, https://www.thegospelcoalition.org/blogs/justin-taylor/incredible-testimony-former-gymnast-confronts-sexual-abuser-court/.

5. Denhollander, "Read Rachael Denhollander's Full Victim Impact Statement About Larry Nassar"; Rachael Denhollander, "The Price I Paid for Taking on Larry Nassar," *New York Times*, January 26, 2018, https://www.nytimes.com/2018/01/26/opinion/sunday/larry-nassar-rachael-denhollander.html.

6. Joshua Pease, "The Sin of Silence: The Epidemic of Denial About Sexual Abuse in the Evangelical Church," *Washington Post*, May 31, 2018,https://www.washingtonpost.com/news/posteverything/wp/2018/05/31/feature/the-epidemic-of-denial-about-sexual-abuse-in-the-evangelical-church/.

7. Jamie Dean, "A Time to Speak," *World*, March 1, 2018, https://world.wng.org/2018/03/a_time_to_speak.

8. Rachael Denhollander, "My Larry Nassar Testimony Went Viral: But There's More to the Gospel Than Forgiveness," *Christianity Today*, January 31, 2018, https://www.christianitytoday.com/ct/2018/january-web-only/rachael-denhollander-larry-nassar-forgiveness-gospel.html.

9. Denhollander, "My Larry Nassar Testimony Went Viral."

10. Denhollander, "My Larry Nassar Testimony Went Viral."

11. Beth Moore (@bethmoorelpm), "This @CTmagazine interview," Twitter, January 31, 2018, 2:12 p.m., https://twitter.com/BethMooreLPM/status/958795199366483969?s=20.

12. Denhollander, "My Larry Nassar Testimony Went Viral."

13. Marie M. Fortune, *Sexual Violence: The Unmentionable Sin* (New York: Pilgrim, 1983).

14. Judith Herman, *Trauma and Recovery* (New York: Basic, 2015).

15. David Augsburger, *Caring Enough to Forgive* (Scottdale, PA: Herald, 1981), 52.

16. Carolyn H. Heggen, *Sexual Abuse in Christian Homes and Churches* (Scottdale, PA: Herald, 1993), 127–28.

17. Pamela Cooper-White, *The Cry of Tamar: Violence Against Women and the Church's Response*, 2nd ed. (Minneapolis: Fortress, 2012), 251.

18. Psalms 103:6; Isaiah 19:20; Luke 1:46–55; 4:18; Matthew 25:35–45.

19. L. Gregory Jones, *Embodying Forgiveness: A Theological Analysis* (Grand Rapids, MI: Eerdmans, 1995), 35–69.

20. Kenneth Burke, *Attitudes Toward History*, 3rd ed. (Berkeley: University of California Press, 1984), 229.

21. Albert R. Jonsen and Stephen Toulmin, *The Abuse of Casuistry: A History of Moral Reasoning* (Berkeley: University of California Press, 1988), 92.

22. Blaise Pascal, *Pensées and Provincial Letters* (New York: Modern Library, 1941); Jonsen and Toulmin, *The Abuse of Casuistry*, 35.

23. Jonsen and Toulmin, *The Abuse of Casuistry*, 91–92.

24. Jonsen and Toulmin, *The Abuse of Casuistry*, 93–96.

25. Jonsen and Toulmin, *The Abuse of Casuistry*, 96–100.

26. Paul Lynch, "Something Completely Different: Notes Toward a Burkean Ethics," *KB Journal: The Journal of the Kenneth Burke Society* 5, no. 1 (2008): https://kbjournal.org/paul_lynch.

27. Kenneth Burke, *Language as Symbolic Action: Essays on Life, Literature, and Method* (Berkeley: University of California Press, 1966), 15–18.

28. Lynch, "Something Completely Different."

29. Jonsen and Toulmin, *The Abuse of Casuistry*, 92.

30. Jeffrey M. Ringer, *Vernacular Christian Rhetoric and Civil Discourse: The Religious Creativity of Evangelical Student Writers* (New York: Routledge, 2016), 79.

31. Denhollander, "Read Rachael Denhollander's Full Victim Impact Statement About Larry Nassar."

32. Carol Winkelmann, *The Language of Battered Women: A Rhetorical Analysis of Personal Theologies* (Albany: SUNY Press, 2004), 136–39.

33. Heggen, *Sexual Abuse in Christian Homes and Churches*, 45–46.

34. Beth Moore, "What About the Church's Silence?" *Religion News Service*, January 31, 2018, https://religionnews.com/2018/01/31/what-about-the-churchs-silence/.

35. Denhollander, "My Larry Nassar Testimony Went Viral," emphasis in the original.

36. Denhollander, "My Larry Nassar Testimony Went Viral."

37. Lynn Heitritter and Jeanette Vought, *Helping Victims of Sexual Abuse: A Sensitive Guide for Counselor, Victims, and Families* (Minneapolis: Bethany House, 1989), 204–5. Gospel passages may be read in ways that productively disrupt such privatized notions. For example, Heitritter and Vought suggest that the command of Jesus to forgive someone "seventy times seven times" establishes forgiveness as an activity grounded more in divine agency than in sheer human will, relieving survivors of a community imperative to feel any particular way.

38. Denhollander, "My Larry Nassar Testimony Went Viral"; D. B. Allender, *The Wounded Heart: Hope for Adult Victims of Childhood Sexual Abuse* (Colorado Springs: Navpress, 1990). Denhollander echoes Fortune (*Sexual Violence*, 208) in lamenting the emptying of forgiveness as an effectual term in the context of sexual violence. Allender particularly critiques this meaningless version of forgiveness when Christians direct it toward victims of childhood sexual abuse.

39. Denhollander, "My Larry Nassar Testimony Went Viral."

40. Herman, *Trauma and Recovery*, 173–95.

41. Stenberg, "'Tweet Me Your First Assaults,'" 133.

42. Cooper-White, *The Cry of Tamar*, 253–54. This point about decision-making is important to survivors, because they often prioritize regaining a sense of agency.

43. Moore, "What About the Church's Silence?"

44. Bob Smietana. "Pastors Seldom Preach About Domestic Violence," LifeWay Research, June 27, 2014, https://lifewayresearch.com/2014/06/27/pastors-seldom-preach-about-domestic-violence/.

45. Moore, "What About the Church's Silence?"

46. Beth Daniell, *A Communion of Friendship: Literacy, Spiritual Practice, and Women in Recovery* (Carbondale: Southern Illinois University Press, 2003); Winkelmann, *The Language of Battered Women*; Sylvia Scribner, "Literacy in Three Metaphors," *American Journal of Education* 93, no. 1 (1984): 6–21.

47. Daniell, *A Communion of Friendship*, 126–48; Winkelmann, *The Language of Battered Women*, 212–15.

48. Denhollander, "My Larry Nassar Testimony Went Viral."

49. Caleb Lindgren, "Evangelicals' Favorite Heresies Revisited by Researchers," *Christianity Today*, September 28, 2016, https://www.christianitytoday.com/news/2016/september/evangelicals-favorite-heresies-state-of-theology-ligonier.

html. Holding beliefs traditionally identified as heresies, as antinomianism has often been labeled, is not a particularly uncommon phenomenon. Lindgren's article discusses LifeWay Research survey findings from 2014 and 2016 that documented that evangelicals "had a surprising level of confusion surrounding core Christian doctrine." This practice of noting blended theological thinking within their rhetorical enclave is common among evangelical leaders and institutions (see Worthen, *Apostles of Reason*).

50. Denhollander, "My Larry Nassar Testimony Went Viral."

51. Moore, "What About the Church's Silence?"

52. Moore, "What About the Church's Silence?" This position is in keeping with casuistic methods; absent any exigent circumstance, rhetors need not devote time to deliberate on a clearly wrong and harmful choice (see Jonsen and Toulmin, *The Abuse of Casuistry*, 307).

53. Moore, "What About the Church's Silence?"

54. Moore's concerns echo both Burke's understanding that overstretching contributes to demoralization and Pascal's claims that casuistry leads to loosened morals.

55. Frances T. Gench, *Back to the Well: Women's Encounters with Jesus in the Gospels* (Louisville, KY: Westminster John Knox, 2004), 152–54; Gail O'Day, "John 7.53–8.11: A Study in Misreading," *Journal of Biblical Literature* 111, no. 4 (1992): 631–40.

56. O'Day, "John 7.53–8.11," 634–35.

57. Moore, "What About the Church's Silence?"

58. Susan Brooks Thistlethwaite, "Every Two Minutes: Battered Women and Feminist Interpretation," in *Feminist Interpretation of the Bible*, ed. Letty M. Russell (Philadelphia: Westminster, 1985), 96–110. Abuse survivors' own comments echo Moore's questions. They often view John 7:53–8:11 in a favorable light, citing it as an excerpt with which they strongly identify. Thistlethwaite observes that, within this story, "women who have suffered physical violence hear that whatever human law or custom may legitimate violence against women, it cannot stand face to face with the revelation of God's affirmation of all humanity" (101–2). This interpretive practice echoes Winkelmann: abuse survivors may critique uses of scripture, but they often rely on sacred texts and a relationship with God for a sense of agency and justice (136–44).

59. Matthew 18:6–7, qtd. in Moore, "What About the Church's Silence?"

60. Denhollander, "Read Rachael Denhollander's Full Victim Impact Statement About Larry Nassar."

61. Denhollander, "My Larry Nassar Testimony Went Viral."

62. Moore, "What About the Church's Silence?"

63. Moore, "What About the Church's Silence?"

64. Herman, *Trauma and Recovery*, 72–73.

65. Herman, *Trauma and Recovery*, 135, 178; Heitritter and Vought, *Helping Victims of Sexual Abuse*, 213–15.

66. Herman, *Trauma and Recovery*, 73, 209–11.

67. Denhollander, "My Larry Nassar Testimony Went Viral."

68. Marie M. Fortune, *Keeping the Faith: Guidance for Christian Women Facing Abuse* (New York: HarperCollins, 1987). Jesus describes repentance as part of the process for Christian forgiveness: rebuke of the sinner, repentance by the sinner, forgiveness toward the sinner (Luke 17:1–4). Fortune interprets this passage, delineating a taxonomy of responses by abuse aggressors: remorse, simply feeling guilty; bargaining, requiring a victim to extend forgiveness; and repentance, fundamentally changing behavior (53–54).

69. Moore, "What About the Church's Silence?"

70. Denhollander, "My Larry Nassar Testimony Went Viral."

71. Herman, *Trauma and Recovery*, 189.

72. Kristin Bumiller, *In an Abusive State: How Neoliberalism Appropriated the Feminist Movement Against Sexual Violence* (Durham, NC: Duke University Press, 2008), 55.

73. Cooper-White, *The Cry of Tamar*, 257; Heggen, *Sexual Abuse in Christian Homes and Churches*, 129. A frequently used Greek term for forgiveness in the New Testament is *aphiemi*. With meanings related to releasing, remitting, separating, or leaving, the emphasis is on forgiveness as a foundational aspect of God's nature more than on an achievement through human exertion.

74. Immanuel Baptist Church, "We Were Rachael's Church," May 31, 2018. https://immanuelky.org/articles/we-were-rachaels-church/.

Chapter 4

1. Bob Allen, "SNAP Cries Foul Over Baptist Press Reporting," *Good Faith Media*, March 27, 2007, https://goodfaithmedia.org/snap-cries-foul-over-baptist-press-reporting-cms-8710/.

2. Paige Patterson, qtd. in Bob Allen, "SBC Seminary President Labels Clergy Sex-Abuse Victims' Group 'Evil-Doers,'" *Good Faith Media*, February 15, 2008, https://goodfaithmedia.org/sbc-seminary-president-labels-clergy-sex-abuse-victims-group-evil-doers-cms-12262/.

3. Paige Patterson, "Paige Patterson (SBC) Advice to Victims of Domestic Violence," *Internet Archive*, March 20, 2008. https://archive-org.ezproxy.baylor.edu/details/PaigePattersonsbcAdviceToVictimsOfDomesticViolence.

4. Danni Moss, "Paige Patterson's Views on Domestic Violence," *Because It Matters*, February 25, 2008, https://dannimoss.wordpress.com/clergy-abuse-links/abuse-in-the-church/paige-pattersons-views-on-domestic-violence/.

5. Darlene Parsons, "A Call for Paige Patterson's Resignation from the Ministry," *Wartburg Watch*, June 16, 2009, http://thewartburgwatch.com/2009/06/16/a-call-for-paige-pattersons-resignation-from-the-ministry/.

6. Ruth A. Tucker, *Black and White Bible, Black and Blue Wife: My Story of Finding Hope After Domestic Abuse* (Grand Rapids, MI: Zondervan, 2016).

7. Anna L. Peterson, "Religious Narratives and Political Protest," *Journal of the American Academy of Religion* 64 (1996): 43.

8. Lori Beaman-Hall and Nancy Nason-Clark, "Translating Spiritual Commitment into Service: The Responses of Evangelical Women to Wife Abuse," *Canadian Women's Studies/Les Cahiers De La Femme* 17 (1997): 58–61; Joanne C. Brown and Rebecca Parker, "For God so Loved the World?" in *Christianity, Patriarchy, and Abuse: A Feminist Critique*, ed. Joanne C. Brown and Carole B. Bohn (New York: Pilgrim, 1989), 1–30; Myra N. Burnett, "Suffering and Sanctification: The Religious Context of Battered Woman's Syndrome," *Pastoral Psychology* 44 (1996): 145–49; Kathleen Ferraro and John M. Johnson, "How Women Experience Battering: The Process of Victimization," *Social Problems* 30 (1983): 325–39; Anne L. Horton, Meland M. Wilkins, and Wendy Wright, "Women Who Ended Abuse: What Religious Leaders and Religion Did for These Victims," in *Abuse and Religion: When Praying Isn't Enough*, ed. Anne L. Horton and Judith A. Williamson (Lexington, MA: D.C. Heath, 1988), 235–46; Nancy Nason-Clark, *The Battered Wife: How Christians Confront Family Violence* (Louisville: Westminster John Knox, 1997).

9. Darwin L. Thomas and Marie Cornwall, "Religion and Family in the 1980s: Discovery and Development," *Journal of Marriage and the Family* 52, no. 4 (1990): 983–92.

10. Vicky Whipple, "Counseling Battered Women from Fundamentalist Churches," *Journal of Marital and Family Therapy* 13, no. 3 (1987): 251.

11. Nancy T. Ammerman, *Baptist Battles: Social Change and Religious Conflict in the Southern Baptist Convention* (New Brunswick, NJ: Rutgers University Press, 1990); Margaret E. de Alminana and Lois E. Olena, eds., *Women in Pentecostal and Charismatic Ministry: Informing a Dialogue on Gender, Church and Ministry* (Leiden: Brill, 2016); Molly Worthen, *Apostles of Reason: The Crisis of Authority in American Evangelicalism* (New York: Oxford University Press, 2014).

12. Jacqueline Jones Royster and Gesa E. Kirsch, *Feminist Rhetorical Practices: New Horizons for Rhetoric, Composition, and Literacy Studies* (Carbondale: Southern Illinois University Press, 2012), 397.

13. John Storey, *Texas Baptist Leadership and Social Christianity, 1900–1980* (College Station: Texas A&M University Press, 1987); Henry May, *Protestant Churches in Industrial America* (New York: Harper and Brothers, 1949); Keith Harper, *The Quality of Mercy: Southern Baptists and Social Christianity, 1890–1920* (Tuscaloosa: University of Alabama Press, 1996). May and Storey make similar distinctions. Harper, however, in his discussion of social Christianity among Southern Baptists, wonders if such distinctions obscure more than they clarify.

14. Storey, *Texas Baptist Leadership and Social Christianity, 1900–1980*, 28.

15. Walter B. Shurden, *The Baptist Identity: Four Fragile Freedoms* (Macon, GA: Smyth and Helwys, 1993).

16. Fisher Humphreys, *The Way We Were: How Southern Baptist Theology*

Has Changed and What It Means to Us All (Macon, GA: Smyth and Helwys, 2002), 35–50.

17. Martin E. Marty, "Baptistification Takes Over," *Christianity Today*, September 2, 1983, 33–36.

18. Carl L. Kell and L. Raymond Camp, *In the Name of the Father: The Rhetoric of the New Southern Baptist Convention* (Carbondale: Southern Illinois University Press, 1999).

19. Susan M. Shaw, "Gracious Submission: Southern Baptist Fundamentalists and Women," *NWSA Journal* 20, no. 1 (2008): 51–77.

20. Susan M. Shaw, *God Speaks to Us, Too: Southern Baptist Women on Church, Home, and Society* (Lexington: University Press of Kentucky, 2008).

21. *Resolution on Ordination and the Role of Women in Ministry*, Kansas City: Southern Baptist Convention, June 1984, https://www.sbc.net/resource-library/resolutions/resolution-on-ordination-and-the-role-of-women-in-ministry/.

22. Emily M. Cope, "Learning Not to Preach: Evangelical Speaker Beth Moore and the Rhetoric of Constraint," in *Rhetoric, History, and Women's Oratorical Education: American Women Learn to Speak*, ed. David Gold and Catherine Hobbs (New York: Routledge, 2013), 217–38.

23. Aesha Adams-Roberts, Rosalyn C. Eves, and Liz Rohan, "'With the Tongue of [Wo]men and Angels': Apostolic Rhetorical Practices Among Religious Women," in *Renovating Rhetoric in Christian Tradition*, ed. Elizabeth Vander Lei, Thomas Amorose, Beth Daniell, and Anne Ruggles Gere (Pittsburgh, PA: University of Pittsburgh Press, 2014), 45.

24. Adams-Roberts, Eves, and Rohan, "'With the Tongue of [Wo]men and Angels,'" 53–54.

25. Adams-Roberts, Eves, and Rohan, "'With the Tongue of [Wo]men and Angels,'" 57.

26. Adams-Roberts, Eves, and Rohan, "'With the Tongue of [Wo]men and Angels,'" 58.

27. Brian Fehler, "Re-Defining God: The Rhetoric of Reconciliation," *Rhetoric Society Quarterly* 33, no. 1 (2003): 105–26.

28. 2 Corinthians 5:17–20.

29. *Resolution on Racial Reconciliation on the 150th Anniversary of the Southern Baptist Convention*, Atlanta: Southern Baptist Convention, June 1995. https://www.sbc.net/resource-library/resolutions/resolution-on-racial-reconciliation-on-the-150th-anniversary-of-the-southern-baptist-convention/.

30. Jennifer Harvey, *Dear White Christians: For Those Still Longing for Racial Reconciliation* (Grand Rapids, MI: Eerdmans, 2014), 2–3.

31. Harvey, *Dear White Christians*, 5.

32. Robert P. Jones, *The End of White Christian America* (New York: Simon & Schuster, 2016), 191.

33. Jones, *The End of White Christian America*, 192.

34. Jones, *The End of White Christian America*, 191.

35. Pamela Cooper-White, *The Cry of Tamar: Violence Against Women and the Church's Response*, 2nd ed. (Minneapolis: Fortress, 2012), 260.

36. Robert McAfee Brown, "The Problems (and Possibilities) of Reconciliation," *Open Hands* 8, no. 3 (1993): 4–5.

37. Cooper-White, *The Cry of Tamar*, 260–61.

38. Ed Stetzer, "Paige Patterson and Doing the Right Thing for the SBC, Again," *Christianity Today*, April 30, 2018, https://www.christianitytoday.co/edstetzer/2018/may/paige-patterson-end-of-era.html.

39. Walter B. Shurden, qtd. in Fisher Humphreys, *The Way We Were*, 43.

40. Beth Moore, "A Letter to My Brothers," *LPM Blog*, May 3, 2018, https://blog.lproof.org/2018/05/a-letter-to-my-brothers.html.

41. Moore, "A Letter to My Brothers."

42. Moore, "A Letter to My Brothers."

43. Moore, "A Letter to My Brothers."

44. Moore, "A Letter to My Brothers."

45. Moore, "A Letter to My Brothers."

46. Moore, "A Letter to My Brothers."

47. Sandra H. Polaski, *Paul and the Discourse of Power* (Sheffield, England: Sheffield Academic, 1993), 27.

48. Moore, "A Letter to My Brothers."

49. Luke 8.

50. John 20:15.

51. These ordinary communications were preserved and eventually canonized as sacred texts, becoming part of Christian scripture.

52. Tom Gjelten, "Southern Baptist Women Protest Church Leader's Comments," *All Things Considered*, May 7, 2018,https://www.npr.org/2018/05/07/609180867/southern-baptist-women-protest-churchs-doctrine.

53. Gjelten, "Southern Baptist Women Protest Church Leader's Comments."

54. Karen Swallow Prior, qtd. in Gjelten, "Southern Baptist Women Protest Church Leader's Comments."

55. "Letter to SWBTS Board of Trustees," May 6, 2018, https://swbtsletter.com/.

56. "Letter to SWBTS Board of Trustees."

57. "Letter to SWBTS Board of Trustees."

58. "Letter to SWBTS Board of Trustees."

59. "Letter to SWBTS Board of Trustees."

60. "Letter to SWBTS Board of Trustees."

61. "Letter to SWBTS Board of Trustees."

62. SWBTS Board of Trustees.

63. Albert Mohler, "The Humiliation of the Southern Baptist Convention," *Christianity Today*, May 23, 2018, https://www.christianitytoday.com/ct/2018/may-web-only/al-mohler-humiliation-of-southern-baptist-convention-metoo.html.

64. Bob Allen, "#AlMohlerToo: Did a Southern Baptist Power Broker Just

Get Woke?" *Baptist News Global*, May 30, 2018, https://baptistnews.com/article/almohlertoo-did-a-southern-baptist-power-broker-just-get-woke/#.XzvPKS05RPM; Christa Brown, *This Little Light: Beyond a Baptist Preacher Predator and His Gang* (Cedarburg, WI: Foremost, 2009).

65. Jonathan Edwards, *The Religious Affections* (Carlisle: Banner of Truth Trust, 2001), 237.

66. Edwards, *The Religious Affections*, 265–66.

67. Kevin Ueckert, "Statement by Kevin Ueckert, Chairman of the Board of Trustees," Southwestern Baptist Theological Seminary, June 1, 2018, https://swbts.edu/news/releases/statement-kevin-ueckert-chairman-board-trustees/.

68. Ueckert, "Statement by Kevin Ueckert, Chairman of the Board of Trustees."

69. Beth Moore (@bethmoorelpm), "'Raise her up,'" Twitter, June 1, 2018, 11:43 p.m., https://twitter.com/BethMooreLPM/status/1002772781338066944?s=20.

Chapter 5

1. SWBTS Board of Trustees, "Statement Regarding Dr. Paige Patterson," *Southwestern Baptist Theological Seminary*, May 23, 2018, https://swbts.edu/news/releases/statement-regarding-dr-paige-patterson/.

2. Robert Downen, Lise Olsen, and John Tedesco, "Abuse of Faith: 20 Years, 700 Victims; Southern Baptist Sexual Abuse Spreads as Leaders Resist Reforms," *Houston Chronicle*, February 10, 2019, https://www.houstonchronicle.com/news/investigations/article/Southern-Baptist-sexual-abuse-spreads-as-leaders-13588038.php.

3. Beth Moore (@bethmoorelpm), "We understand," Twitter, February 10, 2019, 4:12 p.m., https://twitter.com/BethMooreLPM/status/1094720702190678016?s=20.

4. Beth Daniell, *A Communion of Friendship: Literacy, Spiritual Practice, and Women in Recovery* (Carbondale: Southern Illinois University Press, 2003).

5. Daniell, *A Communion of Friendship*, 118.

6. Daniell, *A Communion of Friendship*, 119.

7. Anne Ruggles Gere, *Intimate Practices: Literacy and Cultural Work in U.S. Women's Clubs, 1880–1920* (Champaign: University of Illinois Press, 1997).

8. Deborah Brandt, *Literacy in American Lives* (New York: Oxford University Press, 2001).

9. Brandt, *Literacy in American Lives*, 119–21.

10. Katherine H. Adams, *A History of Professional Writing Instruction in American Colleges* (Dallas, TX: Southern Methodist University Press, 1993).

11. Katherine H. Adams, *A Group of Their Own: College Writing Courses and American Women Writers, 1880–1940* (Albany: SUNY Press, 2001).

12. Daniell, *A Communion of Friendship*, 122–24.

13. Daniell, *A Communion of Friendship*, 123–24; Janice Haaken, *Pillar of Salt: Gender, Memory, and the Perils of Looking Back* (New Brunswick, NJ: Rutgers University Press, 1998).

14. Jean Bessette, *Retroactivism in the Lesbian Archives: Composing Pasts and Futures* (Southern Illinois University Press, 2017), 59–60.

15. Bessette, *Retroactivism in the Lesbian Archives*, 56.

16. Bessette, *Retroactivism in the Lesbian Archives*, 42.

17. Valerie Palmer-Mehta, "The Subversive Power of Survivor Rhetoric: An Innovative Archive of Survivor Discourse in *New York* Magazine," *Women's Studies in Communication* 41, no. 2 (2018): 164.

18. Ann Cvetkovich, *An Archive of Feelings: Trauma, Sexuality, and Lesbian Public Culture* (Durham, NC: Duke University Press, 2003), 7–8.

19. Daniell, *A Communion of Friendship*, 119.

20. Ekaterina Haskins, "Between Archive and Participation: Public Memory in a Digital Age," *Rhetoric Society Quarterly* 37, no. 4 (2007): 401–22.

21. Emma A. Jane, "'Your a Ugly, Whorish Slut': Understanding E-bile," *Feminist Media Studies* 14, no. 4 (2014): 531–46; Adrienne Shaw, "The Internet Is Full of Jerks Because the World Is Full of Jerks: What Feminist Theory Teaches Us about the Internet," *Communication and Critical/Cultural Studies* 11, no. 3 (2014): 273–77.

22. Rosemary Clark, "'Hope in a Hashtag': The Discursive Activism of #WhyIStayed," *Feminist Media Studies* 16, no. 5 (2016): 788–804; Carrie Renschler, "Rape Culture and the Feminist Politics of Social Media," *Girlhood Studies* 7, no. 1 (2014): 65–82; Sherri Williams, "#SayHerName: Using Digital Activism to Document Violence Against Black Women," *Feminist Media Studies* 16, no. 5 (2016): 923–25.

23. Stenberg, "'Tweet Me Your First Assaults,'" 133.

24. Clark, "'Hope in a Hashtag.'"

25. Moore, "We understand."

26. Hannah Bunker (@hannahbunker), "I had," Twitter, February 11, 2019, 8:09 a.m., https://twitter.com/hannahbunker/status/1094961550576795650?s=20.

27. Jen Hatmaker, (@JenHatmaker), "I could," Twitter, February 11, 2019, 2:58 p.m., https://twitter.com/JenHatmaker/status/1095064557582802947?s=20.

28. Beth Moore (@bethmoorelpm), "We understand," Twitter, February 11, 2019, 4:56 p.m., https://twitter.com/BethMooreLPM/status/1095094210364096514?s=20.

29. Jen Hatmaker, (@JenHatmaker), "He plays," Twitter, February 11, 2019, 7:30 p.m., https://twitter.com/JenHatmaker/status/1095132902088687616?s=20.

30. Rachael Denhollander (@R_Denhollander), "Grieving," Twitter, February 10, 2019, 4:26 p.m., https://twitter.com/R_Denhollander/status/1094724290799435776?s=20.

31. Beth Moore (@bethmoorelpm), "And I," Twitter, February 10, 2019, 4:27 p.m., https://twitter.com/BethMooreLPM/status/1094724559763324929?s=20.

32. Referring to Isaiah 61:3.

33. Beth Moore (@bethmoorelpm), "Yes," Twitter, February 10, 2019, 7:38 a.m., https://twitter.com/BethMooreLPM/status/1094953949189361664?s=20.

34. 1 Samuel 24:1–7; 26:5–11.

35. Psalms 105:14–15; 1 Chronicles 16:21–22.

36. Carol Winkelmann, *The Language of Battered Women: A Rhetorical Analysis of Personal Theologies* (Albany: SUNY Press, 2004), 136–44.

37. Beth Moore (@bethmoorelpm), "How magical," Twitter, February 11, 2019, 8:08 p.m., https://twitter.com/BethMooreLPM/status/1095142671973314563?s=20.

38. Hannah Bunker (@hannahbunker), "Those words," Twitter, February 11, 2019, 8:33 p.m., https://twitter.com/hannahbunker/status/1095148800845467648?s=20.

39. Beth Moore, "Why I Removed Some of My Commentary from a Chapter of Praying God's Word," LPM Blog, July 6, 2019, https://blog.lproof.org/2019/07/why-i-removed-some-of-my-commentary-from-a-chapter-of-praying-gods-word.html.

40. Beth Moore (@bethmoorelpm), "Y'all," Twitter, April 27, 2019, 8:29 a.m., https://twitter.com/BethMooreLPM/status/1122130756317347840?s=20.

41. Beth Moore (@bethmoorelpm), "I'm doing," Twitter, April 27, 2019, 8:45 a.m., https://twitter.com/BethMooreLPM/status/1122134785244184576?s=20.

42. Owen Strachan (@ostrachan), "Complementarians disagree," Twitter, May 8, 2019, 4:22 p.m., https://twitter.com/ostrachan/status/1126235933349765120?s=20

43. Albert Mohler (@albertmohler), "We have," Twitter, May 31, 2019, 11:14 a.m., https://twitter.com/albertmohler/status/1134493428371329026?s=20.

44. Beth Moore, (@bethmoorelpm), "Beware of Bible," Twitter, June 19, 2019, 7:44 a.m., https://twitter.com/BethMooreLPM/status/1141325817508765702?s=20.

45. Beth Moore (@bethmoorelpm), "The moment," Twitter, June 23, 2019, 8:09 a.m., https://twitter.com/BethMooreLPM/status/1142781613505486848?s=20.

46. Beth Moore (@bethmoorelpm), "They rotate," Twitter, July 2, 2019, 6:59 a.m., https://twitter.com/BethMooreLPM/status/1146025618036969472?s=20.

47. Beth Moore, *Praying God's Word: Breaking Free from Spiritual Strongholds* (Nashville, TN: B&H, 2009), 279.

48. Beth Moore (@bethmoorelpm), "After taking," Twitter, July 4, 2019, 3:29 p.m., https://twitter.com/BethMooreLPM/status/1146878644398301185?s=20.

Conclusion

1. Michael-John DePalma, Jeffrey Ringer, and Jim Webber, "(Re)Charting the (Dis)Courses of Faith and Politics, or Rhetoric and Democracy in the Burkean Barnyard," *Rhetoric Society Quarterly* 38, no. 3 (2008): 329.

2. DePalma, Ringer, and Webber, "(Re)Charting the (Dis)Courses of Faith and Politics."

3. Patricia Roberts-Miller, *Voices in the Wilderness: Public Discourse and the Paradox of Puritan Rhetoric* (Tuscaloosa: University of Alabama Press, 1999).

4. Donna Freitas, *Sex and the Soul: Juggling Sexuality, Spirituality, Romance, and Religion on America's College Campuses* (New York: Oxford University Press, 2008), 229.

5. Susan Brooks Thistlethwaite, "Every Two Minutes: Battered Women and Feminist Interpretation," in *Feminist Interpretation of the Bible*, ed. Letty M. Russell (Philadelphia: Westminster, 1985), 313.

6. Beth Moore, "A Letter to My Brothers," *LPM Blog*, May 3, 2018, https://blog.lproof.org/2018/05/a-letter-to-my-brothers.html.

7. Rachael Denhollander, "My Larry Nassar Testimony Went Viral: But There's More to the Gospel Than Forgiveness," *Christianity Today*, January 31, 2018, https://www.christianitytoday.com/ct/2018/january-web-only/rachael-denhollander-larry-nassar-forgiveness-gospel.html.

8. James D. Hunter, *To Change the World: The Irony, Tragedy, and Possibility of Christianity in the Late Modern World* (New York: Oxford University Press, 2010), 25–26.

9. Rachael Denhollander, "I'm a Sexual Assault Survivor." *Vox*, October 16, 2018, https://www.vox.com/first-person/2018/10/15/17968534/kavanaugh-vote-supreme-court-sexual-assault-christine-blasey-ford.

10. Beth Daniell, *A Communion of Friendship: Literacy, Spiritual Practice, and Women in Recovery* (Carbondale: Southern Illinois University Press, 2003), 120–21. Such an act is reminiscent of Oprah Winfrey evangelizing with another book by Walker: *The Color Purple*. When it came out, she bought as many copies as she could to give away, so people would read and talk about it.

WORKS CITED

Adams, Carol J. "Foreword: Diving into the Wreck." In *Women, Religion, Revolution*, edited by Xochitl Alvizo and Gina Messina, xv–xix. Cambridge, MA: Feminist Studies in Religion, 2018.

Adams, Katherine H. *A Group of Their Own: College Writing Courses and American Women Writers, 1880–1940*. Albany: SUNY Press, 2001.

———. *A History of Professional Writing Instruction in American Colleges*. Dallas, TX: Southern Methodist University Press, 1993.

Adams-Roberts, Aesha, Rosalyn C. Eves, and Liz Rohan. "'With the Tongue of [Wo]men and Angels': Apostolic Rhetorical Practices among Religious Women." In *Renovating Rhetoric in Christian Tradition*, edited by Elizabeth Vander Lei, Thomas Amorose, Beth Daniell, and Anne Ruggles Gere, 45–58. Pittsburgh, PA: University of Pittsburgh Press, 2014.

Ahmed, Sara. *The Cultural Politics of Emotion*. Edinburgh: Edinburgh University Press, 2004.

Alcoff, Linda, and Laura Gray. "Survivor Discourse: Transgression or Recuperation?" *Signs: Journal of Women in Culture and Society* 18, no. 2 (1993): 260–90.

Alexander, M. Jacqui. *Pedagogies of Crossing: Meditations on Feminism, Sexual Politics, Memory, and the Sacred*. Durham, NC: Duke University Press, 2005.

Allen, Bob. "#AlMohlerToo: Did a Southern Baptist Power Broker Just Get Woke?" *Baptist News Global*, May 30, 2018. https://baptistnews.com/article/almohlertoo-did-a-southern-baptist-power-broker-just-get-woke/#.XzvPKS05RPM.

———. "SBC Seminary President Labels Clergy Sex-Abuse Victims' Group 'Evil-Doers.'" *Good Faith Media*, February 15, 2008. https://goodfaithmedia.org/sbc-seminary-president-labels-clergy-sex-abuse-victims-group-evil-doers-cms-12262/.

———. "SNAP Cries Foul over Baptist Press Reporting." *Good Faith Media*, March 27, 2007. https://goodfaithmedia.org/snap-cries-foul-over-baptist-press-reporting-cms-8710/.

Allender, D. B. *The Wounded Heart: Hope for Adult Victims of Childhood Sexual Abuse*. Colorado Springs: Navpress, 1990.

Ammerman, Nancy T. *Baptist Battles: Social Change and Religious Conflict in the Southern Baptist Convention*. New Brunswick, NJ: Rutgers University Press, 1990.

Anderson, Charles M., and Marian M. MacCurdy. *Writing and Healing: Toward an Informed Practice*. Urbana, IL: NCTE, 2000.

Anderson, Dianna. *Damaged Goods: New Perspectives on Christian Purity*. New York: Jericho, 2015.

Augsburger, David. *Caring Enough to Forgive*. Scottdale, PA: Herald, 1981.

Aristotle. *Rhetoric*. In *The Rhetoric and Poetics of Aristotle*, translated by W. Rhys Roberts, Reprint, New York: Modern Library, 1984.

Bailey, Sarah Pulliam. "'Still the Best Candidate': Some Evangelicals Still Back Trump Despite Lewd Video." *Washington Post*, October 8, 2016. https://www.washingtonpost.com/news/acts-of-faith/wp/2016/10/08/still-the-best-candidate-some-evangelicals-still-back-trump-despite-lewd-video/?utm_term=.93e997ea5a42.

———. "'We're All Sinners': Jerry Falwell, Jr. Defends Donald Trump after Video of Lewd Remarks." *Washington Post*, October 10, 2016. https://www.washingtonpost.com/news/acts-of-faith/wp/2016/10/10/jerry-falwell-jr-the-gop-establishment-could-be-behind-donald-trump-video-leak/.

———. "Why Women Want Moore." *Christianity Today* 54, no. 8 (2010): 20–25.

Balmer, Randall. *Blessed Assurance: A History of Evangelicalism in America*. Boston: Beacon, 1999.

———. *Thy Kingdom Come: How the Religious Right Distorts the Faith and Threatens America; An Evangelical's Lament*. New York: Basic, 2006.

Bambara, Toni Cade. *The Salt Eaters*. New York: Vintage, 1981.

Barr, Beth Allison. *The Making of Biblical Womanhood: How the Subjugation of Women Became Gospel Truth*. Grand Rapids, MI: Brazos, 2021.

Bass, Ellen, and Laura Davis. *The Courage to Heal: A Handbook for Healing*. Washington, DC: Child Welfare League of America, 1988.

Beaman-Hall, Lori, and Nancy Nason-Clark. "Translating Spiritual Commitment into Service: The Responses of Evangelical Women to Wife Abuse." *Canadian Women's Studies/Les Cahiers De La Femme* 17 (1997): 58–61.

Beaty, Katelyn. "'No More': Evangelical Women Are Done with Donald Trump and His Misogyny." *Washington Post*, October 13, 2016. https://www.washingtonpost.com/news/acts-of-faith/wp/2016/10/13/no-more-evangelical-women-are-done-with-donald-trump-and-his-misogyny/.

Bebbington, David. *Evangelicalism in Modern Britain: A History from the 1730s to the 1980s*. London: Unwin Hyman, 1989.

Believed. Episode 7, "What Have You Done?" Aired December 3, 2018, on Michigan Radio. https://believed.michiganradio.org/larry-nassar-what-have-you-done/.

Bernstein, Elizabeth. "Militarized Humanitarianism Meets Carceral Feminism: The Politics of Sex, Rights, and Freedom in Contemporary Antitrafficking Campaigns." *Signs: Journal of Women in Culture and Society* 36, no. 1 (2010): 45–71. doi:10.1086/652918

Bessette, Jean. *Retroactivism in the Lesbian Archives: Composing Pasts and Futures*. Southern Illinois University Press, 2017.

Bevacqua, Maria. *Rape on the Public Agenda: Feminism and the Politics of Sexual Assault*. Boston: Northeastern University Press, 2000.

Bielo, James S. *Words upon the Word: An Ethnography of Evangelical Group Bible Study*. New York: New York University Press, 2009.

Bizzell, Patricia, and Bruce Herzberg. *The Rhetorical Tradition: Readings from Classical Times to the Present.* Boston: Bedford/St. Martin's, 2001.

Block, Sharon. *Rape and Sexual Power in Early America.* Chapel Hill: University of North Carolina Press, 2006.

Bohner, Gerd, et al. "Rape Myth Acceptance: Cognitive, Affective, and Behavioural Effects of Beliefs That Blame the Victim and Exonerate the Perpetrator." In *Rape: Challenging Contemporary Thinking,* edited by Miranda Horvath and Jennifer Brown, 17–45. London: Willan, 2009.

Bonhoeffer, Dietrich. *The Cost of Discipleship.* Translated by R. H. Fuller. New York: Macmillan, 1963.

Booth, Wayne C. *The Rhetoric of RHETORIC: The Quest for Effective Communication.* Malden, MA: Blackwell, 2004.

Borg, Marcus J. *Speaking Christian: Why Christian Words Have Lost Their Meaning and Power—and How They Can Be Restored.* Kindle ed., New York: HarperCollins, 2011.

Borrowman, Shane, ed. *Trauma and the Teaching of Writing.* Albany: SUNY Press, 2005.

Bowler, Kate. *The Preacher's Wife: The Precarious Power of Evangelical Women Celebrities.* Oxford: Oxford University Press, 2019.

Brandt, Deborah. *Literacy in American Lives.* New York: Oxford University Press, 2001.

Brewer, Connie. *Escaping the Shadows, Seeking the Light: Christians in Recovery from Childhood Sexual Abuse.* San Francisco: Harper, 1991.

Brison, Susan J. "Trauma Narratives and the Remaking of the Self." In *Acts of Memory: Cultural Recall in the Present,* edited by Mieke Bal, Jonathan Crewe, and Leo Spitzer, 37–54. Hanover, NH: University Press of New England, 1999.

Brock, Rita N., and Rebecca A. Parker. *Proverbs of Ashes.* Boston: Beacon, 2001.

Brohl, Kathryn. *Working with Traumatized Children: A Handbook for Healing.* Washington, DC: Child Welfare League of America, 1996.

Brown, Brené. *Daring Greatly: How the Courage to Be Vulnerable Transforms the Way We Live, Love, Parent, and Lead.* New York: Gotham, 2012.

———. *I Thought It Was Just Me (But It Isn't).* New York: Avery, 2007.

Brown, Christa. *This Little Light: Beyond a Baptist Preacher Predator and His Gang.* Cedarburg, WI: Foremost, 2009.

Brown, Joanne C., and Rebecca Parker. "For God so Loved the World?" In *Christianity, Patriarchy, and Abuse: A Feminist Critique,* edited by Joanne C. Brown and Carole B. Bohn, 1–30. New York: Pilgrim, 1989.

Brown, Robert McAfee. "The Problems (and Possibilities) of Reconciliation." *Open Hands* 8, no. 3 (1993): 4–5.

Brownmiller, Susan. *Against Our Will: Men, Women and Rape.* Ballantine, 1975.

Bryan, Clint, and Mohammed Albakry. "A Little Bit Transparent with One Another: Constructing Vulnerability in the Evangelical Discourse of Women Preachers." *Culture and Religion* 16, no. 4 (2015): 392–411.

Bull, Chris, and John Gallagher. *Perfect Enemies: The Religious Right, the Gay Movement, and the Politics of the 1990s*. New York: Crown, 1996.

Bumiller, Kristin. *In an Abusive State: How Neoliberalism Appropriated the Feminist Movement Against Sexual Violence*. Durham, NC: Duke University Press, 2008.

Burke, Kenneth. *Attitudes Toward History*. 3rd ed. Berkeley: University of California Press, 1984.

———. *Language as Symbolic Action: Essays on Life, Literature, and Method*. Berkeley: University of California Press, 1966.

———. *The Rhetoric of Religion: Studies in Logology*. Berkeley: University of California Press, 1970.

Burke, Tarana. "The Inception." JustBe. https://justbeinc.wixsite.com/justbeinc/the-me-too-movement-cmml.

Burnett, Myra N. "Suffering and Sanctification: The Religious Context of Battered Woman's Syndrome." *Pastoral Psychology* 44 (1996): 145–49.

Burstow, Bonnie. *Radical Feminist Therapy: Working in the Context of Violence*. London: Sage, 1992.

Burton, Vicki Tolar. *Spiritual Literacy in John Wesley's Methodism: Reading, Writing, and Speaking to Believe*. Waco, TX: Baylor University Press, 2008.

Carey, Tamika L. *Rhetorical Healing: The Reeducation of Contemporary Black Womanhood*. Albany: SUNY Press.

Caruth, Cathy. *Trauma: Explorations in Memory*. Baltimore, MD: Johns Hopkins University Press, 1995.

———. *Unclaimed Experience: Trauma, Narrative, and History*. Baltimore, MD: Johns Hopkins University Press, 1996.

Clark, Naomi. "Circulation Across Structural Holes: Reverse Black Boxing the Emergence of Religious Right Networks in the 1970s." In *Circulation, Writing and Rhetoric*, edited by Laurie Gries and Colin Brooke. Louisville: University of Colorado Press, 2018. 152–69.

Clark, Rosemary. "'Hope in a Hashtag': The Discursive Activism of #WhyIStayed." *Feminist Media Studies* 16, no. 5 (2016): 788–804.

Clingan, Ralph G. *Against Cheap Grace in a World Come of Age: An Intellectual Biography of Clayton Powell, 1865–1953*. New York: Peter Lang, 2002.

Cochran, Pamela D. H. *Evangelical Feminism: A History*. New York: New York University Press, 2005.

Coleman, Monica A. *The Dinah Project: A Handbook for Congregational Response to Sexual Violence*. Cleveland, OH: Pilgrim, 2004.

Cooper-White, Pamela. *The Cry of Tamar: Violence Against Women and the Church's Response*. 2nd ed. Minneapolis: Fortress, 2012.

Cope, Emily M. "Learning Not to Preach: Evangelical Speaker Beth Moore and the Rhetoric of Constraint." In *Rhetoric, History, and Women's Oratorical Education: American Women Learn to Speak*, edited by David Gold and Catherine Hobbs, 217–38. New York: Routledge, 2013.

Cope, Emily Murphy, and Jeffrey M. Ringer. "Coming to (Troubled) Terms: Methodology, Positionality, and the Problem of Defining 'Evangelical Christian.'" In *Mapping Christian Rhetorics: Connecting Conversations, Charting New Territories*, edited by Jeffrey Ringer and Michael-John DePalma, 103–24. New York: Routledge, 2015.

Crenshaw, Kimberlé. "Demarginalizing the Intersection of Race and Sex: A Black Feminist Critique of Antidiscrimination Doctrine, Feminist Theory, and Antiracist Politics." *University of Chicago Legal Forum* 1, no. 8 (1989): 139–67.

Crouse, Janice. "Facing an Unwelcome Truth." *Christianity Today*, October 2005. 87.

———. *Strategies for Reclaiming America's Culture*. Washington, DC: Beverly LaHaye Institute, 2000.

Crowe, Allison, and Christine E. Murray. "Stigma from Professional Helpers Toward Survivors of Intimate Partner Violence." *Partner Abuse* 6, no. 2 (2015): 157–79. doi:10.1891/1946-6560.6.2.157

Crowley, Sharon. *Toward a Civil Discourse: Rhetoric and Fundamentalism*. Pittsburgh, PA: University of Pittsburgh Press, 2006.

Cutrer, Corrie. "A Time of Justice." *Christianity Today*, May 21, 2002, 19–20.

———. "Witnesses Accused of Failing to Report Abuse." *Christianity Today*, December 3, 2001, 23–24.

Cvetkovich, Ann. *An Archive of Feelings: Trauma, Sexuality, and Lesbian Public Culture*. Durham, NC: Duke University Press, 2003.

Dadas, Caroline. "Making Sense of #MeToo: Intersectionality and Contemporary Feminism," *Peitho* 22, no. 3 (Spring 2020): http://cfshrc.org/article/making-sense-of-metoo-intersectionality-and-contemporary-feminism/.

Daniell, Beth. *A Communion of Friendship: Literacy, Spiritual Practice, and Women in Recovery*. Carbondale: Southern Illinois University Press, 2003.

Davis, Angela Y. *Women, Race and Class*. Toronto: Vintage, 1984.

Dawsey, Josh. "Trump Derides Protections for Immigrants from 'Shithole' Countries." *Washington Post*, December 19, 2018. https://www.washingtonpost.com/politics/trump-attacks-protections-for-immigrants-from-shithole-countries-in-oval-office-meeting/2018/01/11/bfc0725c-f711-11e7-91af-31ac729add94_story.html.

de Alminana, Margaret E., and Lois E. Olena, eds. *Women in Pentecostal and Charismatic Ministry: Informing a Dialogue on Gender, Church and Ministry*. Leiden: Brill, 2016.

D'Emilio, John, and Estelle B. Freedman. *Intimate Matters: A History of Sexuality in America*. New York: Harper & Row, 1988.

Dean, Jamie. "A Time to Speak." *World*, March 1, 2018. https://world.wng.org/2018/03/a_time_to_speak.

Denhollander, Rachael. "I'm a Sexual Assault Survivor." *Vox*, October 16, 2018. https://www.vox.com/first-person/2018/10/15/17968534/kavanaugh-vote-supreme-court-sexual-assault-christine-blasey-ford.

———. "My Larry Nassar Testimony Went Viral: But There's More to the Gospel Than Forgiveness." *Christianity Today*, January 31, 2018. https://www.christianitytoday.com/ct/2018/january-web-only/rachael-denhollander-larry-nassar-forgiveness-gospel.html.

———. "The Price I Paid for Taking on Larry Nassar." *New York Times*, January 26, 2018. https://www.nytimes.com/2018/01/26/opinion/sunday/larry-nassar-rachael-denhollander.html.

———. "Read Rachael Denhollander's Full Victim Impact Statement about Larry Nassar." *CNN*, January 30, 2018. https://www.cnn.com/2018/01/24/us/rachael-denhollander-full-statement/index.html.

DePalma, Michael-John. "Reimagining Rhetorical Education: Fostering Writers' Civic Capacities through Engagement with Religious Rhetorics." *College English* 79, no. 3 (2017): 251–75.

DePalma, Michael-John, Jeffery Ringer, and Jim Webber. "(Re)Charting the (Dis) Courses of Faith and Politics, or Rhetoric and Democracy in the Burkean Barnyard." *Rhetoric Society Quarterly* 38, no. 3 (2008): 311–34.

Desser, Daphne. "Fraught Literacy: Competing Desires for Connection and Separation in the Writings of American Missionary Women in 19th Century Hawai'i." *College English* 69 no. 5 (2007): 443–69.

———. "Teaching Writing in Hawai'i after Pearl Harbor and 9/11: How to 'Make Meaning' and 'Heal' Despite National Propaganda." In *Trauma and the Teaching of Writing*, edited by Shane Borrowman, 85–97. Albany: SUNY Press, 2005.

Devlin, Rachel. *A Girl Stands at the Door: The Generation of Young Women Who Desegregated America's Schools*. New York: Hachette, 2018.

Dobson, James. "Dr. James Dobson on Donald Trump's Christian Faith." *Family Talk*, July 21, 2016. http://drjamesdobson.org/news/dr-james-dobson-on-trumps-christian-faith-em.

Douglas, Kelly Brown. "Black Body/White Soul: The Unsettling Intersection of Race, Sexuality, and Christianity." In *Body and Soul: Rethinking Sexuality as Justice Love*, edited by Marvin M. Ellison and Sylvia Thorson-Smith, 99–111. Cleveland, OH: Pilgrim, 2003.

Downen, Robert, Lise Olsen, and John Tedesco. "Abuse of Faith: 20 Years, 700 Victims: Southern Baptist Sexual Abuse Spreads as Leaders Resist Reforms." *Houston Chronicle*, February 10, 2019. https://www.houstonchronicle.com/news/investigations/article/Southern-Baptist-sexual-abuse-spreads-as-leaders-13588038.php.

Downs, Douglas. "True Believers, Real Scholars, and Real True Believing Scholars: Discourses of Inquiry and Affirmation in the Composition Classroom." In *Negotiating Religious Faith in The Composition Classroom*, edited by Elizabeth Vander Lei and Bonnie Lenore Kyburz, 39–55. Portsmouth, NH: Heinemann, 2005.

Drescher, Elizabeth. *Choosing Our Religion: The Spiritual Lives of America's Nones.* New York: Oxford University Press, 2016.

DuBois, Joshua. "Powerful Evangelical Women Split from Male Church Leaders to Slam Trump." *Daily Beast,* October 10, 2016. https://www.thedailybeast.com/powerful-evangelical-women-split-from-male-church-leaders-to-slam-trump.

Du Mez, Kristin Kobes. *Jesus and John Wayne: How White Evangelicals Corrupted a Faith and Fractured a Nation.* New York: W. W. Norton, 2020.

Dworkin, Andrea. *Letters from a War Zone: Writings, 1976–1989.* Chicago: Lawrence Hill, 1993.

Edwards, Jonathan. *The Religious Affections.* Carlisle, PA: Banner of Truth Trust, 2001.

Episcopal Church. *The Book of Common Prayer and Administration of the Sacraments and Other Rites and Ceremonies of the Church: Together with the Psalter or Psalms of David According to the Use of the Episcopal Church.* New York: Seabury, 1979.

Fehler, Brian. "Re-Defining God: The Rhetoric of Reconciliation." *Rhetoric Society Quarterly* 33, no. 1 (2003): 105–26.

Feldmeth, Joanne Ross, and Midge Wallace Finley. *We Weep for Ourselves and Our Children.* San Francisco: Harper, 1990.

Ferraro, Kathleen, and John M. Johnson. "How Women Experience Battering: The Process of Victimization." *Social Problems* 30 (1983): 325–39.

Field, Samantha. "How We Teach Purity Culture Isn't the Problem: Purity Culture Itself Is the Problem." *Rewire News,* October 24, 2016. https://rewirenewsgroup.com/article/2016/10/24/teach-purity-culture-isnt-problem-purity-culture-problem/.

Fortune, Marie M. *Keeping the Faith: Guidance for Christian Women Facing Abuse.* New York: HarperCollins, 1987.

———. *Sexual Violence: The Unmentionable Sin.* New York: Pilgrim, 1983.

Foucault, Michel. *The History of Sexuality, Vol. I.* Trans. Robert Hurley. New York: Random House, 1990.

Fraser, Nancy. "Rethinking the Public Sphere: A Contribution to the Critique of Actually Existing Democracy." *Social Text,* no. 25/26 (1990): 56–80.

Freitas, Donna. *Sex and the Soul: Juggling Sexuality, Spirituality, Romance, and Religion on America's College Campuses.* New York: Oxford University Press, 2008.

Furnham, Adrian. "Belief in a Just World: Research Progress over the Past Decade." *Personality and Individual Differences* 34, no. 5 (2003): 795–817.

Gavey, Nicola. *Just Sex? The Cultural Scaffolding of Rape.* New York: Routledge, 2005.

Gench, Frances T. *Back to the Well: Women's Encounters with Jesus in the Gospels.* Louisville, KY: Westminster John Knox, 2004.

Gere, Anne Ruggles. *Intimate Practices: Literacy and Cultural Work in U.S. Women's Clubs, 1880–1920.* Champaign: University of Illinois Press, 1997.

Giles, Thomas. "Coping with Sexual Misconduct in the Church." *Christianity Today*, January 11, 1993, 48–49.

Gilyard, Keith. *Composition and Cornel West: Notes Toward a Deep Democracy*. Carbondale: Southern Illinois University Press, 2008.

Ginsberg, Ruth Bader. *Brief* of the ACLU et al. as Amicus Curiae. Coker v Georgia, No 75-5444, (1976).

Gjelten, Tom. "Southern Baptist Women Protest Church Leader's Comments." *All Things Considered*, May 7, 2018. https://www.npr.org/2018/05/07/609180867/southern-baptist-women-protest-churchs-doctrine.

Godbeer, Richard. *Sexual Revolution in Early America*. Baltimore, MD: Johns Hopkins University Press, 2002.

Goodburn, Amy. "It's a Question of Faith: Discourses of Fundamentalism and Critical Pedagogy in the Writing Classroom." *JAC* 18, no. 2 (1998): 333–53.

Goodstein, Laurie. "Donald Trump Reveals Evangelical Rifts That Could Shape Politics for Years." *New York Times*, October 17, 2016. https://www.nytimes.com/2016/10/17/us/donald-trump-evangelicals-republican-vote.html.

Gorney, Cynthia. *Articles of Faith: A Frontline History of the Abortion Wars*. New York: Simon & Schuster, 1998.

Graham, Ruth. "Larry Nassar's First Accuser Is Taking on Another Big Target—This Time, Within Her Own Evangelical Community." *Slate*, March 9, 2018. https://slate.com/human-interest/2018/03/larry-nassars-first-accuser-rachael-denhollander-is-now-taking-on-a-big-target-within-her-evangelical-community.html.

———. "These Evangelical Women Speaking Out Against Trump Have More Influence Than You Think." *Slate*, October 12, 2016. https://slate.com/human-interest/2016/10/the-evangelical-women-speaking-out-against-trump-have-more-influence-than-you-think.html.

Grimké, Sarah. *Letters on the Equality of the Sexes, and the Condition of Woman*. Boston: Isaac Knapp, 1838.

Griswold, Eliza. "Silence Is Not Spiritual: The Evangelical #MeToo Movement." *New Yorker*, June 15, 2018. https://www.newyorker.com/news/on-religion/silence-is-not-spiritual-the-evangelical-metoo-movement.

Grönlund, Kimmo, Kaisa Herne, and Maija Setälä. "Does Enclave Deliberation Polarize Opinions?" *Political Behavior* 37, no. 4 (2015): 995–1020.

Haag, Matthew. "Thousands of Immigrant Children Said They Were Sexually Abused in U.S. Detention Centers, Report Says." *New York Times*, February 27, 2019. https://www.nytimes.com/2019/02/27/us/immigrant-children-sexual-abuse.html.

Haaken, Janice. *Pillar of Salt: Gender, Memory, and the Perils of Looking Back*. New Brunswick, NJ: Rutgers University Press, 1998.

Habermas, Jürgen. *The Structural Transformation of the Public Sphere: An Inquiry into a Category of Bourgeois Society*. Trans. Thomas Burger with Frederick Lawrence. Cambridge, MA: MIT Press, 1989.

Hall, David D., ed. *The Antinomian Controversy: 1636–1638*. 2nd ed. Durham, NC: Duke University Press, 1990.

Hardesty, Nancy A. *Women Called to Witness: Evangelical Feminism in the Nineteenth Century*. 2nd ed. Knoxville: University of Tennessee Press, 1999.

Harper, Keith. *The Quality of Mercy: Southern Baptists and Social Christianity, 1890–1920*. Tuscaloosa: University of Alabama Press, 1996.

Harvey, Jennifer. *Dear White Christians: For Those Still Longing for Racial Reconciliation*. Grand Rapids, MI: Eerdmans, 2014.

Haskins, Ekaterina. "Between Archive and Participation: Public Memory in a Digital Age." *Rhetoric Society Quarterly* 37, no. 4 (2007): 401–22.

Hatmaker, Jen. *7: An Experimental Mutiny Against Excess*. Nashville: B&H, 2012.

———. "My Saddest Good Friday in Memory: When Treasured Things Are Dead." Jen Hatmaker. April 14, 2017. http://jenhatmaker.com/blog/2017/04/14/my-saddest-good-friday-in-memory-when-treasured-things-are-dead.

Hauser, Gerard A. *Vernacular Voices: The Rhetoric of Publics and Public Spheres*. Columbia: University of South Carolina Press, 1999.

Haverluck, Michael F. "Jeffress: Trump Still Best Choice After Lewd Tape." *OneNewsNow*, October 10, 2016. https://onenewsnow.com/politics-govt/2016/10/10/jeffress-trump-still-best-choice-after-lewd-tape.

Heggen, Carolyn H. *Sexual Abuse in Christian Homes and Churches*. Scottdale, PA: Herald, 1993.

Heitritter, Lynn, and Jeanette Vought. *Helping Victims of Sexual Abuse: A Sensitive Guide for Counselor, Victims, and Families*. Minneapolis: Bethany House, 1989.

Herman, Judith. *Trauma and Recovery*. Reprint, New York: Basic, 2015.

Hogg, Charlotte. "Including Conservative Women's Rhetorics in an 'Ethics of Hope and Care.'" *Rhetoric Review* 34, no. 4 (2015): 391–408.

Horton, Anne L., Meland M. Wilkins, and Wendy Wright. "Women Who Ended Abuse: What Religious Leaders and Religion Did for These Victims." In *Abuse and Religion: When Praying Isn't Enough*, edited by Anne L. Horton and Judith A. Williamson, 235–46. Lexington, MA: D. C. Heath, 1988.

Huang, Jon, Samuel Jacoby, Michael Strickland, and K. K. Rebecca Lai. "Election 2016: Exit Polls." *New York Times*, November 8, 2016. https://www.nytimes.com/interactive/2016/11/08/us/politics/election-exit-polls.html.

Humphreys, Fisher. *The Way We Were: How Southern Baptist Theology Has Changed and What It Means to Us All*. Macon, GA: Smyth and Helwys, 2002.

Hunter, James D. *To Change the World: The Irony, Tragedy, and Possibility of Christianity in the Late Modern World*. New York: Oxford University Press. (2010).

INCITE! Women of Color Against Violence, eds. *Color of Violence: The INCITE! Anthology*. Cambridge, MA: South End, 2006.

———. *The Revolution Will Not Be Funded: Beyond the Non-Profit Industrial Complex*. Durham, NC: Duke University Press, 2007.

Ingersoll, Julie. *Evangelical Christian Women*. New York: New York University Press, 2005.

Jane, Emma A. "'Your a Ugly, Whorish Slut': Understanding E-bile." *Feminist Media Studies* 14, no. 4 (2014): 531–46.

Janis, Irving L. *Victims of Groupthink*. New York: Houghton Mifflin, 1972.

Janoff-Bulman, Ronnie, Christine Timko, and Linda L. Carli. "Cognitive Biases in Blaming the Victim." *Journal of Experimental Social Psychology* 21, no. 2 (1985): 161–77.

Johnston, Lori. "She Helped Bring Down Larry Nassar." *Washington Post*, January 25, 2018. https://www.washingtonpost.com/news/acts-of-faith/wp/2018/01/24/she-helped-bring-down-larry-nassar-at-his-sentencing-for-sex-crimes-she-spoke-about-her-faith/?utm_term=.82cd7f21b6d2.

Jones, L. Gregory. *Embodying Forgiveness: A Theological Analysis*. Grand Rapids, MI: Eerdmans, 1995.

Jones, Robert P. *The End of White Christian America*. New York: Simon & Schuster, 2016.

Jones, Serene. *Trauma and Grace: Theology in a Ruptured World*. Louisville, KY: Westminster John Knox, 2009.

Jonsen, Albert R., and Stephen Toulmin. *The Abuse of Casuistry: A History of Moral Reasoning*. Berkeley: University of California Press, 1988.

Jordan-Lake, Joy. "Conduct Unbecoming a Preacher." *Christianity Today*, February 19, 1992, 26–32.

Joy, Emily. "#ChurchToo." Emily Joy Poet. http://emilyjoypoetry.com/churchtoo.

Karpowitz, Christopher F., Chad Raphael, and Allen S. Hammond IV. "Deliberative Democracy and Inequality Two Cheers for Enclave Deliberation Among the Disempowered." *Politics and Society* 37, no. 4 (2009): 576–615.

Kell, Carl L., and L. Raymond Camp. *In the Name of the Father: The Rhetoric of the New Southern Baptist Convention*. Carbondale: Southern Illinois University Press, 1999.

Larson, Jane E. "'Even a Worm Will Turn at Last': Rape Reform in Late Nineteenth-Century America." *Yale Journal of Law and the Humanities* 9, no. 1 (1997): 1–71.

Lazarus, Margaret, and Renner Wunderlich, producers. *Rape Culture*. Cambridge Documentary Films, 1975.

Lelek, Barbie. "Young Children Have Questions for the President." *Big Spring Herald*, February 1990.

Lenz, Lyz. "Recovering from I Kissed Dating Goodbye: A Roundtable." The Toast, June 8, 2016, https://the-toast.net/2016/06/08/recovering-from-i-kissed-dating-goodbye-a-roundtable/.

Lerner, Gerda. *The Grimké Sisters from South Carolina: Pioneers for Women's Right and Abolition*. New York: Oxford University Press, 1998.

"Letter to SWBTS Board of Trustees." Swbtsletter.com, May 6, 2018. https://swbtsletter.com/.

Leys, Ruth. *Trauma: A Genealogy*. Chicago: University of Chicago Press, 2000.

Lindgren, Caleb. "Evangelicals' Favorite Heresies Revisited by Researchers." *Christianity Today*, September 28, 2016. https://www.christianitytoday.com/news/2016/september/evangelicals-favorite-heresies-state-of-theology-ligonier.html.

Lindley, Susan H. *You Have Stept Out of Your Place: A History of Women and Religion in America*. Louisville, KY: Westminster John Knox, 1996.

Lindsay, D. Michael. *Faith in the Halls of Power: How Evangelicals Joined the American Elite*. New York: Oxford University Press, 2007.

Luhrmann, T. M. *When God Talks Back: Understanding the American Evangelical Relationship with God*. New York: Vintage, 2012.

Lupton, Robert D. *Toxic Charity: How Churches and Charities Hurt Those They Help (and How to Reverse It)*. New York: HarperOne, 2011.

Lynch, Paul. "Something Completely Different: Notes Toward a Burkean Ethics." *KB Journal: The Journal of the Kenneth Burke Society* 5, no. 1 (2008): https://kbjournal.org/paul_lynch.

Maddux, Kristy. "Finding Comedy in Theology: A Hopeful Supplement to Kenneth Burke's Logology." *Philosophy & Rhetoric* 39, no. 2 (2006): 208–32.

Mahmood, Saba. *The Politics of Piety: The Islamic Revival and the Feminist Subject*. Princeton, NJ: Princeton University Press, 2005.

Mannon, Bethany. "Xvangelical: The Rhetorical Work of Personal Narratives in Contemporary Religious Discourse." *Rhetoric Society Quarterly* 49, no. 2 (2019): 142–62.

Mansbridge, Jane. "Using Power/Fighting Power: The Polity." In *Democracy and Difference: Contesting the Boundaries of the Political*, edited by Seyla Benhabib, 46–66. Princeton, NJ: Princeton University Press, 1996.

Mansbridge, Jane, James Bohman, Simone Chambers, and David Estlund, et al. "The Place of Self-Interest and the Role of Power in Deliberative Democracy." *Journal of Political Philosophy* 18, no. 1 (2010): 64–100.

Martin, Stephanie A. *Decoding the Digital Church: Evangelical Storytelling and the Election of Donald J. Trump*. Tuscaloosa: University of Alabama Press, 2021.

Marty, Martin E. "Baptistification Takes Over." *Christianity Today*, September 2, 1983, 33–36.

Marsh, Charles. *Strange Glory: A Life of Dietrich Bonhoeffer*. New York: Alfred A. Knopf, 2014.

Martínez, Jessica, and Gregory A. Smith. "How the Faithful Voted: A Preliminary 2016 Analysis." Pew Research Center, November 9, 2016. https://www.pewresearch.org/fact-tank/2016/11/09/how-the-faithful-voted-a-preliminary-2016-analysis/.

Matthews, Nancy A. *Confronting Rape: The Feminist Anti-Rape Movement and the State*. London: Routledge, 1994.

Mattingly, Carol. *Well-Tempered Women: Nineteenth-Century Temperance Rhetoric*. Carbondale: Southern Illinois University Press, 1998.

May, Henry. *Protestant Churches in Industrial America.* New York: Harper and Brothers, 1949.

McGuire, Danielle L. *At the Dark End of the Street: Black Women, Rape, and Resistance; A New History of the Civil Rights Movement from Rosa Parks to the Rise of Black Power.* New York: Alfred A. Knopf, 2010.

Merritt, Jonathan. "The Politics of Jen Hatmaker: Trump, Black Lives Matter, Gay Marriage and More." *Religion News Service,* October 25, 2016. https://gazette.com/news/the-politics-of-jen-hatmaker-trump-black-lives-matter-gay/article_d8f7ec19-9447-521d-87d2-6bd5187a6d61.html.

Mohler, Albert. "The Humiliation of the Southern Baptist Convention." *Christianity Today,* May 23, 2018. https://www.christianitytoday.com/ct/2018/may-web-only/al-mohler-humiliation-of-southern-baptist-convention-metoo.html.

Montgomery, Leslie. *Were It Not for Grace: Stories from Women After God's Own Heart.* Nashville, TN: B&H, 2005.

Moore, Beth. "Do You Want to Get Well?" Living Proof Ministries, July 25, 2016. https://subsplash.com/livingproofwithbethmoore/lb/mi/+8efddcb.

———. "A Letter to My Brothers." *LPM Blog,* May 3, 2018. https://blog.lproof.org/2018/05/a-letter-to-my-brothers.html.

———. "Overcoming Sexual Abuse." In *Were It Not for Grace: Stories From Women After God's Own Heart,* edited by Leslie Montgomery. Nashville, TN: B&H, 2005.

———. *Praying God's Word: Breaking Free from Spiritual Strongholds.* Nashville, TN: B&H, 2009.

———. "What About the Church's Silence?" *Religion News Service,* January 31, 2018. https://religionnews.com/2018/01/31/what-about-the-churchs-silence/.

———. "Why I Removed Some of My Commentary from a Chapter of *Praying God's Word.*" LPM Blog, July 6, 2019. https://blog.lproof.org/2019/07/why-i-removed-some-of-my-commentary-from-a-chapter-of-praying-gods-word.html.

Moorti, Sujata. *The Color of Rape: Gender and Race in Television's Public Spheres.* New York: SUNY Press, 2002.

Moss, Danni. "Paige Patterson's Views on Domestic Violence." *Because It Matters.* February 25, 2008. https://dannimoss.wordpress.com/clergy-abuse-links/abuse-in-the-church/paige-pattersons-views-on-domestic-violence/.

Mountford, Roxanne. *The Gendered Pulpit: Preaching in American Protestant Spaces.* Carbondale: Southern Illinois University Press, 2003.

Nason-Clark, Nancy. *The Battered Wife: How Christians Confront Family Violence.* Louisville, KY: Westminster John Knox, 1997.

Nelson, Katherine S. "My Justice Is Her Justice: Toward a New Vision of Survivorhood." In *Queering Sexual Violence: Radical Voices from Within the Anti-Violence Movement,* edited by Jennifer Patterson. Kindle ed., New York: Riverdale Avenue, 2016.

Newman, Elana. "Narrative, Gender, and Recovery from Childhood Sexual Abuse."

In *Survivor Rhetoric: Negotiations and Narrativity in Abused Women's Language*, edited by Christine Shearer-Cremean and Carol L. Winkelmann, 23–41. Toronto: University of Toronto Press, 2004.

Noll, Mark. *The Scandal of the Evangelical Mind*. Grand Rapids, MI: Eerdmans, 1994.

O'Day, Gail. "John 7.53–8.11: A Study in Misreading." *Journal of Biblical Literature* 111, no. 4 (1992): 631–40.

Odem, Mary E. *Delinquent Daughters Protecting and Policing Adolescent Female Sexuality in the United States, 1885–1920*. Chapel Hill: University of North Carolina Press, 1995.

Paasch, Hannah. "Sexual Abuse Happens in #ChurchToo—We're Living Proof." *HuffPost*, December 4, 2017. https://www.huffpost.com/entry/sexual-abuse-churchtoo_n_5a205b30e4b03350e0b53131.

Palmer-Mehta, Valerie. "The Subversive Power of Survivor Rhetoric: An Innovative Archive of Survivor Discourse in *New York* Magazine." *Women's Studies in Communication* 41, no. 2 (2018): 159–82.

Parsons, Darlene. "A Call for Paige Patterson's Resignation from the Ministry." *Wartburg Watch*, June 16, 2009. http://thewartburgwatch.com/2009/06/16/a-call-for-paige-pattersons-resignation-from-the-ministry/.

Pascal, Blaise. *Pensées and Provincial Letters*. New York: Modern Library, 1941.

Pashman, Manya B., and Jeff Coen. "After Year of Inquiries, Willow Creek Pastor Denies Misconduct Allegations." *Chicago Tribune*, March 23, 2018. https://www.chicagotribune.com/news/breaking/ct-met-willow-creek-pastor-20171220-story.html.

Patterson, Jennifer, ed. *Queering Sexual Violence: Radical Voices from Within the Anti-violence Movement*. Kindle ed., New York: Riverdale Avenue, 2016.

Patterson, Paige. "Paige Patterson (SBC) Advice to Victims of Domestic Violence." Internet Archive, March 20, 2008. https://archive-org.ezproxy.baylor.edu/details/PaigePattersonsbcAdviceToVictimsOfDomesticViolence.

Pavia, Catherine Matthews. "The 'My Online Friends' Religious Enclave: Expanding the Definition and Possibilities of Enclaved Discourses." *Rhetoric Review* 39, no. 1 (2020): 88–100.

Payne, Michelle. *Bodily Discourses: When Students Write about Abuse and Eating Disorders*. Portsmouth, NH: Boynton/Cook, 2000.

Pease, Joshua. "The Sin of Silence: The Epidemic of Denial about Sexual Abuse in the Evangelical Church." *Washington Post*, May 31, 2018. https://www.washingtonpost.com/news/posteverything/wp/2018/05/31/feature/the-epidemic-of-denial-about-sexual-abuse-in-the-evangelical-church/.

Perkins, Priscilla. "'A Radical Conversion of the Mind': Fundamentalism, Hermeneutics, and the Metanoic Classroom." *College English* 63, no. 5 (2001): 585–611.

Peterson, Anna L. "Religious Narratives and Political Protest." *Journal of the American Academy of Religion* 64 (1996): 27–44.

Phillips, Joshua Daniel, and Rachel Alicia Griffin. "Crystal Mangum as Hypervisible Object and Invisible Subject: Black Feminist Thought, Sexual Violence, and the Pedagogical Repercussions of the Duke Lacrosse Rape Case." *Women's Studies in Communication* 38, no. 1 (2015): 36–56.

Polaski, Sandra H. *Paul and the Discourse of Power*. Sheffield, England: Sheffield Academic Press, 1993.

Probyn, Elspeth. *Blush: Faces of Shame*. Minneapolis: University of Minnesota Press, 2005.

Rambo, Shelly. *Spirit and Trauma: A Theology of Remaining*. Louisville, KY: Westminster John Knox, 2010.

Rentschler, Carrie. "Rape Culture and the Feminist Politics of Social Media." *Girlhood Studies* 7, no. 1 (2014): 65–82.

Resolution on Ordination and the Role of Women in Ministry. Kansas City: Southern Baptist Convention, June 1984. http://www.sbc.net/resolutions/1088/resolution-on-ordination-and-the-role-of-women-in-ministry.

Resolution on Racial Reconciliation on the 150th Anniversary of the Southern Baptist Convention. Atlanta: Southern Baptist Convention, June 1995. http://www.sbc.net/resolutions/899/resolution-on-racial-reconciliation-on-the-150th-anniversary-of-the-southern-baptist-convention.

Ringer, Jeffrey M. *Vernacular Christian Rhetoric and Civil Discourse: The Religious Creativity of Evangelical Student Writers*. New York: Routledge, 2016.

Ritchie, Andrea J. *Invisible No More: Police Violence Against Black Women and Women of Color*. Boston: Beacon, 2017.

Roberts-Miller, Patricia. *Deliberate Conflict: Argument, Political Theory, and Composition Classes*. Carbondale: Southern Illinois University Press, 2004.

———. "Dissent as 'Aid and Comfort to the Enemy': The Rhetorical Power of Naïve Realism and Ingroup Identity." *Rhetoric Society Quarterly* 39, no. 2 (2009): 170–88.

———. *Voices in the Wilderness: Public Discourse and the Paradox of Puritan Rhetoric*. Tuscaloosa: University of Alabama Press, 1999.

Robinson, Marilynne. *Gilead*. London: Virago, 2004.

Rothaus, Kyndall R. "Christians Need Consistency in Principles of Inclusion, Compassion." *Waco Tribune-Herald*, December 10, 2016. https://www.wacotrib.com/opinion/columns/guest_columns/kyndall-rae-rothaus-guest-columnist-christians-need-consistency-in-principles/article_f9ca5e87-2990-55f9-b810-099c00cceb24.html.

Royster, Jacqueline Jones, and Gesa E. Kirsch. *Feminist Rhetorical Practices: New Horizons for Rhetoric, Composition, and Literacy Studies*. Carbondale: Southern Illinois University Press, 2012.

Runn, Courtney. "The Year of Jen Hatmaker." *Texas Monthly*, October 4, 2017. https://www.texasmonthly.com/articles/year-jen-hatmaker/

Schechter, Susan. *Women and Male Violence*. Boston: South End, 1982.

Schreiter, Robert. *Constructing Local Theologies*. Maryknoll, NY: Orbis, 1985.

Scribner, Sylvia. "Literacy in Three Metaphors." *American Journal of Education* 93, no. 1 (1984): 6–21.

Sedgwick, Eve Kosofsky, and Adam Frank, eds. *Shame and Its Sisters: A Silvan Tompkins Reader*. Durham, NC: Duke University Press, 1995.

Serisier, Tanya. "Speaking Out Against Rape: Feminist (Her)Stories and Anti-Rape Politics." *Lilith: A Feminist History Journal*, no. 16 (2007): 84–95.

Shaver, Lisa. *Beyond the Pulpit: Women's Rhetorical Roles in the Antebellum Religious Press*. Pittsburgh, PA: University of Pittsburgh Press, 2012.

———. *Reforming Women: The Rhetorical Tactics of the American Female Moral Reform Society, 1834–1854*. Pittsburgh, PA: University of Pittsburgh Press, 2018.

Shaw, Adrienne. "The Internet Is Full of Jerks Because the World Is Full of Jerks: What Feminist Theory Teaches Us about the Internet." *Communication and Critical/Cultural Studies* 11, no. 3 (2014): 273–77.

Shaw, Susan M. *God Speaks to Us, Too: Southern Baptist Women on Church, Home, and Society*. Lexington: University Press of Kentucky, 2008.

———. "Gracious Submission: Southern Baptist Fundamentalists and Women." *NWSA Journal* 20, no. 1 (2008): 51–77.

Shearer-Cremean, Christine, and Carol Winkelman, eds. *Survivor Rhetoric: Negotiations and Narrativity in Abused Women's Language*. Toronto: University of Toronto Press, 2004.

Shurden, Walter B. *The Baptist Identity: Four Fragile Freedoms*. Macon, GA: Smyth and Helwys, 1993.

Sills, Sophie, Chelsea Pickens, Karishma Beach, Lloyd Jones, Octavia Calder-Dawe, Paulette Benton-Greig, and Nicola Gavey. "Rape Culture and Social Media: Young Critics and a Feminist Counterpublic." *Feminist Media Studies* 16, no. 6 (2016): 935–51.

Simonson, Peter. "Reinventing Invention, Again." *Rhetoric Society Quarterly* 44, no. 4 (2014): 299–322.

Smietana, Bob. "Megachurch Pastor John Ortberg Kept a Family Member's Attraction to Children Secret. Then His Son Blew the Whistle." Religion News Service, July 6, 2020, https://religionnews.com/2020/07/06/megachurch-pastor-john-ortberg-family-member-attraction-to-children-secret-menlo-church-daniel-lavery-whistelblower.

———. "Pastors Seldom Preach About Domestic Violence." LifeWay Research, June 27, 2014. https://lifewayresearch.com/2014/06/27/pastors-seldom-preach-about-domestic-violence/.

Smith, Andrea. *Native Americans and the Christian Right: The Gendered Politics of Unlikely Alliances*. Durham, NC: Duke University Press, 2008.

Southwestern Baptist Theological Seminary (SWBTS) Board of Trustees. "Statement Regarding Dr. Paige Patterson." Southwestern Baptist Theological Seminary, May 23, 2018. https://swbts.edu/news/releases/statement-regarding-dr-paige-patterson/.

Southwestern Baptist Theological Seminary (SWBTS) Board of Trustees Executive Committee. "Statement by the Southwestern Theological Seminary." Southwestern Baptist Theological Seminary, May 30, 2018. https://swbts.edu/news/releases/statement-southwestern-theological-seminary/.

Stenberg, Shari J. "Liberation Theology and Liberatory Pedagogies: Renewing the Dialogue." *College English* 68, no. 3 (2006): 271–90.

———. "'Tweet Me Your First Assaults': Writing Shame and the Rhetorical Work of #NotOkay." *Rhetoric Society Quarterly* 48, no. 2 (2018): 119–38.

Sterling, Dorothy. *Ahead of Her Time: Abby Kelley and the Politics of Antislavery*. New York: W. W. Norton, 1991.

Stetzer, Ed. "Paige Patterson and Doing the Right Thing for the SBC, Again." *Christianity Today*, April 30, 2018. https://www.christianitytoday.com/edstetzer/2018/may/paige-patterson-end-of-era.html.

Storey, John. *Texas Baptist Leadership and Social Christianity, 1900–1980*. College Station: Texas A&M University Press, 1987.

Summers, Gertrude, and Nina S. Feldman. "Blaming the Victim Versus Blaming the Perpetrator: An Attributional Analysis of Spouse Abuse." *Journal of Social and Clinical Psychology* 2, no. 4 (1984): 339–47.

Sunstein, Cass. *Going to Extremes: How Like Minds Unite and Divide*. Oxford: Oxford University Press, 2009.

Swavola, Elizabeth, Kristine Riley, and Ram Subramanian. *Overlooked: Women and Jails in an Era of Reform*. Vera Institute of Justice. 2016.

Taylor, Justin. "The Incredible Testimony as a Former Gymnast Confronts Her Sexual Abuser in Court." Gospel Coalition, January 24, 2018. https://www.thegospelcoalition.org/blogs/justin-taylor/incredible-testimony-former-gymnast-confronts-sexual-abuser-court/.

Terrell, JoAnne M. *Power in the Blood? The Cross in the African American Experience*. Eugene, OR: Wipf and Stock, 2005.

Thistlethwaite, Susan Brooks. "Every Two Minutes: Battered Women and Feminist Interpretation." In *Feminist Interpretation of the Bible*, edited by Letty M. Russell, 96–110. Philadelphia: Westminster, 1985.

Thomas, D. L., and M. Cornwall. "Religion and Family in the 1980s: Discovery and Development." *Journal of Marriage and the Family* 52, no. 4 (1990): 983–92.

Thompson, Becky. *A Promise and a Way of Life: White Antiracist Activism*. Minneapolis: University of Minnesota Press, 2001.

Thomson-Bunn, Heather. "Mediating Discursive Worlds: When Academic Norms and Religious Belief Conflict." *College English* 79, no. 3 (2017): 276–96.

Tierney, Kathleen J. "The Battered Women Movement and the Creation of the Wife Beating Problem." *Social Problems* 29, no. 3 (1982): 207–20.

Tucker, Ruth A. *Black and White Bible, Black and Blue Wife: My Story of Finding Hope After Domestic Abuse*. Grand Rapids, MI: Zondervan, 2016.

Turner, Laura. "How Long Can Evangelical Women Stay Behind Donald Trump?" *Politico*, October 12, 2016. https://www.politico.com/magazine/

story/2016/10/donald-trump-evangelical-women-2016-videotape-214346.

Ueckert, Kevin. "Statement by Kevin Ueckert, Chairman of the Board of Trustees." Southwestern Baptist Theological Seminary, June 1, 2018. https://swbts.edu/news/releases/statement-kevin-ueckert-chairman-board-trustees/.

Vander Lei, Elizabeth. "'Ain't We Having Fun Yet?': Teaching Writing in a Violent World." In *Renovating Rhetoric in Christian Tradition*, edited by Elizabeth Vander Lei et al., 89–104. Pittsburgh, PA: University of Pittsburgh Press, 2014.

Vander Lei, Elizabeth, Thomas Amorose, Beth Daniell, and Anne Ruggles Gere, eds. *Renovating Rhetoric in Christian Tradition*. Pittsburgh, PA: University of Pittsburgh Press, 2014.

Waldenfels, Hans. "Contextual Theology." In *Dictionary of Mission: Theology, History, Perspectives*, edited by Karl Muller, Theo Sundermeier, Stephen B. Bevans, and Richard H. Bliese, 82–87. Maryknoll, NY: Orbis, 1985.

Warner, Michael. *Publics and Counterpublics*. New York: Zone, 2002.

Warner, Michael, Jonathan Van Antwerpen, and Craig Calhoun, eds. *Varieties of Secularism in a Secular Age*. Cambridge, MA: Harvard University Press, 2010.

Weddle, Kendra, and Jann Aldredge-Clanton. *Building Bridges: Letha Dawson Scanzoni and Friends*. Eugene, OR: Cascade, 2018.

"We Were Rachael's Church." Immanuel Baptist Church, May 31, 2018. https://immanuelky.org/articles/we-were-rachaels-church/.

Whipple, Vicky. "Counseling Battered Women from Fundamentalist Churches." *Journal of Marital and Family Therapy* 13, no. 3 (1987): 251–58.

Williams, Daniel K. "The Partisan Trajectory of the American Pro-Life Movement: How a Liberal Catholic Campaign Became a Conservative Evangelical Cause." *Religions* 6 (2015): 451–75.

Williams, Delores S. *Sisters in the Wilderness: The Challenge of Womanist God-Talk*. Maryknoll, NY: Orbis, 1993.

Williams, Mark Alan. "Transformations: Locating Agency and Difference in Student Accounts of Religious Experience." *College English* 77, no. 4 (2015): 338–63.

Williams, Sherri. "#SayHerName: Using Digital Activism to Document Violence Against Black Women." *Feminist Media Studies* 16, no. 5 (2016): 923–25.

Winkelmann, Carol. *The Language of Battered Women: A Rhetorical Analysis of Personal Theologies*. Albany: SUNY Press, 2004.

Winston, Kimberly. "Popular Christian Author Eric Metaxas Stands by Donald Trump." *Religion News Service*, October 12, 2016. https://religionnews.com/2016/10/12/popular-christian-author-eric-metaxas-stands-by-donald-trump/.

Woodruff, Betsy. "Evangelical Leaders Shrug at Donald Trump's Lewd Comments." *Daily Beast*, October 7, 2016. https://www.thedailybeast.com/evangelical-leaders-shrug-at-donald-trumps-lewd-comments.

Worthen, Molly. *Apostles of Reason: The Crisis of Authority in American Evangelicalism*. New York: Oxford University Press, 2014.

Zaeke, Susan. *Signatures of Citizenship: Petitioning, Antislavery, and Women's Political Identity*. Chapel Hill: University of North Carolina Press, 2003.

Zapotosky, Matt. "Judge Strikes Down Trump Administration Effort to Deny Asylum for Migrants Fleeing Gang Violence, Domestic Abuse." *Washington Post*, December 19, 2018. https://www.washingtonpost.com/world/national-security/judge-strikes-down-trump-administration-effort-to-deny-asylum-for-migrants-fleeing-gag-violence-domestic-abuse/2018/12/19/61687d00-03b1-11e9-b6a9-0aa5c2fcc9e4_story.html.

INDEX

abortion: and evangelical community/leadership, 14; and feminist activism against sexual and domestic violence, 34, 38–39, 58
Abortion Speak Out, Washington Square United Methodist Church, 34
Abyssinian Baptist Church, Harlem, 50
Adams, Carol J., *Woman-Battering*, xiv
Adams-Roberts, Aesha, 89
agency: gained by sexual abuse survivors through sacred texts, 148n58; grace, and social transformation, xiv, 52; and values recommitment, 5, 9
age of consent, nineteenth-century, 33–34, 39
Al-Anon, xii–xiii, xiv, xxiii, 52, 107, 127
Aldredge-Clanton, Jann, 40
American Female Moral Reform Society (AFMRS), 32–34, 39, 41
Anderson, Dianna, 14, 55, 58
anti-CRT/I campaign, 30, 105, 106, 115, 118
Antinomian Controversy, 28–31
antinomianism, 22, 147n49; demoralized forgiveness or cheap grace, 82; and differing standards for in-group and out-group members, 75–76, 115; and evangelical responses to sexual violence, 69
anti-rape movement: and movement to destigmatize abortion, 34; and rape as war, 13; rape crisis centers and legal changes toward rape, 12, 35; replication of dominant racial attitudes, 36
anti-violence movement, 33–38; appropriation by racialized state power, 37–38; professionalization and social services approach, 35–36; replication of dominant racial attitudes, 36; state and national networks and legislative campaigns, 35
"apostolic" and "prophetic" rhetoric, 89–90, 108, 122
archives, survivor-generated: of abuse and healing, 108, 110–15, 113; affect-transforming and community-forming functions, 108; photographs, memories, and scriptures, 108, 113, 115
atonement theology, 4–5, 121
Augsburger, David, 68

Balmer, Randall, 8–9, 14, 39
Bambara, Toni, *The Salt Eaters*, xiii
"Baptistification," 88
Bass, Ellen, and Laura Davis, *Courage to Heal, The*, xxiii
Bauman, Belinda, 44, 53
Beaty, Katelyn, 48
Believed, NPR podcast series on Larry Nassar, 65
Bernstein, Elizabeth, 47
Boston Globe, Investigative Staff of the, *Betrayal* (book), 104
Biden, Joseph R., Jr., 139n41
Black Liberation movement: police brutality and sexual violence against activists, 34, 37, 126; propaganda against by segregationists, 25, 30
Black men: constituting more than 80 of executions for rape between 1700 and 1820, 30–31; trope of Black male rapist, 36–37
Black women: historical movement against sexual violence and

lynching, 36–37; and rape culture, 13; sexual and labor exploitation of in slavery, 4; sexualization of, 14; and sexualized violence in police encounters, 13; spirituality-informed fiction, xii, 53; tensions with white women activists, 33
Bonhoeffer, Dietrich: *The Cost of Discipleship*, 50–51; distinction between "cheap grace" and "costly grace," 21, 48–52, 55, 64, 75; and "justification of the sinner," 61
Borg, Marcus J., 51–52
Bowler, Kate, 18, 51
Brock, Rita Nakashima, 4, 17
Brock, Rita Nakashima, and Rebecca Ann Parker, *Proverbs of Ashes: Violence, Redemptive Suffering, and the Search for What Saves Us*, 4
Brown, Brené: on confession, 51–52; TED Talk on Shame, 18
Brown, Christa, 85
Brownmiller, Susan, 12, 35, 36, 138n33
Bunker, Hannah, 111, 115
Burke, Kenneth, 4, 5, 69, 70, 148n54
Burke, Tarana, 7, 43

Camp, L. Raymond, 89
"carceral feminism," 47
Carey, Tamika L., *Rhetorical Healing: The Reeducation of Contemporary Black Womanhood*, xii–xiii
"casuistic stretching," 6, 69, 70–72, 73, 148
"casuistic tightening": and enclave deliberation, 6, 65, 69, 71, 120, 124; and forgiveness, grace, and sin, 22, 76–82, 120–21
casuistry, as case-based approach to practical ethics, 65, 148n52
"cheap grace": distinction from "costly grace," 48–49, 120; and expressive justice, 121; and instant forgiveness for in-group members, 76, 124, 128; and political alliances, 35; resistance to confession and repentance, 51–52
"Chicago Declaration," 39
Christianity Today, 22, 48, 66, 67–68, 73, 92
Christians for Biblical Equality (CBE), 40–41, 42
#ChurchToo, xi, 7, 15, 20, 22, 28, 42–44, 53, 83, 85, 113, 114, 123, 127, 128; as enclave version of #MeToo, 28; GC2 summit, 44–45
civil rights movement. *See* Black Liberation movement
Clergy Consultation Service, 34
Clinton, Hillary, 46, 55
Combahee River Collective (CRC), 37
Committee for Equal Justice for the Rights of Mrs. Recy Taylor, 37
commonplaces. *See* proverbs of ashes
community preservation/boundary policing, evangelical/Baptist communities, 42, 47, 55, 106, 109–10, 124
complementarianism, evangelical/Southern Baptist communities, 30, 41–42, 44, 57, 89, 96–97, 115, 117–18, 122–23, 144n53
Conservative Resurgence, 84, 118, 123
contamination concerns, White Christian America, 3, 24–28, 30, 106, 110, 117–18, 139n43
"contextual theology," 4, 20, 69
Cooper-White, Pamela, 55, 68, 92
Cope, Emily M., 56, 89
"costly grace": distinction from "cheap grace," 48–52, 64, 75; and evangelical activist women, 57–58, 60–61, 63, 120–21; and sacrifice of strong social order, 53–54
Council for Biblical Manhood and Womanhood, 41
COVID-19, and domestic violence, ix
Crenshaw, Kimberlé, 28

criminal justice system: incarceration practices, and feminist and anti-violence concerns, 38; and racial discrimination, 36
critical race theory and intersectionality (CRT/I), 105–6
Crowley, Sharon, xiv, 6, 63
Cvetkovich, Ann, xiv, 16, 17, 26

Dadas, Caroline, 28
Daniell, Beth: *A Communion of Friendship*, xii–xiii, xiv, xxi, xxiii, 107, 121, 127; and literacy as grace, 52–53, 59
Davis, Angela: Pacifica Radio program, 36; *Women, Race, and Class*, 36
DC Rape Crisis Center, 12
deliberative democratic discourse, 10–11, 48
Denhollander, Rachel, xxi, 15, 20, 21–22, 83; and accountability of in-group sexual aggressors in evangelical communities, 20, 65, 68–69, 75–76, 127; biblicism, 72–73; *Christianity Today* interview, 66–67, 73; and community preservationism, 124; and 2019 Ethics of Religious Liberty Committee convention, 105, 106, 118; on grace and forgiveness, 69, 70–72, 74, 79–82, 112, 147n38; reinvention of proverbs of ashes, 69, 72, 75, 123, 128; and repentance as involving intention and impact, 80–81; responses to Moore's Twitter archive on abuse, 104, 113–14; as survivor of childhood sexual abuse and abuse by Nasser, 66; victim impact statement at sentencing of Larry Nassar, 21–22, 66–69, 79–82
DePalma, Michael-John, 122
Desser, Daphne, 16–17
divine grace: and forgiveness, 77, 147n37; as remedy for sin, 49–50. *See also* grace
Dobson, James, 40, 135n78, 144n63
domestic violence: and COVID-19, ix; victim stigmatization in encounters with helping professionals, 13. *See also* trauma, and sexual and domestic violence
domestic violence shelters, 1960s and 1970s, 35
Downen, Robert, Lise Olsen, and John Tedesco, "Abuse of Faith" series, responses of evangelical women and survivors of childhood sexual abuse, 22, 105–6, 108, 111–15, 124

Edwards, Jonathan, and "evangelical humiliation," 101
election. *See* salvation
enclave deliberation: and "casuistic tightening," 71, 120; and costly rhetorical grace over cheap grace, 64, 121; denominational-specific, 22, 87; and differences among participants, 7; and group polarization, 11; and groupthink, 11; and #MeToo movement, 42–43; and the public sphere, 9–12; and religious conviction, 123; and repentance, 125; and rhetorical invention, 6–7; and sexual and domestic violence, x, xiv, 2–3. *See also* faithful deliberation, rhetorical invention for
evangelical community/leadership: and complementarian gender lines, 41–42, 57, 115; concern with purity culture, and failure to confront rape culture, 3, 50, 54, 58; conflation of sexual violence and sexuality, 54, 56, 69, 75, 77–78; defined, x, 7–8; differing responses to sexual violence and rape, 48–49; heteronormative marriage as only acceptable form of sexuality, 75, 123–24; impediments to LGBTQ+ rights, 14, 75; and in-group

trust and forgiveness of accused sexual aggressors, ix, 55, 58, 62, 68–69, 71–72, 75–76, 115, 124, 128; opposition to private school desegregation, 8–9, 39, 139n43; responses to Trump's *Access Hollywood* remarks, 48, 54–56, 95; theological and political diversity, 8, 88; in 2016 US presidential election, x. *See also* community preservation/boundary policing, evangelical/Baptist communities; contamination concerns, White Christian America; proverbs of ashes; purity culture; rape culture
evangelical feminism: Evangelicals for Social Action (ESA), 39; Evangelical Women's Caucus (EWC), 39–41, 115–16, 139n47; interactions with public sphere and evangelical subculture, 42, 139–40n50; sex and marriage guides, 39; in the tradition of earlier evangelical women, 39–40
evangelical women activists. *See* evangelical feminism; faithful deliberation, rhetorical invention for; Southern Baptist women; White Christian America, historical precedents to twenty-first century
evangelism, and reshaping boundaries of Christian communities, 100, 110
Eves, Rosalyn C., 89
"expressive justice," 35, 81, 116, 121

faithful deliberation, rhetorical invention for, 6–9; and action for community-internal change, 2–3; challenges to "cheap grace," 31–32, 35; and community boundaries and resistance to change, 35; and feminist rhetorical ethics of hope and care, 5, 19–20, 87, 122–25; fruits of, 82–83; possibilities for, 120–21; redefining of "proverbs of ashes" about abuse and violence, ix–x, xiii, 3–4, 20, 26, 32, 49, 53–56, 64, 69, 72, 75, 120, 123, 128; and repentance, 125; and values recommitment, 5. *See also* enclave deliberation; proverbs of ashes
Falwell, Jerry, 22, 97
Falwell, Jerry, Jr., 22, 55, 56, 97
fellowship: and archive of abuse and healing, 110–15, 120–21; and encounters with difference, 109–10; through scriptural reinterpretation, 114–15
feminism: 1960s and 1970s, 34; and nineteenth-century evangelical revivals, 32; and post-traumatic stress disorders in women abuse victims, 16; rape and domestic violence movements, 13, 34
feminist/womanist theology: assessments of religiously supported violence, 5, 87; theological reflection, 19–20. *See also* faithful deliberation, rhetorical invention for
Fisher, Frank, 50
Ford, Christine Blasey, 127
forgiveness: as *aphiemi*, 149n73; "fantasy of," "magical," or "instant," 68, 74, 120; as proverbs of ashes, 69, 72–75, 78, 147n38; revitalized, 68
Fortune, Marie, 42, 68, 147n38, 149n68
Founders Ministries, *By What Standard?*, 118

Gere, Anne Ruggles, xxiii
Gilyard, Darrell, 85, 113–14
Ginsburg, Ruth Bader, 47
Godbeer, Richard, 31
grace: and agency and social transformation, xiv, 52; as Christian theological concept, 49; distinction between "cheap grace" and "costly grace," 48–49; literacy as, 52–53; as remedy for

sin, 49–50. *See also* "cheap grace"; "costly grace"
Graham, Billy, 105
Great Commandment, 45
Great Commission, 44–45
Grimké, Sarah and Angelina, 32, 121, 125; attacks by clergy on their public abolitionist lectures, 25, 30; campaign against sexual exploitation of slaves, 24–26; responses to clergymen's cult of white womanhood, 25–26; "Social Intercourse of the Sexes," 24–25

Habermas, Jürgen, 9–10
Hall, David D., 30
Hamer, Fannie Lou, 126–27
Hardesty, Nancy A., 32
Harper, Lisa Sharon, 44, 53, 141n70
Harris, Joshua, *I Kissed Dating Goodbye*, 15
Hatmaker, Jen, xi, xxi, 20, 102, 117, 128; and affirmation of LGBTQ+ rights, 116; and Austin New Church, 60; backlash against her "costly grace," 29, 63; challenge to in-group trust of evangelical leadership, 62; and the "Christian Machine," 63–64; and costly rhetorical grace as tool for perceptual shift, 49, 60–61, 63–64, 121; "IF:Gathering," 51, 59; reply to Moore's Twitter post on abuse, 112; response to Trump's *Access Hollywood* comments on sexual abuse, 16, 21, 47–48, 59–62; signatory of #SilenceIsNotSpiritual statement, 60; and values articulation, 56
healing: in emotionally connected groups, 23; listening and, 19, 45, 107–8; rhetorical, xii–xiii, 16–17
Herman, Judith, 16, 17–18, 68, 74, 81
Hogg, Charlotte, 20
Humphreys, Fisher, 88, 123
Hutchinson, Anne, 28–30
Hybels, Bill, 44, 131n32

Immanuel Baptist Church (IBC), "We Were Rachael's Church," 82–83
immigrants: Trump's equation of with racialized sexual violence, 47. *See also* migrant children, vulnerability to sexual abuse as result of family separation policy
independent fundamental Baptist (IFB), multiple instances of sexual abuse among institutions, 104–5
Ingersoll, Julie, 41
intention, and repentance, 80, 149n68
intersectionality, 6, 26, 28, 30, 34, 35, 38 105–6

Jeffress, Robert, 54, 55, 56, 62
Jesus, 17, 24, 42, 44, 51, 64, 66, 70, 74, 93, 95, 98, 102; death as atonement for sins of humanity, 4–5, 7; fellowship, 110; forgiveness, 147n37; grace, 49, 50, 72; and healing, xiii, 82; John 7:53–8:11 (*Pericope Adulterae*), 76–79; reconciliation, 90–91, 99–100; and repentance, 52, 57–58, 144n63, 149n68; use of antithesis, 61
Job, 1–2, 3–4, 5, 13
John 7:53–8:11 (*Pericope Adulterae*), 76–79
Jones, L. Gregory, 50, 52, 69
Jones, Robert P., 91–92
Jones, Serene, 53
Jonsen, Albert R., 70–71
Joy, Emily, 15, 43–44, 53, 123, 141n70
just-world hypothesis, 12–13, 30, 73

Kell, Carl L., 89
Kirsch, Gesa E., 19
#KissShameBye, 15

LaHaye, Tim and Beverly: *The Act of*

Marriage, 39; *Left Behind* series, 139n46
Lavery, Danny M., 15
Lerner, Melvin, 12
LGBTQ+ community, xxi, 35, 37, 58, 108; and evangelical leadership, 13–14, 15, 40, 75, 115–16, 144n54; Moore's theology of LGBTQ+ sexuality, 23, 106, 116–18; and rape culture, 13
LifeWay Research, 7, 57, 63, 92, 147n49
literacy, as grace, 52–53
literacy communions, 107–8
Lively, Megan, 113
Living Proof Ministries, ix, 21, 56, 76, 92, 109
Lord's Supper (or communion, fellowship), 106, 108–9
Luther, Martin, 28–30
Lynch, Paul, 70

MacArthur, John, ix, xv
Maddux, Kristi, 5
Mahaney, C. J., 15, 67, 76
Mahmood, Saba, 20
Mannon, Bethany, 59–60
Marty, Martin E., 88, 123
Mattingly, Carol, 44, 88
Merritt, Jonathan, 116
Metaxas, Eric, 55–56
#MeToo movement: and knowledge-action gap, xiv–xv; mainstreaming of, x–xii, 2, 17, 21, 57, 64, 87, 113; and parallel developments in religious contexts, 7, 28; and reshaping of public and evangelical discourse, 8, 20, 22, 32, 42–45, 85, 87, 102, 127–28
migrant children, vulnerability to sexual abuse as result of family separation policy, 37–38, 139n40
Milano, Alyssa, 7, 42–43
Mohler, Al, 67, 117; "The Humiliation of the Southern Baptist Convention," 86, 100–102; opposition to database of abusers, 127–28
Mollenkott, Virginia Ramey, 40, 139–40n50
Moore, Beth, xxi, 20, 24; "Abuse of Faith" response, and social media posts from survivors of childhood sexual abuse, 22, 105–6, 108, 111–15, 124; antithesis, 95–96; backlash against for responses to religious controversies, 29, 32, 105–6, 116, 118–19; biblicism, 72, 76–79, 82; call for accountability of in-group sexual aggressors in evangelical communities, ix, 68–69, 74–75, 87, 102; and "casuistic tightening" of forgiveness and grace, 69, 70–72, 76–82, 148n54; and complementarianism, 22–23, 57, 117, 125; and costly rhetorical grace, 42, 49, 57–58, 63; departure from the Southern Baptist Convention, 87; *Esther: It's Tough Being a Woman*, 115; and fellowship as seeking out difference, 23, 118; on forgiveness and biblical principles, 71–72, 78–79; and Hatmaker, 64; "A Letter to My Brothers," 86, 92–96, 102, 125; and Living Proof Ministries, ix, 56; *LPM Blog*, 92–93; and misogyny, 21–22, 48, 87, 93–96, 118, 124; and narrow boundaries of evangelical communities, 109–10, 143n48; and *Pericope Adulterae* (John 7:53–8:11), 76–79; and rape culture and sexual violence as sin, 58; reconciliation, rhetoric of, 93–96; reinvention of proverbs of ashes, 69, 72–73, 123, 128; repentance over conflict avoidance, 57, 59; response to Denhollander's impact statement, 67–68; response to Trump's *Access Hollywood* comments about sexual abuse of women, xi, 47–48, 56–59; revision of *Praying God's Word*, 117–18; social media activism,

16, 21, 22, 42, 86, 92–93, 102, 105–6, 108, 111–15; strategies to define oratorical career as not preaching, 56–57, 89, 144n53; as survivor of childhood sexual abuse, 57, 59; on "the church's silence," 31; theology of LGBTQ+ sexuality, 23, 116–18; and values articulation, 56; "What about the Church's Silence?," 125, 148n52
Moore, Russell: and ERLC panel on sexual abuse, 105, 118; racial reconciliation agenda, 91, 118
Morgan, Marabel, *The Total Woman*, 39

Nassar, Larry, criminal trial and sentencing for sexual assault, 21, 65–66, 67, 68, 72, 75, 79–82, 118
National Council of Negro Women, 37
New York Radical Feminists (NYRF): 1971 Rape Speak-out on Rape, 34, 37; and term "rape culture," 12
#NotOkay, 111

Ortberg, John, III, 15
Ortberg, John, Jr., 15

Paasch, Hannah, 43–44, 53, 123
Pacifica Radio, 36, 138n34
Parker, Rebecca Ann, 4, 17
Parks, Rosa, 37
Pascal, Blaise, 70, 148n54
"Pastoral Letter of the General Association of Congregational Ministers of Massachusetts, The," 25
Patterson, Paige, 17, 22, 44, 87, 92–93; inappropriate responses to clergy misconduct and sexual assault victims, 84–86, 100, 102, 113–14, 127; influence within SBC, 84–86, 89; and "Letter to SWBTS Board of Trustees" from SBC women members, 86, 96–100, 122, 124; termination from SWBTS, 85–86, 100–102, 104
Paul, St., 28, 71, 90–92, 96, 98, 152n51
Pavia, Catherine M., 6–7
Pentecostalism, 87, 90
Pericope Adulterae (John 7:53–8:11), 76–79
Powell, Adam Clayton, 50
Pressler, Paul, sexual assault lawsuit against, 84, 105
Prior, Karen Swallow, xxi, 20, 22, 97, 128
Probyn, Elspeth, 18
proverbs of ashes, 1, 2, 102, 121, 122, 126; and casuistic stretching, 65, 73; and conflation of sexual violence with sexuality, 54, 69, 75, 77; defined, 9; forgiveness as, 68–69, 72–75, 147n38, 378; and "instant forgiveness," 54–55; minimization of trauma, xv, 3, 20, 49, 75, 86, 120; reinforcement of rape culture, 3, 12, 18, 49, 61; reinvention of through rhetorical work, ix–x, xiii, 3–4, 9, 20, 26, 32, 45, 49, 53–56, 64, 69, 72, 75, 114, 119, 120, 123, 128; within white evangelical subcultures, 3, 21
public sphere, and deliberative democratic discourse, 9–11, 32, 37, 42–45, 123, 132n37
Puritanism, 27, 123; doctrines of signs and preparation, 29; religious and social disputes, and politics, 28–30; and same-sex intimacy, 31
purity culture, 9, 12, 14–15, 18, 19, 20, 24, 25–26, 27, 28, 31, 32, 38, 45, 48, 60–61, 126; and conflation of sexual violence with sexuality, 124; conflation of womanhood with whiteness, 30, 53–54, 124; and cult of true womanhood, 25; in evangelical communities, 3, 43–44, 50, 54, 58, 59, 64, 98, 123–24, 135n78; and women's bodies as shameful, 3

rape: and eighteenth-century

reinforcement of patriarchal white supremacy, 30–31; as a political issue, 12; as tool of lynching, 36–37; and trope of Black male rapist, 36–37; as war, 16. *See also* anti-rape movement; rape culture
rape culture, 12–14; commonplaces reinforcing, 3, 12, 18, 49, 61; delegitimization of survivors' discourse, 13; and just-world hypothesis, 12–13, 73; and LGBTQ+ community, 13; as sin, 58; and trivialization of sexual trauma and violence, 3, 12, 31; and women of color, 13; and Women's Christian Temperance Union (WCTU), 33
Rauschenbusch, Walter, 88
reconciliation, rhetoric of, 5, 51, 89–92, 120–21, 123–24; and Christian engagement with racial injustice, 91–92; focus on pain and transformation, 90; St. Paul and, 90–91
Redstockings, 34
Reed, Ralph, 54, 55, 56. 62
repentance: and "cheap grace," 51, 91–92; and commitment to implementing change, 80, 92, 149n68; and community transformation, 54; and "costly grace," 57–58; and faithful deliberation, 125
researchers, positionality and responsibilities, xiv–xv
revenge fantasy, 17–18, 81–82
rhetorical healing, xii–xiii, 16–17
rhetorical invention. *See* faithful deliberation, rhetorical invention for; proverbs of ashes
Ringer, Jeffrey M., xiv, 6, 48, 56, 71, 122
Rivera, Sylvia, 35
Roberts-Miller, Patricia, 10, 11, 30, 132n37, 135n78
Roe vs. Wade, 38–39
Rohan, Liz, 89
Roman Catholic Church, and clerical abuse of children, 85, 104
Rothaus, Kyndall Rae, 54, 58, 144n54
Royster, Jacqueline Jones, 19
Russell, Diana, 36

salvation, 7, 28–29, 32, 49–50, 94, 128
Scanzoni, Letha, 40, 139–40n50
Scanzoni, Letha, and Virginia Ramey Mollenkott, *Is the Homosexual My Neighbor*, 40
school desegregation, and white fears of moral contamination by Black students, 8–9, 39, 139n43
Scottsboro Boys, 36–37, 138n33
scriptural reinterpretation, and fellowship, 114–15
Sension, Nicholas, 31
Sessions, Jeff, 37–38
sexual violence: and Black activist women, 36–37; and Black liberation movement, 34, 126; conflation with sexuality, 54, 56, 69, 75, 77–78, 124. *See also* rape; survivors, of sexual abuse; trauma, and sexual and domestic violence
shame, of abuse survivors, 18
Shange, Ntozake, 53
Shaver, Lisa, 32
Shaw, Susan, 89
Shurden, Walter B., 88
#SilenceIsNotSpiritual, xi, 7, 20, 22, 42, 44, 53, 60, 83, 85; as enclave version of #MeToo, 28
Simonson, Peter, 6
sin: defined, 49; and forgiveness and repentance, 77–82; rape culture and sexual violence as, 58; "sexual sins," 76–78; from standpoint of harm, 77–78
skepticism, 8, 11, 125–27
Smith, Andrea, 40, 41
social Christianity: distinction from

Social Gospel, 87–88, 150n13; and Southern Baptists, 87–88, 92, 94, 122
social media writing, of sexual assault survivors, 18. *See also* archives, survivor-generated; Denhollander, Rachel; Hatmaker, Jen; Moore, Beth
Southeastern Baptist Theological Seminary (SEBTS), 84, 97
Southern Baptist community: boundary policing: and doctrinal line-drawing, 115–19; and evangelism, 100, 110; and fellowship, 106; four freedoms, 88, 91; and institutional autonomy, 96; lack of support for LGBTQ+ community, 115; opposition to CRT/I, 115; and preaching of women, 116–17; and Prohibition movement, 8; and reconciliation, 91; and social Christianity, 87–88, 92, 94, 100, 122. *See also* community preservation/ boundary policing; complementarianism, evangelical/ Southern Baptist communities; contamination concerns, White Christian America; evangelical community/leadership; Southern Baptist Convention (SBC); Southern Baptist women
Southern Baptist Convention (SBC), ix, 14, 22, 42, 56; "Abuse of Faith" documentation of sexual abuse by affiliated personnel and leaders, 105; and authoritarianism, 87, 123; and autonomy of women, 89; *The Baptist Faith and Message*, 89, 96, 98, 109; boundary policing; and CRT/I, 118; Ethics of Religious Liberty Committee (ERLC), 91, 105; and responses to sexual and domestic violence, 84–87, 96–100; rhetoric of reconciliation, 124. *See also* community preservation/boundary policing; complementarianism, evangelical/ Southern Baptist communities; evangelical community/leadership; Patterson, Paige
Southern Baptist women: conflicted relationship to nontraditional roles and feminism, 89; and gender complementarianism, 96–97, 115, 122–23; history of varying freedoms and constraints within SBC, 87; and importance of evangelism, 99–100; "Letter to SWBTS Board of Trustees," 86, 96–100, 122, 124; and preaching, 116–17; and rhetoric of reconciliation, 86–87, 92, 97–98; and social Christianity, 124. *See also* faithful deliberation, rhetorical invention for
Southwestern Baptist Theological Seminary (SWBTS), 84; Patterson's inappropriate responses to clergy misconduct and sexual assault victims, 84–86, 100, 102, 113–14; termination of Paige Patterson, 85–86, 100–102, 104
Sovereign Grace Churches (SGC), 15, 76; child sexual abuse allegations surrounding, 66–67, 83
Spotlight (film), 85, 104
Stenberg, Shari, 12, 18, 74
Stetzer, Ed, 92, 93, 97
Storey, John, 87–88, 150n13
survivors, of sexual abuse, 74, 147n42; archives of abuse and healing, 110–15; centering of, 20, 27, 106, 121–22. *See also* rape culture; trauma, and sexual and domestic violence
Survivors Network of those Abused by Priests (SNAP), 85

Taylor, Recy, 37
Terrell, JoAnne Marie, 4–5, 17
theological reflection, and deliberation and invention, 5, 19–21, 26, 49, 75, 120

Thigpen, Tiffany, 113–14
Thistlethwaite, Susan Brooks, 124, 148n58
Till, Emmett, kidnapping and murder, 36, 138n33
Toulmin, Stephen, 70–71
transgender women, sexualized violence against in police encounters, 13
trauma, and sexual and domestic violence: collective trauma, 16; and listening, 19, 45, 107–8; minimized through religious rhetoric, 3, 12, 31, 54; and perceptions of "others," 13; as "unclaimed experience," 19. *See also* archives, survivor-generated; healing; survivors, of sexual abuse
true womanhood, cult of, 3, 14, 25, 39
Trump, Donald J., x, 41; call for reinstatement of death penalty, 46; equation of immigrants with racialized sexual violence, 47; fueling of hatred toward Central Park Five, 46–47; sexual assault discourses, and evangelical responses, xi, 16, 21, 46–62, 95; support of White Christian America, xi, 8, 47, 56, 62–63, 144n63

Ueckert, Kevin, 98, 102

values articulation, and rhetoric reinvention, 48, 56, 65
Violence Against Women Act (VAWA), 37–38
Violent Crime Control and Law Enforcement Act of 1994, 38

Walker, Alice, 53; *The Color Purple*, xii, 156n10; *The Temple of My Familiar*, xii, 127
Warner, Michael, 9
Warren, Kay, 81
Warren, Rick, 81
Weddle, Kendra, 40
Wells, Ida B., and rape as tool of lynching, 36–37
Welter, Barbara, 14
Wheelwright, John, 29
White Christian America, 5, 8; contamination concerns, 3, 24–28, 30, 106, 110, 117–18, 139n43; reconciliation efforts to address racial injustices, 91–92; religious rhetoric, and boundary policing, 37–38; resistance to school desegregation, 8–9, 39, 139n43; support for Trump, xi, 8, 47, 56, 62–63; "White Christian Strategy," 56, 64. *See also* evangelical community/leadership; Southern Baptist community; White Christian America, historical precedents to twenty-first century
White Christian America, historical precedents to twenty-first century, 21; Antinomian Controversy, 28–31; anti-violence movement, 33–38; discursive rules, boundaries, and responses to sexual and domestic trauma, 25–28; evangelical feminism, 38–42; evangelical women's activism, nineteenth century, 24–26, 30–33, 38; Puritan beginnings, 28–31. *See also* Grimké, Sarah and Angelina; White Christian America
Willard, Frances, 36, 96
Williams, Delores, 4, 5, 17
Winkelmann, Carol L., 53, 148n58
Winthrop, John, *A Short Story of the Rise, reign, and ruine of the Antinomians, Familists & Libertines, that infected the Churches of New England*, 30
women of color, and rape culture, 13. *See also* Black women
Woman's Christian Temperance Union (WCTU), 32–34, 39, 41; and age of

consent campaigns, 33–34, 39; and rape culture, 33
women's liberation movement. *See* feminism
Woodson, Jules, 113
writing: as healing activity and political resource, 16; of shame, 18; and survivor-generated archives, 108, 110–15, 113. *See also* Denhollander, Rachel; Hatmaker, Jen; Moore, Beth

"Xvangelical," 60

Zaeke, Susan, 32